DATE DUE

SHADOW CHASERS

The Woolfolk Tragedy Revisited

SHADOW CHASERS

The Woolfolk Tragedy Revisited

Carolyn DeLoach

Eagles Publishing

Newnan, Georgia

First edition, entitled "The Woolfolk Tragedy" published by Anneewakee River Press.
Second edition entitled "Shadow Chaser: The Woolfolk Tragedy Revisited" published by
Eagles Publishing; 384 Bullsboro Dr., #339; Newnan, GA 30263

The paper in this book meets the guidelines for permanence and durability of the
Committee on Production Guidelines for Book Longevity of the Council on Library
Resources.

First Edition Library of Congress Catalog Card Number: 96-95336
Second Edition Library of Congress Catalog Card Number:00-132304

Cataloging Data
DeLoach, Carolyn, 1951 -
The Shadow Chasers: The Woolfolk Tragedy Revisited./Carolyn DeLoach

Newnan, GA: Eagles Publishing, c2000
400 p.: ill.; 22 cm.
Includes bibliographical references (p.389 - 394)

Hardcover ISBN: 0-9700656-0-4
Softcover ISBN: 0-9700656-1-2

1. Woolfolk, Tom, 1860-1890. 2. Mass murder -Georgia-Bibb
County--History. 3. Case studies-19th century.

364.1524 DELOA

Eagles Publishing, hardcover edition/March 2000
Eagles Publishing, softcover edition/March 2000
Printed in the United States of America
05 04 03 02 01 00   6 5 4 3 2

In Memory of

…the Captain, Mattie,
Aunt Temp, Dick, Pearl, Annie,
Rosebud, Charlie, Little Mattie,
Flo, Lillie,
… and Tom.

May they all rest in peace.

TABLE OF CONTENTS

The Characters

AUTHOR'S NOTE: The following individuals were real people. Their participation in the various aspects of this case is well documented. Their conversations, impressions, and actions have been recreated in this book and adhere as closely as possible to the original records.

The Accused:
Thomas G. Woolfolk--age 27, son of Richard F. Woolfolk, Bibb County Georgia.

The Victims:
Richard F. Woolfolk--age 54, father, murdered.
Mattie E. Howard Woolfolk--age 41, step-mother, murdered.
Richard F. Woolfolk, Jr.--age 20, step-brother, murdered.
Pearl Woolfolk--age 17, step-sister, murdered.
Annie Woolfolk--age 10, step-sister, murdered.
Rosebud Woolfolk--age 7, step-sister, murdered.
Charlie Woolfolk--age 5, step-brother, murdered.
Little Mattie Woolfolk--age 18 mos., step-sister, murdered.
Temperance West--age 84, Mattie Woolfolk's great-aunt, murdered.

Hazzard District, Bibb County Georgia:
Emma Jones--cook, Woolfolk Farm.
Aaron Jones--Emma Jones' husband, sharecropper, Woolfolk Farm.
London and Luanna Cooper--sharecroppers, Yates Farm.
Greene Lockett--age 43, overseer, Woolfolk Farm.
Fanny Lockett--wife of Greene Lockett, Woolfolk Farm.
Anderson and Ann James--sharecroppers, Gibson Farm.
Sarah Hardin--washwoman, Woolfolk Farm.
John Jeff, Tom Banks, Silas Woolfolk--fieldhands, Woolfolk Farm.
Henry Brown--neighbor, witness for prosecution.

Howard's District:
William H. Smith--age 38, Woolfolk sawmill foreman.
Samuel Chambless--age 60, farmer.
Benjamin Howard--age 76, Mattie H. Woolfolk's father.
Charles and John Howard--Mattie H. Woolfolk's brothers.

Macon, Georgia:
Montgomery Morgan Folsom--correspondent Piedmont Region,
The Atlanta Constitution, The New York Times.

George W. Gustin--Judge, Macon Circuit Court.
John L. Hardeman--Solicitor General, 1887-88.
William H. Felton--State Representative, Solicitor General, 1889.
Dupont Guerry--Attorney for the Prosecution.
Joseph Hall--Attorney for the Prosecution.
George Westcott--Sheriff, Bibb County.
William Hodnett--Coroner, Bibb County.
Nathan Birdsong--Jailer, Bibb County.
John Clay--Undertaker, Bibb County.
Daniel Adams--Clerk of Superior Court, Bibb County.

Athens, Georgia:
Floride Woolfolk Edwards--age 33, Tom's oldest sister.
Fannie Crane--Tom's aunt.
Love A. (L.A.) Shackleford--Tom's cousin.
John Cobb Rutherford--Attorney for the Defense.

Hawkinsville, Georgia:
Lillie Woolfolk Cowan--age 30, Tom's sister.
Henry P. Cowan--Lillie's husband.

Jones County, Georgia:
Thomas Jefferson Woolfolk--brother of Richard F. Woolfolk.
Georgia Bird Woolfolk--wife of Tom Woolfolk.
Thomas Bird--father of Georgia Bird Woolfolk.

Houston County, Georgia:
John Washington Woolfolk--brother of R. F. Woolfolk.
Melton L. Cooper--Sheriff, Houston County.
Alexander Lawton Miller--Attorney for the Defense.
Clinton C. Duncan--Attorney for the Defense.
Winter Wimberly--Attorney for the Defense.

The Others:
Paschal J. (Pea Jay) Moran--reporter, The Atlanta Constitution.
James T. Nisbet--private secretary to Governor John B. Gordon.
Frank R. Walker--Attorney for the Defense.
George W. Kitchen--Sheriff of Cherokee County.
Samuel Pennington--Witness for the defense.
Dr. James Holly--Witness for the prosecution.
Simon Cooper
Jackson Dubose   --graduates of Georgia's Convict-lease System
John Owens

Illustrations

INTRODUCTION TO THE
SECOND EDITION

When the first edition of this book was released several years ago under the title of *The Woolfolk Tragedy* I was repeatedly asked the same two questions. People wanted to know how I stumbled upon this case and why I stayed with it for more than twenty years. I would like to answer both questions now.

While a student at Tift College in Forsyth, Georgia, I was fascinated with the school's history. The late Dr. Eugenia Stone had just finished writing her book on the school, and all of her records were still locked up in the library. One night I could no longer resist the temptation. I took the librarian's key to Dr. Stone's office and went inside.

Hours later I reemerged filled with awe at the volumes of records I had just perused. I was also completely committed to locating two students whose names I came across in the records.

You see, I stumbled upon a diary of a teacher that was kept at the school during the Civil War. She wrote of a company of young men from the county getting ready to go north to Virginia and to war. They marched down the lane to the school, and the girls greeted them on the verandah. She wrote that Mattie Howard gave a speech and Lizzie Murphy presented them with the company's new battle flag.

The names of those two students literally jumped from the pages. For reasons I have never been able to explain I knew I simply had to locate them. I had to find out what happened to them. I had to know who they married, where they lived, and where they were buried.

Because Lizzie Murphy was listed as being from Monroe County, the same county my college was located, I searched for her first. I enthusiastically learned the art of searching courthouse records and grave yards, and in no time I located where she grew up. I learned who she married and where she was buried.

I had achieved my goal and so, innocently, I set out for Mattie Howard. I had only two pieces of information on her. I knew she had married Richard Woolfolk and was from Howard's District in Bibb County.

Using the same approach I had used to find Lizzie, I went to Howard's District and asked a nice lady if she knew where the Woolfolk Place was located. She gave me directions to Highway 74, to Hazzard District and to Mr. Ralph Whitten.

This elderly gentleman kindly pointed out the hill where the Woolfolk house once stood. I explored the house site, marveled at the well, the huge holly tree, and the ruins of the chimneys.

Once back down the hill, Mr. Whitten asked if I was investigating the murders. I had absolutely no idea what he was talking about and told him so.

"Well now, I don't think I ever run into someone who ain't never heard of the Woolfolk tragedy," he said. Pointing towards the hill, he continued, "That woman you're looking for? Her, her husband, and all their kids were killed up there. The oldest son did it. He went crazy one night and killed ever last one of'em. I got the old newspaper in the house. It came with the land deed. Wanna see it?"

Back at the house, the old man brought out a box containing land deeds and an old newspaper. Folded for a century, the old document was nothing more than four quartered sections of a once complete paper. The front page heralded the tragic murder of the Woolfolk family and the arrest of Tom, the oldest son. It contained detailed information about the coroner's investigation as well as a floor-plan of the murder scene.

Although fascinated, I was nonetheless finished. I had found what had happened to Mattie. It was a much more tragic ending than Lizzie's, but my quest was complete. I had found both of them.

I actually do not remember which of us was first to notice that it was the anniversary of the murders. Even that, however, did not really intrigue me beyond a momentary sense of the 'willies' and a few goose bumps.

The newspaper was in desperate need of salvaging and so I offered to get it laminated back at the college. Mr. Whitten entrusted it to me and I was on my way. Unfortunately, the laminating machine was broken and repair was not in the near future. I called him and he reassured me it was all right. The last thing he said was that he was in no hurry.

When I finally went back to Hazzard District to return the newly laminated newspaper to Mr. Whitten, I found his house closed up. A young boy who was mowing the yard informed me that the old man had died.

In my effort to locate a relative of the old man so I could return the paper, I soon discovered that every one I talked to in the area knew about the murders but no one had the same story. I was told the family members were killed as they slept, that Tom drugged them first, and then raped his sister. I was told that he was a blithering maniac.

I had read the original newspaper and found I knew more than the locals. I was curious. How could the facts of such a famous case become so skewed with time?

Thus far I knew that the family had been killed by an axe. I had read the coroner's detailed report in that old newspaper. I knew that the oldest son Tom was arrested and tried for the crime. The State's case against him was built on the murder of the baby. No one, it was argued quite successfully, needed to kill a baby during a robbery. The child was completely defenseless and could not identify anyone later. The baby was killed, the State said, because Tom was trying to wipe out all of the other children. He wanted to inherit his father's 'riches'. The State won and Tom was executed. Case closed.

Still curious, I went to the Georgia State Archives in Atlanta and checked out microfilm of the Atlanta Constitution for the fall of 1887. As I was fast forwarding the film to the August issues, I inadvertently over shot my target month and stopped the film on September. The headlines immediately caught my attention. Someone else had been arrested for the murder of the family. This person, however, had confessed.

I was dumbfounded. I read his statement over and over. When he explained why the baby was killed I knew he was telling the truth. That one little statement placed the baby beneath the mother and had the baby dying before her. The coroner's report confirmed it.

The man had to have been there.

I was hooked. If there had been a confession from someone other than the oldest son, I had to know what happened. I had to know what events led up to Tom being found guilty and executed.

History is written by the winners. Every person born and raised in the south knows this. I wanted to know why the legend of the Woolfolk Tragedy was so far off from reality.

With that first visit to the Archives I began my research. At no point was Tom's guilt or innocence an issue with me. I simply wanted to know what brought him to the gallows.

I never intended to write a book much less have it published. I treated it as a hobby. I was never obsessed. I was always able to walk away from it until I would stumble upon another lead or another interesting fact.

After a while, however, I had no more leads and thought I had come to the end of my search. It had taken me over twenty years to accumulate enough information for me to be able to get a realistic account of what happened. When I thought I had it all, I self-published *The Woolfolk Tragedy*.

That first book, however, was not the ending for me and this case, but only the beginning. Among those ten thousand readers who purchased a copy were people who had more information, some rare photos, and new leads on the actual murderers.

Interest was still strong about the case. People were still asking for the book. And I was still coming upon more information. I had no choice but to re-release it.

This second edition is everything I wanted the first edition to be. The editing is tighter. There are more details and some incredibly rare photos. I have received the full endorsement of the Howard, Woolfolk, and Cowan descendents. It is for them that I present to you this book. Enjoy.

Carolyn DeLoach
Darien, Georgia
April, 2000

FIRST EDITION
AUTHOR'S NOTES

No one knows exactly what happened during the early morning hours of August 6, 1887, in rural Bibb County, Georgia. All those privy to the tragedy have long since died. What is known with certainty is that Captain Richard Franklin Woolfolk and his family, a total of five adults and four children, were murdered. The bloody slaughter of this prominent Southern family rocked the State of Georgia almost from its moral and social foundation.

Newspapers from across the country rushed reporters to the scene. The sensation generated by the brutal crime, the emotionally charged funeral, the trials, and the execution held the public spellbound for three years. It was well documented.

These reporters recorded what they saw and heard. They hounded anyone remotely associated with the case, from the victims' relatives to the officials, neighbors, as well as prisoners in cells adjacent to the accused. Some investigated beyond the interviews and public information. Others, wanting to keep the masses obsessing over the case and purchasing more of their papers, unscrupulously wrote lies, rumors, and distortions.

Photographers and artists documented every scene imaginable. Pictures of the murdered victims, the funeral, inside and outside the courthouses, and the gallows were sold as souvenir postcards on the streets of Atlanta and Macon. Memorabilia collected from this case became treasured keepsakes passed from generation to generation.

For over a century this massacre has lived in oral history, anniversary news and magazine articles, and even played out on the stage at a local dinner theater.

In some parts of middle Georgia, the very name WOOLFOLK will still conjure up images of a manical axe murderer rampaging through the dark house, viciously dispensing his bloodlust upon his helpless, sleeping family.

An indepth study of the primary records revealed volumes of critical information long since forgotten and ignored. In many cases, what is considered factual reports were actually derived from local legend and folkloric-styled myths.

In recent years, we have seen and experienced the feeding frenzy of the news media when a sensational murder and trial occur. The hysteria, the public focus, the literal addiction for information on the case was no different a hundred years ago.

This is the story of the murder, the trials, and the execution. It is based on eyewitness accounts, trial testimonies, and exhaustive coverage by the news reporters. Every fact was retrieved from newspaper accounts, official papers, on site investigation, and some secondary sources. Every statement concerning critical facts in the case is, in almost all instances, a direct quote.

This is a true story written as accurately and as objectively as possible. Every important fact, every quotation, every shred of information presented in this book was documented in the original records. It is a story told by the actual participants, in their own words.

Only two characters should be considered composites of sorts–Montgomery Morgan Folsom and Paschal J. Moran who used the pseudonym "Pea Jay". Both men did in fact exist and both did work for The Atlanta Constitution. They both covered this case. The majority of the activity and dialogue credited to them are theirs. It would not have been possible, however, to have individually credited all the named and unnamed journalists whose information will also be found here. Folsom, therefore, represents those reporters who wrote as objectively as possible during this period of intense public hysteria fueled daily by reporters such as "Pea Jay".

I take no literary credit for what you are about to read. I am nothing more that a chronicler, a giver of information. The true authors are the reporters who, more than a hundred years ago, became obsessed with the story and went after the truth. Their words were published by their respective newspapers and exist today on microfilm. Thus, I give full credit to the Atlanta Constitution, the Watchman Banner from Athens, the Augusta Chronicle, the Perry Home Journal and the Macon Telegraph for this story.

To understand the events, I had to become a student of Georgia's social, economic, political, racial, and legal history. I studied thousands of articles and documents, the actual locations, records on local weather and events, the geography, the topography, and the personalities involved.

I have done my best to recreate the events surrounding this family and this case during the period of 1887-1890. Some local residents who grew up with this story may not agree with the facts in this book. Their memories are usually founded on local legend and the oral tradition passed down from their ancestors. Over time, these memories became diluted, altered, or faded. Thus, the reason for this book–to get the original facts of this case written as accurately and comprehensively as possible.

My purpose in doing so is simple. These people lived. This event happened. It is not fiction. It is a part of our collective past and, heaven forbid, we should continue to change history or simply forget.

Carolyn DeLoach
Atlanta, Georgia
December, 1996

FIRST AND SECOND EDITION ACKNOWLEDGMENTS

I literally stumbled upon the story of the Woolfolk murders more than twenty years ago as a student at Tift College in Forsyth, Georgia. Mattie E. Howard Woolfolk, the murdered mother, was an alumna. During these last two and a half decades studying this case became a hobby where I received valuable advice, assistance, and encouragement from many, many people. I have to say I could not have done it without them.

My love and appreciation to my father and mother, the late B. Hoyt DeLoach and Betty Belmont DeLoach; to my sisters and brother, Barbara Ann Bray, Susan Allen, Tricia Scott, James Hoyt DeLoach and their families. Their love, support, patience, and faith in me made all the difference. My love to D. Ashton Bray. Through her incredible strength of will power and creative spirit I have a brilliant light by which to follow.

My sincere appreciation to the late Ralph Whitten for sparking my curiosity and to Dr. Ruth G. Jones for encouraging me to write that first chapter. Thanks to Cathy Patterson for twenty years of helping me search hundreds of graveyards, dusty libraries, and blinding microfilm.

To Cathy McHenry for her patience and encouragement as well as her skillful editing. To my friend and comrade in Georgia history Guelda Hay for her endless love and support. To Sandy Kallas, John Bell, Jim & Pam Cole, Launda Cowart DeLoach for their contributions. To Martha Forlines, Kay McGhee and Stephanie Humphries for just being there when I needed them most. Thanks to Dr. Kevin and Carolyn Robinson.

To Mitzi Hall and her daughters; to Susan Alexander, Lori Jones, Laura James, Carol Welch, Page Allen, Debbie McAdoo, Gail Stamin, Toni Ralston, Judy Schneible, Beverly Reynolds, June Cartrell, Erin McAlister, Pam McIntyre, Dottie Row, Marty Galione,

21

Ginger Branton, Judy White, Jan Blanchart, Patti Morgan, Terri Walker, Debbie Press, Pat Hussein, Cherry J'Neese and Teresa Tyson for their proof reading and editing assistance.

Thanks to Lydia Wood my new copy editor and to Mitch Foster, Mark Walker, Patrick Webster, William Hobbs, Gabriel Cusumano, Michael Hamilton and Steven Parker for their technical support. To Jennifer Westall, Jennifer Moorer, thanks for your enthusiasm. Thanks to Susan Kanellos and Bobbi Riley for their invaluable production guidance, graphic design and typesetting assistance. Also thanks to Billy C. Horne, the late Bobby J. Stokes, Rev. Alan Wheeler, Genivieve Wynegar, Judy Sapp, Alice Bullock, Inez Southwell, Harold Green, Martha and Bobby Sims, Sherry Culverhouse, Helen Hanson, Alton Bird, Barbara and Don Turner for their input.

My love to my good friend Toni Ralston and appreciation to the late Celestine Sibley for that glorious pat on the back. Thanks to Anthony, Linda and Casey at Eagles Publishing for encouraging me to get back into the business of being a writer. To Ginny, Caroline, Suzanne and Marianna in Valona for allowing me a quiet place to recharge my spirits. To all those wonderful students and staff at McIntosh County Academy for letting me hide out as a chemisty teacher for a little while.

To Margaret McBride, thank you, thank you, thank you.

And now, finally-- to Barbara Anchors, Lily Norris Owen, Thomas Cowan, George Cowan, and Louise Arrington, all descendents of Lillie Woolfolk Cowan; to Zack E. Ryan, great grandson of Floride Woolfolk Edwards Shackleford; to Johnny Woolfolk, great grandson of John Washington Woolfolk, and his family; to Vickie Folsom Eggleston, great granddaughter of Montgomery Morgan Folsom, and her family; to Carlton H. Smith, grandson of William H. Smith; to Clifford Byrd, grand nephew of Georgia Bird Woolfolk; to Elaine Irby and William Chambless, descendents of Samuel Chambless; to Jessie Balkcom, widow of Mark Balkcom, descendent of Charles Howard; to Lovick and Ann Culverhouse, descendents of Randolph Gilbert; to Bessie Mell Lane, great grandniece of John Cobb Rutherford; to Millie C. Stewart, great granddaughter of Thomas Jefferson Woolfolk and her family--thank you all so very much for your warm support, encouragement, trust and valuable assistance. I hope in some small way I have succeeded in giving you back a part of your past.   **CD**

FOREWORD TO FIRST EDITION

When Carolyn DeLoach brought her manuscript to me, my first reaction was, admittedly, "Oh no, not another horror story about the Woolfolks!"

I was an adult before I learned the ugly little family secret of the Woolfolk murder. You see, we, the younger members of the family, were shielded by our elders and from the Macon Telegraph. It was not until I began working on my family tree that I discovered my personal connection. One can imagine my surprise when I learned that, as a child, I knew people who were living in Macon during this whole, tragic affair. Many of them were my relatives. No one talked about it.

Since 1987, writers have annually plagued me and other family members about our knowledge of the crime and trial. Each time, the resulting articles sensationalized the gore. Full of errors, these articles were painful to read and I personally wanted no part of any of it ever again.

During her research, Carolyn did not approach local residents or historians and, out of respect for the family, she did not contact descendants. Instead, she went to the original records and conducted an objective twenty year search.

It was not until she exhausted the records that she approached me with a manuscript. As the great granddaughter of Thomas Jefferson Woolfolk, the murdered Richard Franklin Woolfolk's brother, as well as a regional historian and genealogist, I was, she was told, the one to read her manuscript for accuracy. With serious reservation, I agreed to look it over.

Immediately, I was drawn into the events as a participant. I was seeing, hearing, feeling it all as if I were actually there, standing beside my ancestors and the other residents of this region, experiencing this tragic drama as it unfolded.

Carolyn has taken the facts of the investigation and trials, and has cleverly woven them into a "page turning" story of the actual events surrounding this horrendous tragedy and its aftermath. The names are real and the facts are correct.

At last, the truth is out and now the Woolfolk family, especially Tom Woolfolk, can rest in peace!

Millie C. Stewart
Macon, Georgia

Thomas G. Woolfolk

SHADOW CHASERS

CHAPTER ONE
"They're all dead."

Before the rains, Tobesofkee Creek was a meandering branch lazily engraving its serpentine path down from the fertile fields of lower Monroe County through the backcountry of Bibb County before fading quietly into the mightier Ocmulgee River.

Then the rains came.

The four and a half-day downpour transformed the quiet creek into a deluging formless, moving swamp. The bottomland of Hazzard District and the Tobesofkee seeped together to form an oversized murky hog wallow.

Everything–man and beast, fowl and foliage–was soaked through.

The early August flood of 1887 saturated crops and badly eroded fields as the run-off rushed aimlessly downward towards the rising river. The farmers' rich Georgia soil became a thick, brick-red mud that oozed between the fieldhands' toes, caked on the white man's boots and ruined the shoes of the womenfolk.

Inside everything was damp. Nothing escaped the heavy moisture suspended in the air. Wet boots cluttered doorways. Damp and dirty clothes were draped on backs of chairs to dry.

Emma Jones stirred. The silver rays of a bright full moon gradually illuminated her bedroom then faded again in the clouded night. She turned over and closed her eyes. There were hours yet before dawn and work.

The incessant barking of a dog in the distance continued to annoy her. She closed her eyes and waited patiently for the Captain or one of his boys to hush it up. Instead, the lone hound was joined by a loud, frenzied chorus. The snarling, yapping, howling brought Emma to her feet.

"What's goin' on up there?" She groaned aloud.

Her husband, Aaron, grumbled an incoherent response and stirred slightly. He was not fully awake.

Emma remembered that Miz Mattie, the Captain's wife, kept a lantern lit every night in the main hall of the big house. She knew if she looked up at the summit of the terraced hill there would be the lights and shadows of activity.

There was no light.

The young woman stood at the window. Her eyes were transfixed upon the distant grayness of the Captain's house. The hounds continued their relentless barking proclaiming to the countryside that something was terribly wrong at the Woolfolk house.

As if a bolt of lightning had suddenly cut a brilliant jagged path through the night sky, a scream, followed immediately by another, ripped the darkness at the top of the hill and shot a flash of terror through the startled woman standing alone at a window in her cabin a thousand yards away.

There was still no light.

A third scream and a loud, guttural "OH LORD!" seemed to thunder down the hill and penetrate her room. Emma caught her breath.

She knew the voice.

"Miz Mattie," she whispered as sounds of slapping and screams of terror and pain exploded from the Woolfolk house.

Aaron, finally disturbed by the commotion, joined her as she ran into the front room of their small two room shack. His brute strength nearly ripped the front door off its rusty hinges.

The couple stood in the doorway and listened. Dogs barking and cows bellowing were the only sounds. The lone structure at the top of the hill stood silent in the darkness.

Off in the distance someone called out for Anderson James, a neighbor. Then silence. Experience told Aaron to take Emma inside the cabin and turn his back to the trouble. He learned the lesson early in life. Stay out of white folks' business. The farm laborer gently pulled his anxious wife back inside, closed the door, and latched it.

The mustard plaster, though scalding his skin, soothed London Cooper's aches and pains. The old man was content as his wife, Luanna, fussed over him. Years of hard, back breaking labor on the Yates' farm were finally claiming their toll, and the late night, early morning treatments had become a family ritual.

Cooper ignored Luanna as she walked about the room complaining. The floor boards groaned with each step. In the distance, cows began to bellow and dogs barked furiously.

"Hush up, woman!" He growled, removing the plaster pack and rolling over to look out the window by his bed. "Listen!"

Luanna leaned out the window and listened. "You hear that. That's d'Woolfolk's dawgs." She said. "What you s'pose goin' on up there?"

"Woman, I told you t'HUSH!"

"GREENE!" The faint voice called out to him. "Greene Lockett!" The shouting grew louder and louder until it exploded inside his head. "My gawd man, git up!"

A sharp rapping at the door jolted him to his feet.

The night air was damp and muggy. His mind reeled as he fumbled clumsily to light a lantern.

The knocking continued.

"Who's out there?" he shouted.

"You know damn well who. Open this door."

Fanny, Lockett's young wife, began whimpering. "Baby, please don't open that doe," she begged.

"I's got to," he whispered back.

Lockett squinted his eyes against the glare of the lantern light and opened the door. Before him stood the short, sturdy figure of Tom Woolfolk, the Captain's eldest son, trembling in his underwear and socks. His milky skin was aglow.

"Mistah Tom?"

"You gotta help me," Tom cried. "Get a gun...they're killin' Pa!"

Fanny anxiously peered out from behind the door and muffled her cry with her fist.

"Did ya hear me, man? I said ya gotta help me!" He grabbed him roughly by the arm.

Lockett pulled away and looked over Tom's shoulder. "Where's yo brother, Mistah Tom? Where's Mistah Dick?"

Tom was shaking. His hands trembled as he ran his fingers through his disheveled hair.

"Gawd man...I dunno..."

"Mistah Tom?" Lockett asked. "You ain't drunk is ya?"

Tom ignored the question and rambled on. "Someone's in the house."

Lockett interrupted abruptly, "Who's in your house?"

"Listen to me...you damn fool. I'm tryin' to tell you someone's up there now in the house. I heard'em. They hit Pa and woulda got me. You gotta help me."

Lockett's son joined him at the door. Tom remained rooted to the doorstep.

"Mistah Woolfolk, there ain't nothin' I can do. You know I been bad sick."

Tom said nothing.

Lockett, familiar with the look of utter contempt, simply avoided the man's eyes, a self-protecting habit. You don't look white people right in the eyes. They don't like it.

Tom slammed his fist against the door facing. Fanny jumped.

"Damn it all," he shouted. "We gotta do somethin'. Get me some help."

"Mistah Woolfolk...I been too sick to ride no mule. I can't help you none."

Tom's fingernails cut into the wood. His knuckles were white. His eyes were opened wide and reflected a wildness Lockett had never before seen. Nervously, he jerked his head around and barked at the young boy standing behind him. "Run over to d'Smith's and d'Yates'. Tell'em to git over here quick...tell'em somethin' bad's happened at d'Cap'ns."

The boy brushed roughly against the white man's shoulder as he ran by him on his way around the corner of the shack. Tom regained his balance and turned to face Greene Lockett.

The former slave was forty three years old, brown with skin like old leather, cracked and scarred. His yellow eyes were sunken and bloodshot.

Lockett shuddered. The dim light of the lantern danced shadows about the pale figure standing in front of him.

Rustling of brush forced Tom to whirl around and Lockett to raise his lantern high over their heads.

"Who's out there?" he shouted.

A large form slowly solidified from the darkness. Anderson James, a laborer from the neighboring Gilbert farm, strolled into the light.

"What's all d'ruckus?" he questioned. "Mistah Thomas? I thought I heard you runnin' down d'hill hollerin somethin' 'bout your whole family gettin' killed."

"Anderson...ya gotta help me," Tom said anxiously. "They're killin' pa."

"Great Gawd," James gasped as he slumped down beside a tree.

Lockett listened closely to the noises around them. There were dogs barking and cows bellowing in distant pastures. The night orchestrated sounds not unlike those he had heard many times before.

"Jeezus Christ," Tom groaned. "Come with me Anderson. I'm goin' back up there."

Anderson James reluctantly got to his feet and followed. Lockett kept silent and watched as the two men slowly dissolved into the darkness.

Hazzard District, in the late 1880's, was a sparsely populated rural area of western Bibb County, Georgia. White farmers, though out numbered almost two to one by poor black laborers and sharecroppers, were still the ruling class socially and politically. Emotional and physical scars were clearly visible on faces and bodies in both groups.

The war, having established freedom for the slaves some twenty years earlier, created new socioeconomic problems for the region. Sharecropping and the convict lease system replaced slavery. Financially ruined plantation masters blamed their desperate situations on the loss of a once abundant work force.

Each group lived in constant terror of the other. One wanted revenge while the other anxiously anticipated the coming retribution. Their fears were not without reason. A generation of freed slaves were displaced and trapped in a society of white landowners desperate to reclaim their total dominance. Efforts of coexistence were strained.

It was into this unstable, paranoid environment that Greene Lockett unwillingly sent his boy to sound the alarm. The leader of the white community, Captain Richard F. Woolfolk, had been murdered.

The first white to receive the news and respond was William H. Smith, the Captain's sawmill foreman. He and his wife, Catherine, were awakened by the young Lockett boy hammering excitedly at their back door. Smith hurried him on to Samuel Chambless' farm and then quickly dressed while his son, Carlton, saddled the mare.

William H. and Catherine Burnett Smith
(Photo courtesy of Carlton H. Smith)

"Bill, now be careful," Catherine pleaded. "You don't know what's happened over there at the Captain's place."

"Don't you go and worry yourself none. The Captain's been expectin' trouble." He answered as calmly as he could and checked the chamber of his old pistol. "I'll be awright."

Turning to his son, he continued, "Carlton, soon's you git everythang squared away here I want you to hitch up d'mule and take yer Ma over t'Russellville." He shoved the gun in his belt and mounted.

"Maybe you bedder stop by Burnett's store on the way and let'em know what's happened," he shouted over his shoulder.

Kicking his horse into a full gallop, he left his small farm and raced towards the Captain's rolling thousand acre plantation known as "The Homeplace".

Minutes later, the thirty-eight year old man reined his mare onto the Captain's property. The three-quarter mile lane leading up to the house was canopied by massive oaks lining each side. To the east, beyond the fence, were the fields of the widow of old Randolph Gilbert, Woolfolk's closest white neighbor.

As the news spread, Lockett's shack became the focal point of activity. Men, all sharecroppers and laborers from the Gilbert, Parker, Yates and Woolfolk farms, anxiously milled around the old clapboard dwelling, their womenfolk tucked away safely inside.

Greene sat in the doorway. There was a hush about the group as they cautiously eyed the lone figure squatting against a large oak. Tom Woolfolk had come down the hill a second time.

Keeping his distance he made no attempt in explaining to them what he had done back at the house. They made no effort at finding out. The silence between them was mutual.

The rhythmic clatter of horse hooves brought the laborers instinctively together. Every eye was on Smith as he galloped up to Lockett's house. His horse pranced about with excitement.

Tom, still squatting against the tree trunk, slowly placed both hands on his upper thighs and pushed himself up. Smith was startled to see the Captain's son, scantily clad, calmly walking towards him.

Tom took hold of the reins. Talking softly, he repeatedly glanced over his shoulder.

"It's bad, Bill. Someone stole into Pa's house and killed 'em all."

Smith's eyes shot over to the group of men and then back to Tom. "Where were you?" he asked.

"I was asleep. I heard Pa holler and Ma scream. Someone was waitin' t'git me too so I jumped out my window and ran down here for help. What good it done'em. They're dead."

Greene Lockett approached the two men.

Smith placed his hand on his pistol. "Lockett, how 'bout you comin' with us."

Lockett turned and looked over at his friends standing a short distance away and then back at the men.

"Yassuh, Boss."

Artist sketch of Captain Richard F. Woolfolk's Home

The whitewashed house stood silent against the backdrop of night.

Smith and Lockett stopped short of entering through the gate as Tom walked on up the steps and onto the porch.

"How do you know they're all dead?" Smith whispered.

"Cause I been inside. They're all dead. Ever last one of 'em." Tom glared at the scared black man standing beside Smith's horse. "I came back up here after tryin' to get some help. Anderson James started up with me but he got spooked and ran on off before we even got to the house."

"See anybody?" Smith asked.

"No...but I heard'em good enough. They were on the back porch laughin'. When I heard'em open the back gate I snuk in the front. It was so dark in there I had to feel my way around."

Smith looked intently at the eastern sky. "We got another good hour yet, I figger," he remarked, removing his hat and scratching his head. "Since they're all dead, there ain't nuthin' any of us kin do b'fore it gits light."

"Lockett," he continued, watching a group slowly making their way up the lane. "I don't want no trouble from them, ya hear me?"

"Naw suh. Ya'll ain't gonna have no trouble from us." Lockett answered.

A muffled, shuffling sound from within the house startled the three men. Tom looked at Smith who shook his head indicating he was not ready to go inside.

"I'll go," Tom said finally, and entered the front door. He reappeared seconds later carrying a lantern.

"Need some light. Can't see a damn thing."

Smith cautiously walked to the side of the porch, pulled a match from his vest pocket and handed it up. Tom squatted down at the porch's edge, took the match, struck it on the post and lighted the kerosene wick. Slowly, he reentered the house. The soft glow from his lantern illuminated each room and revealed no signs of life to anyone standing outside in the predawn darkness.

George Yates, another Woolfolk neighbor, galloped up the lane. Smith hurried out to meet him. Lockett waited at the gate and watched as the two men talked in low voices.

A moment later Tom emerged from the house. He raised the glass chimney, blew out the flame and placed the lantern by the door. He then walked down the steps and over to the men at the gate. Yates' horse pranced around. Tom nodded to Yates and then turned to Smith.

"Don't know what we coulda heard. Ain't nobody breathin' in there," he muttered.

"Ya sure?" Lockett asked.

Tom's glare went through him. "I'm sure." Turning back to Smith he continued. "I lifted Ma's head and moved Pearl a bit." He looked down at his hands and began to rub them nervously against his chest. "Got some blood on me," he said quietly. "I'll be at the well."

Yates looked anxiously over at the crowd of men standing a short distance away.

"I'm goin' for help," he said. Pulling his hat tighter onto his head, he jerked his horse around and galloped away. Smith rejoined Lockett. It was going to be a long and lonely wait.

Dawn showed itself in the presence of a gray mist hovering heavily around the house. Greene Lockett could tell the news of the tragedy had spread throughout the countryside. The crowd continued to grow.

Smith, standing alone at the gate, also watched the gathering. He could hear the splashing of water from behind the house as Tom washed at the well.

Lockett quietly walked over. "Mistah Smith?" he asked. "It's awlmost light."

"Yeh, I know. I sent that boy of yern on over t'Chambless' place. We bedder wait a little longer, " he answered. "Yates' rode over to d'Parkers." Smith stopped and listened. Tom had re-entered through the back door and was inside the house. He could only wonder what the man was doing.

Samuel Chambless owned a farm at Lorane, Georgia, that was half the size of the Woolfolk Plantation. Accompanied by his wife, son and several other armed white men the old farmer finally arrived. Smith hurried up to his buggy and helped him down.

"Smith...Thomas," Chambless said, nodding to the two men.

Sixty years old, the old man stood erect as he approached Tom. Although the young man's father had been his close friend for many years, he personally did not like the younger Woolfolk.

"We've been waitin' for ya, Mistah Chambless. Tom, here, says someone broke in and kilt d'Captain, Mattie, and the littl'ins. But I ain't bin inside yet."

"Thomas? This true?"

"Yessir."

"What were you doin' when all this was goin' on?"

"Sleeping."

Chambless listened intently as Tom explained how he had been awakened in the middle of the night by his father's cry but could not see anything in the darkness.

"What about that lantern your ma kept lit at night for the baby?"

"All I know it was pitch black in the house," Tom answered. He then described how he was about to run into his parents' room when his half-brother, Dick, darted past him.

"I heard'im get hit and fall," Tom said excitedly, gesturing wildly. "I knew they were in there waitin' for me...so I jumped out the window by my bed and ran down to Lockett's for some help."

The old man took a long, deep breath and slowly walked over to the front door. "Well son, 'spect its time to get it over with. You, boy!" He barked at Lockett who instinctively jumped to attention.

"I want you to keep everybody outta here. Tom, Smith...y'all come on with me."

"Yassuh, Marse Sam, suh." Lockett responded obediently, nodding, and twisting his hat into a tight wad.

Chambless rested his hand on the porch post and turned to face Tom.

"That blood?" he asked.

Tom brought his hand up to his right ear.

"Yessir, there's blood everywhere in there."

The old man waved at Tom's meager attire. "Better get some britches on," he said and then gave the brass door knob a slow turn.

The door opened with a low, soft groan into a long wide hallway filled with shadows. Chambless lit Lockett's lantern and entered first. Smith followed and almost immediately noticed a faint, sweet odor.

Tom brushed roughly by and pointed to the last door on the left.

"They're in there," he whispered.

The Woolfolk house was a simple, ordinary one story dwelling. Two square rooms were situated on each side of the hall. The door to which Tom had pointed led to the bedroom of his parents.

Chambless stopped and looked quickly into the boys' front bedroom. All seemed in order. He cautiously walked down the hall and stopped to look at blood smeared on the wall to his right. On the floor in front of him was a single set of bloody footprints that tracked through a large congealing puddle and led into the Captain's bedroom.

Smith looked down at Tom's feet. His socks were bloody.

"Whose tracks are these?" Chambless questioned.

"Mine."

"But Tom," Smith whispered, "there's only one set of tracks here."

The old man stepped over the puddle, walked up to the bedroom door, raised the lantern high, and looked in.

Samuel Chambless had fought for the Confederacy with General George Kirby. He witnessed men shot, bayonetted, and cannonballed. As he stood in the doorway of Captain Richard Woolfolk's bedroom, however, he was horrified.

Richard F. Woolfolk, shortly after returning from war. *(Photo courtesy of Millie C. Stewart).*

Twenty-year-old Dick lay sprawled just inside the entrance beside his five-year-old brother, Charlie. Each had been dealt a killing blow with the blade of an axe. Their blood flowed as rivulets into a common pool.

The battered, bloody body of beautiful Pearl was draped across the foot of her parents' bed. Seventeen years old, she was home for a brief visit from college. It looked as if her body had simply been tossed onto the bed. Her feet were dragging the floor.

The bed was a mountain of carnage. Chambless stared in disbelief at the entangled remains of Tom's father and step-mother.

The Captain's body rested on the side of the bed near the wall. Mrs. Woolfolk's position suggested she was struck while sitting up. The walls and floor all around them were splattered with blood and brains.

William Smith felt a sickening taste of bile creep slowly up into his throat. At his feet, a short-handled axe covered with blood, brain tissue, and strands of long black hair leaned against the door jam.

"My dear God," Chambless whispered, desperately trying to maintain his composure.

A single set of bloody tracks led from body to body.

"These yours?" He asked, pointing at the footprints.

The silence in the house was deafening. Tom stood quietly beside the old man and stared at Pearl's body. Smith began to feel nauseous. He had to get out of the house and into the fresh air.

"TOM!" Chambless barked angrily. "Are these your tracks here?"

Tom nodded.

"Did you move any of the bodies?" It was obvious to him someone had placed Pearl on the bed.

"Tom!" Smith nudged him.

Looking slowly around the room Tom spoke softly, "I thought..." He was noticeably confused and began to stammer. "I thought...I remember picking Ma up off the floor. She was lying across Pa and hanging off the other side. Her head was touching the floor by the wall over there. I thought I had..." His voice cracked. "I thought I had put Pearl higher up on the bed. She... she must have slid back down."

Chambless stared closely at the young man's expression.

"Tom?" he asked. "What's it like in the other room?"

Tom said nothing.

"THOMAS!" The old veteran was tired and scared and short on patience. "What's it like in the girls' room?"

"Don't know."

Smith looked painfully confused. "Tom...you said they were all dead by the time I got here."

"They were. I checked each of them for breathing."

Chambless walked across the hall, pushed the door open and stopped short. His shoulders dropped. The lantern hung loosely at his knees.

Smith had seen enough. He had to get away from the stench in the air, away from the blood, but most especially he had to get away from Tom Woolfolk. He knew he could not see any more.

Chambless did not see Smith stumble out the back door. His eyes were fixed on the horrible scene before him. In the double bed on his left were the bodies of two people–an elderly woman and a small child.

The old man recognized Mattie's great-aunt, Temperance West. The elderly woman was lying on her right side with her cheek resting on her two hands as if she was sleeping peacefully. There was no sign of a struggle; she had been murdered in her sleep. From the doorway Chambless could see that her skull was crushed. Grayish-yellow matter oozed from a large gash over her left eye.

The tiny form lying at the foot of the bed was that of little seven-year-old Rosebud. Her small frame was lost in the matted mess of bloody sheets.

The old man took a step further into the room and raised the lantern high over his head. It was still too early in the morning to see clearly. Clothing was scattered about the floor and a chair had been overturned. A lone figure beneath the window between the two beds captured his attention.

Little Annie, only ten years old, had pulled the sheet off her bed during her efforts to escape. Her left arm was hooked on the window sill. The sheet partly covered her mutilated body.

The room seemed frozen in time as a feeling of eternal finality overtook Chambless. All were dead just as Tom said. There was nothing the old man could do for them.

Looking around the room again, Chambless suddenly realized someone was missing.

"Where's the baby?" he asked softly.

Tom remained silent, staring at the body of his sister, Rosebud.

Trembling with rage, Chambless grabbed him by the arm and demanded, "Where is little Mattie? Where's the baby?"

"She sleeps with Ma 'n Pa...in there."

Chambless pushed Tom aside and rushed into the other room. He gently lifted the sheet, held it up for a moment and then let it fall. He blew out the lantern's flame and steadying himself along the wall he walked out of the house.

A mob gathered during his absence. The loud murmur quickly diminished to a hush as Chambless walked out onto the porch. Astonished, the old war veteran removed his hat and wiped the sweat from his brow. He took a deep breath and slowly looked around the yard at the countless number of wagons lining the narrow road.

Horses were tied to every available post. The flower bed he remembered Mattie tending for so many years was trampled. Children played catch in the road while the older folks simply stood watching and waiting. His wife, Amanda, walked away from a group of white neighbors and joined him on the porch.

Two friends of the Woolfolk family walked up. Ben Burnett owned the general store a few miles away and Robert Wright was the local postmaster. Chambless wiped his brow. Shaking his head from side to side, he motioned towards the door.

"They're in there," he said.

All eyes fell on the front door as Tom Woolfolk walked out dressed in a dirty shirt and baggy pants. Ignoring the glares and hostile comments from the mob, the soul survivor of the Woolfolk household appeared to saunter as he walked to the porch's edge to lie down.

Standing at the edge of the crowd, Emma Jones watched him closely. He looked exhausted.

Wright and Burnett entered the house only to quickly return a moment later. The latter held a handkerchief to his nose as sweat trickled down his right cheek.

The small delegation of whites surveyed the crowd and conferred in close conference. Chambless and Burnett finally walked over to Tom who instantly stood up and shoved his hands deep into the pockets of his trousers.

"Son, it don't look too good for you," Chambless spoke in a hushed voice.

"We're gonna have to arrest you and put you inside the house for safe keepin' 'til Sheriff Westcott gets here from Macon." Burnett added.

Tom looked out at the mob that watched his every move and mumbled blankly, "Been lying here thinking about that."

Chambless scribbled a note on the back of a canceled bank draft and handed it down to Greene Lockett standing beside the porch.

"Send a boy to Macon for the Sheriff and the Coroner," he said. "Better have'im go first to the boarding house near the Presbyterian Church on Mulberry Street and fetch Daniel Adams, the Clerk of Court. He'll know where to find'em."

The old farmer then took his prisoner by the elbow and ushered him inside the house. There was no need for the lantern by this time. The sun was up.

CHAPTER TWO
"They didn't have a chance."

Saturday morning, August sixth, had begun like all other Saturdays in Macon, Georgia, as hundreds of wagons loaded with cotton made their way into town for the warehouses and city market on Poplar Street. Merchants were busy setting up their sidewalk displays of farm and garden tools, clothing, dried beef and fowl.

Typical street scene in Macon, Georgia, circa late 1800s
(Photo courtesy of Billy C. Horne)

Street sounds crescendoed with activity as Montgomery Morgan Folsom, reporter for the Atlanta Constitution, stood buttoning his vest at the mirror. His room at the prestigious Lanier House on Mulberry Street offered him a panoramic view of the city.

The 1887 freshet flooded the low lying areas on both sides of the Ocmulgee River forcing the inhabitants to seek higher ground.

Folsom did not mind sending his wife and children south to his family in Hahira and having to leave his home on the east bank. The Lanier House located in the government and business district was ideal for keeping up with the news and events of the area.

The loud rapid cadence of a horse galloping down the street caught his attention. Always curious, the reporter looked out his window in time to see its rider, a black man, dismount and run up the steps of the boarding house at the corner.

A moment later, the Clerk of Court, Daniel Adams, emerged hurriedly pulling on his coat, his breakfast napkin still tucked in his collar. The two men ran down the sidewalk and disappeared through the front door of the court house.

Folsom quickly gathered the tools of his trade–his hat, coat, pencil, reporter's pad–hurried out of the hotel and met the rider as he walked out of the courthouse. Exhausted, the young man sat down on the granite steps. Sweat dripped off his brow. His white shirt was wet and smudged with dirt.

"Mistah, them folks is all dead. They is all dead." He spoke breathing heavily.

"Who's dead?" Folsom asked.

"D'Woolfolks. D'Cappin and his whole damn family was killed last night in their sleep. I just come with the news. Mistah Adams, he's in there right now roundin' up d'Sheriff."

His words spread through the growing crowd, rushing outward in all directions and away from the nucleus of people. The small gathering on the courthouse steps was rapidly transformed into a large crowd anxiously waiting for more word. Although Sanford, the messenger, had brought the information directly from the scene, he was, nonetheless, considered an ignorant farm laborer. So, they waited for someone of authority, white authority, to confirm the news.

They did not have to wait long.

Daniel Adams walked solemnly out onto the steps and spoke to the throng of concerned citizens. "I have here a dispatch brought in by this boy from the farm of Richard Woolfolk. It's addressed to the public at large and reads: 'Captain Woolfolk and his family were murdered last night.'"

Painful reality showed itself on the faces of the crowd as each member individually comprehended what was said.

Women grabbed at their throats and gasped. Others muffled their anguish on their husbands' shoulders while still others wept openly. The men looked at each other in total disbelief. The Woolfolk family was prominent in Macon's aristocratic circle.

The Captain's father, Thomas Woolfolk, played a vital role sixty years earlier in the redevelopment of the area on the eastern banks of the Ocmulgee River that included the old, historic wilderness outpost, Fort Hawkins.

Old Thomas Woolfolk
Photo courtesy of Millie C. Stewart

It was public knowledge that the Captain and his brothers owned valuable property, commercial and private, on both sides of the river. The family was well known state wide.

"I've sent for the coroner," Adams announced trying to calm the crowd.

"Who did it? Do they know?" someone called out.

"Says here they've arrested Tom Woolfolk."

"You don't mean the Captain's own son?" Folsom questioned, looking up from his note pad. He knew Tom Woolfolk. Everyone did. Although young Woolfolk did not possess the social attitude of his family and was considered a scoundrel by most he was liked by those who took the time to know him.

"Yes sir. It says here that they arrested Tom Woolfolk and are holding him for the Sheriff."

Culloden Road was choked with westward traffic as every conceivable conveyance transported the official, the related, the concerned, and the curious to "The Homeplace."

Folsom, wanting to keep close to the sheriff and his deputies, sat on the edge of his seat as William A. Davis, who was giving the reporter a ride, expertly reined his buggy through the congestion.

It was impossible for any of them to imagine the bizarre situation unfolding in Hazzard District.

Montgomery Morgan Folsom
(Photo courtesy of Vickie Folsom Eggleston)

Hundreds of people had already gathered throughout the morning. The Montepelier Springs picnic, for which the Captain chaired the planning committee and Mattie prepared two large baskets of food the night before, literally transferred itself from the nearby springs to the Captain's front yard.

The atmosphere was carnival-like as nearly five hundred people congregated on the terraced hill.

Inside Tom and his neighbors waited. He had been stripped, searched, and questioned. The bodies of his family were as they had been found that morning except bed sheets covered them, more to keep down the flies and to shield the living from the horror of the deaths than out of respect for the deceased.

To insure security and to prevent gawkers, Chambless ordered the windows closed, and the blinds drawn. The air in the house soon became stale and foul.

The old farmer stared anxiously through the blinds. He was worried about the crowd's growing restlessness. Although he did not care for Tom's slovenly ways nor his utter contempt for social status and honor, Chambless knew the responsibility of protecting the young man from a lynch-mob rested on the shoulders of the white men sequestered with him.

Folsom could see the Woolfolk farm house, on a hill, as it glared against the bright sun.

No longer able to drive his buggy through the congestion, Davis suggested they both walk the remaining hundred yards.

Folsom hopped down and began weaving between small clusters of spectators. Women and children picnicked beneath the large, ancient oaks, while their menfolk stood in groups talking softly among themselves. The excitement was contagious.

The reporter tuned his trained ears toward the myriad of conversations floating about him as he worked his way up the lane.

"Wad we waitin' for? We know who dun it."

"That no count Woolfolk. We oughta take care of this business here and now."

"They say he was doin' it to his sister when d'Cap'n and Miz Mattie dey cotched 'im. That's why he had to kill 'em all. Even d'littlins."

"I heard he came back last week, with hat in hand. His wife done run out on him, and not a cent to his name. I always said that boy was nothin but trash. Ain't I always said that?"

Folsom, certain the mob was primed and ready for revenge, was unsure of its true motivation. Either they loved the Captain and his family that much or just hated Tom Woolfolk more. Some, he felt confident, were simply caught up in the growing hysteria brought on by the brutality of the murders.

The intensity of the noon day sun forced dogs, farm animals, and womenfolk deeper into the shade while the sweating male citizenry stood angry and helpless in the lane. The high pitched hum of katydids rattled from the trees and bushes while hordes of gnats congregated in front of faces. As the sound of approaching riders grew louder, everyone turned in unison and watched the sheriff and his party arrive.

The official entourage from Macon consisted of Sheriff George Westcott and four of his deputies, as well as, Coroner William Hodnett, and Solicitor General John L. Hardeman. The men were quiet and closed mouth as the mob made a narrow opening through which they could walk.

It had been hours since Tom made his first run down the hill to Greene Lockett's house. The atmosphere surrounding the murdered family was electrified with suspicion, denial, accusations, paranoia, and horror. Finally, impotence was transformed into action as Westcott took over and began investigating the murders.

By this time, members of Mattie's family had arrived. The Howard's plantation was located a few miles north in Howard's District. Many in the crowd were moved to tears for Mattie's father, Benjamin F. Howard. The old gentleman looked lost and bewildered as his two sons, Charles and John Howard, escorted him out of the house and helped him into a large rocker on the front porch.

Charles Wallace Howard (left) and John Howard (right).
(Photos courtesy of Mrs. Jessie Balkcom)

Sheriff Westcott leaned over and spoke quietly to Howard. The seventy-six year old man nodded and began to rock slowly, his right hand gripping the top of his walking stick. Twisted from arthritis, his left hand trembled as it rested on his lap. His snow white hair hung loose on his shoulders. The old man said nothing, his eyes focused on the edge of the porch in front of him.

Mattie's brothers walked over to the sheriff and told him of their desire for a speedy investigation and promised they would not interfere with his work.

Sam Chambless greeted the officials from Macon with sincere relief and escorted them inside the house.

To assist Coroner Hodnett in his investigation, a twelve-man coroner's jury was immediately sworn in. The Captain's white neighbors and friends constituted the majority. Folsom was also made a member, giving the news correspondent a most coveted position.

Emma Jones, waiting for an opportunity to speak to someone in charge, listened to Luanna Cooper repeat her hysterical monologue to all who would listen. Her husband, Aaron, stood with a group of his friends as they waited and watched the coming and going of white people.

"Then d'cows began bellerin. You know how they act when they smells blood." Luanna's eyes widened, her voice raised to a feverish pitch. "I knew then 'n there, that blood had been spilt up'peer. Miz Mattie 'n her poor chillins. Those lit'l babies, murdered in their sleep like they was. I tell you it just rips at my heart when I think about it."

Ann, Anderson James' wife, stood beside her listening intently. "They say no one heard nothin' comin' from d'house," she said in a near whisper.

"I heard somethin'," Emma remarked as she watched Aaron converse with Green Lockett. Her two friends stared back at her.

"Don't say those thangs, child. You ain't dun no seech thang." Luanna barked.

"But I did."

Ann grabbed Emma by the elbow and hissed, "What did you hear?"

"I heard'em scream. I heard Miz Mattie and the chidren scream as they was gettin' killed. I also heard someone call out for that man o'yours." Emma wrapped her arms tightly about herself and quickly walked over to her husband. "Baby," she said quietly as she touched his elbow, "I's got t'talk to ya."

Aaron waved slightly to Greene and stepped aside with Emma.

"When we gonna tell them what we heard last night?"

"We ain't tellin' no body nuthin'."

"But baby, we's got to tell 'em."

"...not 'til they ask us, we don't. This ain't none our 'fair, ain't none our bidness." Emma's grip tightened on his elbow.

Aaron continued, "And what's we gonna tell'em, that we heard them poor white folks as they was gittin' killed?"

Emma's eyes filled with tears. Aaron looked at his wife and then over at his friends who were watching the couple closely. "We'll tell'em," he whispered finally, patting her hand, "we'll tell'em soon as they come outta that house."

Inside the house, the air was stifling. The smell of the congealed blood and mutilated bodies caused even the hardiest to place a handkerchief to nose and mouth when in the immediate vicinity of the victims.

Coroner Hodnett examined each body closely while Folsom made notes. "By all appearance," Hodnett noted, "the Captain received the first blow of the ax cutting off the top frontal lobe part of his skull. Mattie was then struck as she rose up in the bed. She was hit in the back of the head completely crushing her skull."

The baby was between the two adults. Hodnett noted that an ax wound an inch wide by three inches long ran from the center of the top of the head to the back. The jury was horrified at the pitiful sight. The child was almost unrecognizable.

"Pearl's body was placed here," Hodnett continued. "I would assume she encountered her murderer in her bedroom and then struggled with him in the hallway where she died. That would explain the blood smears on the wall and the puddle of blood out there. It took several blows to stop her," he said, noting the cut on her forehead and one on the side of the face.

"This is the one that probably killed her," Westcott added as he pointed to the large gash over the left eye. "Hit her so hard, knocked her eye out." Jury members looked away. Folsom stared in disbelief.

Hodnett and Westcott knelt beside the two bodies on the floor. Dick's wound appeared to be the most severe with a single blow from the front dissecting the left side of his face. His younger brother received two blows. One was on the very top of his head while the other was over the right eye.

"Look how deep the wounds are," Westcott noted. "This one is a good half inch wide."

"They didn't have a chance," Folsom mumbled to himself as he wrote furiously. Sweat ran along the sides of his face, falling into the pool of dried blood at his feet.

Flies were becoming numerous and bothersome. They fed not only on the blood and brains scattered about the rooms but collected inside the open wounds of the deceased and defiantly flew into the faces of the men.

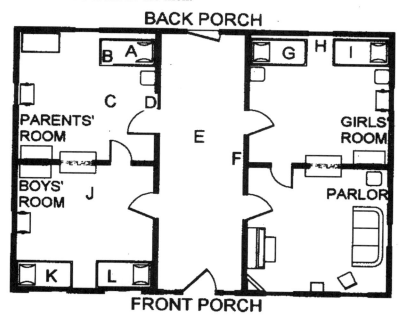

Floor-plan of the murder scene

A--the bodies of the Captain, Mattie, and the Baby; **B**--Pearl's body; **C**--the bodies of Charlie and Dick; **D**--the short handled axe; **E**--pool of blood; **F**--blood smears on wall; **G**--bodies of Aunt Temp and Rosebud; **H**--Annie's body; **I**--bed where Pearl and Annie were sleeping; **J**--wet spot by fireplace; **K**--bed where Dick and Charlie were sleeping; **L**--Tom's bed.

While the coroner, sheriff, and jury examined his family, Tom waited quietly in the parlor. Chambless, Smith, and another farmer, Henry Brown, continued to watch the mob outside. Although the sheriff had officially taken over, the three men knew there were not enough of his men to prevent a lynching should the mob choose to take matters into its own hands.

It had happened before. Memories of the Jim Moore lynching in Macon a year earlier kept the men anxious over the possibility of it happening again. Moore's removal from Sheriff Westcott's jail and execution by a mob was fresh on the minds of nearly everyone inside and outside the house.

The county was still divided over the affair even after the courts brought the participants to trial and convicted them. Some people were inclined to have allowed the law the time necessary to decide the accused man's fate. Many, however, felt the men were justified in rendering immediate vengeance upon the man charged with the rape of an innocent child.

Although civil justice had been returned to southerners after more than a decade of northern control, many whites as well as blacks did not trust the system. Mob justice was a reality that Chambless, Smith, and Brown did not care to encounter, especially for someone the likes of Tom Woolfolk.

In the second room, the twelve-man jury crowded around the officials as the coroner continued dictating to Folsom a description of the elderly woman's single wound.

On the wall near her bed, two double barrel shotguns rested on pegs. Folsom stood staring at them. He looked around the room at the bodies and wondered aloud, "Why use an ax?"

No one appeared to hear him. No one else seemed to notice the two guns.

Between the two beds, the jury was closely examining little Annie's position.

"Looks to me like the murderer hit her from behind as she tried to get out the window. See these two wounds here," he continued, pointing to a cut over her right eye and a smaller one on the left side of her neck. "He probably thought she was killed with these and then later caught her trying to escape and had to finish her off."

"Poor little thing, she almost made it," someone commented.

The men turned their attention to the end of the bed and the body of little Rosebud. Gently turning her over, Hodnett continued, "This child was struck three times. Twice in the face, one over the left ear and the other on the forehead. She then fell over on her face," he said turning her back to her original position, "where she was hit in the back of the skull, here."

It was not necessary for him to point out the wound to them. The blow was given with such force it had opened up the back of her head.

Midafternoon, Solicitor-General Hardeman emerged from the house.

"We gonna hang that murderer now?" a man called out from the rear of the crowd.

"We're conducting an official investigation here. We don't need talk like that. I want all you people who might have heard or saw anything unusual last night to make yourselves known to this man here," he announced resting his hand on Ben Burnett's shoulder. "When your name's called I want you to come inside and tell us what you know."

He then turned walked back into the house.

At first, no one emerged from the crowd until Greene Lockett hurried up the steps. Following his lead, Anderson James stepped forward along with another laborer, John Owens. Emma held onto Aaron's arm as together they walked up with London and Luanna Cooper.

Ben Burnett added their names to the list.

Samuel Chambless, Bill Smith, George Yates, Henry Brown, and Robert Wright, all of whom were still inside with Tom, had already been questioned by the sheriff and the jury.

Tom again had to strip. While his clothes were being examined a small medicine bottle fell out of a pocket of his trousers. The sheriff cautiously opened it and sniffed its contents.

"This chloroform?" He asked, handing it over to Hodnett who was busy studying red stains on Tom's shirt.

Tom reassured him the liquid in the bottle was nothing more than tincture of cantharide he had gotten to take off some warts. Then he offered an explanation for the blood on his shirt sleeve that was causing Hodnett such consternation.

"That probably came from just walkin' around the house."

Jury members nodded their agreement as, by this time, everyone had blood on their shoes and clothing.

When asked about his drinking, Tom insisted he had only one drink at Burnett's store when he went to mail a letter to his wife. He informed the jury he turned in early and was completely sober.

Although Tom was convincing in his reconstruction of the events following his first run down the hill, he contradicted himself on what he was wearing when he discovered the bodies.

He admitted walking through the blood and having to change his socks but could not recall what he did with them or his undershirt. A search of the house was unsuccessful. Westcott ordered his men to keep looking.

All day circumstantial evidence against Tom fed the fire of suspicion towards him. A juror detected an upturned bloody hand print on Tom's upper thigh. From that moment on all persons involved in the investigation were convinced they had the murderer.

"Tom, where did this hand print come from?" The sheriff questioned.

Tom was unable to answer.

"Tom, this is definitely a bloody handprint on your thigh. Are you sure there ain't something you wanna tell us?" He continued.

Tom looked around at the faces of the coroner's jury and mumbled, "No sir, there is nothing more than I already told you. Why don't you ask them coloreds out yonder?"

"Tom, they're going to get their chance to tell us what they know. What I want to know is how did this bloody handprint get on your leg?"

Tom looked around. "I don't know how." He stopped and thought for a moment. "After I came back in and moved some of the bodies I got sick and went out to the toilet. My bowels were all torn up. I musta got blood on my leg when I got up. I thought I'd cleaned my hands but they coulda still been bloody."

Dr. James Holly, the first doctor on the scene, walked up to him and looked at the draw string of his shorts. Westcott joined him. Tom looked down and watched as they examined the string closely.

"How were you able to undo this string and not get any blood on it?" Dr. Holly asked.

Tom did not have an answer.

"Alright Tom, then tell me again what you heard after you got out of the house."

Tom looked up and tears filled his eyes. "I heard the little girls screamin'."

"And you didn't go back to help'em?" a juror asked.

"I didn't know what to do. I knew I didn't have a chance if I stayed...so I ran for help."

"Down to Greene Lockett's house, I know." Westcott finished his sentence for him. "'Bout how far is that, would you say?"

"Not far...a few hundred yards, I guess."

"So you ran down the hill to Lockett's house. What did you do after that?"

"I came back up here."

"Why?" the Sheriff asked.

"Well...I thought maybe I could save the littl'n."

"What did you find?"

"Everybody dead."

A juror spoke up. "How did ya know? Did you feel the dead people in the dark?"

"Yes."

"Now...tell us what you did next," the sheriff continued.

"Since they were all dead, I figured the best thing I could do was go on back down the hill and wait for light and some help."

"Tom," Westcott walked over to the door, "why is there a wet place on the floor in your bedroom?"

"That's where I washed off last night...by the fire..."

"What time was that?"

"Around nine o'clock."

"Can you explain why the floor is still wet?"

"No sir, I can't."

Folsom studied the young man seated on the piano stool. His shoulders were stooped, his arms crossed. He looked as if he was shivering, yet, the room was hot and humid. He was unshaven and his hair was in need of a trim. He seemed to want to cooperate but was unable to answer what the reporter considered critical questions.

"Tom, you've admitted the tracks are yours."

"Yes, they're mine. There was blood everywhere."

"So...why aren't your feet bloody now?"

"Like I already told you, when Smith got here I went around to the back and washed at the well."

"You sure you didn't wash the blood off in your bedroom?"

"I told you I washed last night in my bedroom."

"Then, can you explain why the floor in your room is still wet? It looks like it's been recently scrubbed?"

Tom could not satisfy them with his explanation of bathing the previous night.

"Where's your wife, Georgia?"

"She's with her Pa."

"How is it that you are back here at the Captain's house?"

"Pa sent for me."

"So you came here to work for your father? And how much was he going to pay you?"

"Nine dollars a month."

"When did you get here?"

"About a week ago."

"A week ago," Westcott repeated Tom's answer. "One more question," he said, glancing out the window at the mob. "What did the blows sound like?"

Tom sighed loudly. "Like the flat end of an ax."

Folsom was both impressed and confused at Tom's attitude. In the rooms containing the remains of his family, he appeared composed and reserved. The reporter made note that his demeanor could possibly have been from shock.

Tom answered questions matter-of-factly with a blank expression. However, in his own bedroom, when they first discovered the wet, scrubbed area, he seemed shakened and confused.

He was questioned twice and would not change his story. Other than not being able to present the actual clothing he had on when he discovered the bodies, he seemed, nonetheless, credible in his answers.

While the jurymen were asking Tom their final questions, a deputy walked in and handed the sheriff a bundle.

Sheriff Westcott unfolded the material slowly and held up Tom's undershirt. The room was silent. Pulled out from beneath Tom's bed, the garment still had red stains on the sleeves and chest.

The reaction of the jury prompted Westcott, Hodnett, and Hardeman to confer in private. They immediately decided it would be wise for the sheriff to hurry back to Macon with Tom. Hodnett could finish questioning the remaining witnesses, and the jury could render its decision without the sheriff or Tom being present.

Hodnett walked to the front door and called out for Greene Lockett. Tom, Westcott, and three armed deputies exited the back door. While a large portion of the crowd concentrated its attention on the activity surrounding the black witnesses, the small group climbed aboard a carriage and left the farm via a back road. Although some people saw Tom's exit, they also saw the armed men accompanying him.

No one attempted to interfere.

CHAPTER THREE

"My name is Thomas G. Woolfolk."

Montgomery Folsom knew he could not be at two places at the same time, but he needed to be if he intended to do both his job as a reporter and his civic duty on the coroner's jury. He wanted to follow the Sheriff to Macon but could not leave until the jury rendered its decision.

One by one the witnesses were interviewed. Greene Lockett's uneasiness was obvious as he shifted nervously about in his chair. His testimony was mostly a repeat of Tom's and Smith's. The terrified man then began frantically insisting that Tom had most likely been trying to set the murder on him by getting him inside the house, kill him and then say that he, Greene Lockett, had murdered Tom's family before Tom could stop him.

Emma Jones was calm and articulate as she spoke of the horrible sounds coming from the Woolfolk house that night. Aaron disagreed on the time. Emma was certain it was closer to four in the morning while Aaron thought it was much earlier.

Luanna Cooper's hysterical testimony discredited her as a reliable witness while her husband supported Aaron on the time.

Anderson James was questioned twice. His testimony also confirmed Tom's. The jury, however, had a problem with his explanation of how he just happened to be at Greene Lockett's so early in the morning. Folsom thought it curious that both Tom and Lockett testified Tom said someone was killing his 'ma and pa', while James said he heard Tom say his whole family had been murdered.

The large laborer was ordered to strip. The jury examined his body and clothes closely for blood but found no evidence to implicate him in the murders.

The most damaging testimony against Tom came from another field hand, John Owens.

"You say you actually heard Tom Woolfolk threaten his father?" a juror asked.

"Yassur, I did. I was whitewashin' d'house."

"And when was that?" someone asked.

"Oh...back in March or thereabouts. Mistah Thomas, he come 'round braggin' that d'house 'n property was all his'n and his own blood sisters. He say that if he lived he'd have it all."

Folsom looked up from his notes and asked, "You'd consider that a threat?"

"Yassur. Ya see, he was struttin' 'round talkin' high and mighty 'bout how'z d'place was his'n and his sisters 'n that he was gonna have it."

"But how is that a threat?"

"Well suh, ya see, I was outside there paintin' 'n I heard him'n his pa arguin'. D'Cappin', he went on in d'house. Mistah Tom he stays outside wid me. He was real mad. He say he'd be damned if he let that woman have d'place."

Sheriff Westcott's plan to secret Tom away from the murder scene and the mob failed. The party consisting of Westcott, Deputy W.H. Opry, two armed guards, and the prisoner was immediately recognized as it left the farm road and turned eastward on Culloden Road.

Their entry into the city was also highly visible as their carriage, followed by countless wagons, hacks, buggies, and riders on horseback, turned onto First Street.

Onlookers lined the street. While no one attempted to molest the small group, it became immediately evident to Westcott that the mentality of a lynch mob followed them to Macon.

Tom was escorted unshackled into the jail house. Although he was under arrest, the armed guard accompanying him was there for his personal protection. A throng of people congregated in the yard. Many yelled threats. Some banged on the back door demanding entrance and the few with official business were allowed inside.

Nathan Birdsong, the jailer, led his new prisoner up the stairs to the cell block. "Wait here," he barked. "Just stand over there."

Tom draped his coat over his left arm, leaned against the wall, and waited. Outside, the crowd also waited.

Floride Edwards innocently greeted the messenger with a smile. The young boy seemed anxious but gave no clue for his uneasiness. Flo, as she preferred being called, opened the folded paper and began reading its contents.

As she read, a raw pain began cutting deep within her, increasing in intensity and severity until it exploded in her chest. She felt as if someone savagely reached inside her body, took hold of her heart, and ripped it out.

Her gasp brought her aunt, Fannie Crane, and Fannie's fifteen year old son, James, to her side. L.A. Shackleford, another cousin, entered the parlor in time to assist them both in guiding her to the sofa. Taking the crumpled paper from her hand, he read the message.

"What does it say?" Fannie asked anxiously.

Shackleford had to clear his throat. "To Floride Edwards, in care of Mrs. John R. Crane, 774 Prince Avenue, Athens, Georgia. Regret to inform you of the deaths of your father, stepmother, stepsisters and brothers, and great aunt, Temperance West. Have arrested your brother, Thomas G. Woolfolk, for murder." Shackleford read slowly, his eyes filling with tears. "It's signed G.S. Westcott, Sheriff, Bibb County, Georgia, August 6, 1887, 4:00 p.m."

At the mention of her brother's name, Flo crumbled into a bundle of heart wrenching tearful despair. L.A., whose given name was 'Love', knelt beside her and gently took hold of her hand. He was fond of his cousin. In fact, after the death of her husband, Zachary T. Edwards, in eighty five and her two years of mourning, he was beginning to officially court her.

There was nothing he could do to console her. There was nothing anyone could do to ease the pain of such a loss, the reality of which began to overwhelm the Cranes as well. Shackleford suddenly found himself trying to comfort Flo and her aunt, while James sat helpless and stunned.

"James! Run get Doc Whaley," L.A. ordered. "James!"

The boy loved his cousins. He sat on the edge of a chair and stared at the telegram.

"Jim! We need Doc Whaley!" Shackleford said firmly.

James jerked his head up. "Yeh. Yeh. I'm going right now."

Leaving Shackleford to console the grieving women, the boy ran out the front door and down the block.

Athens, Georgia was stunned by the news. Richard F. Woolfolk and his family were loved and respected by all who knew them. He married his first wife, Susan, the young daughter of Thomas Moore, Superintendent of the Georgia Factory there, in 1854, the same year Woolfolk graduated from the University of Georgia.

They had two daughters, Flo and Lillie, by the time Tom was born June 18, 1860. Susan never recovered from Tom's birth and died in June, 1865.

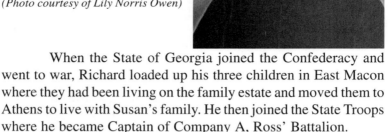

Susan Moore Woolfolk
(Photo courtesy of Lily Norris Owen)

When the State of Georgia joined the Confederacy and went to war, Richard loaded up his three children in East Macon where they had been living on the family estate and moved them to Athens to live with Susan's family. He then joined the State Troops where he became Captain of Company A, Ross' Battalion.

After Sherman's invasion of his home state and the surrender of the Confederacy, Captain Woolfolk returned to find a war torn society under martial law and in total economic chaos. In this depressed environment he opened the first hardware store in Macon called Woolfolk and Co. The business failed.

In 1867, he married Mattie E. Howard, a graduate of the prestigious Monroe Female College in Forsyth, Georgia, and the daughter of wealthy Benjamin F. Howard of Howard's District.

This marriage made it possible for the Captain to re-establish a home and place of prominence as a country gentleman in Bibb County. He and his family continued to maintain close ties to their friends and relatives in Athens.

Sympathizers rushed to the Crane home to offer condolences, assistance, and to receive more information. With his cousin and aunt both overwrought with grief, Love Shackleford became the family spokesman and began making arrangements for Flo to go home to East Macon as soon as possible.

At the Woolfolk farm, anger and sweat marked the faces of the citizens waiting for the coroner's official decision.

After all the witnesses were interviewed, John Hardeman cleared the room and allowed the jury time to consult. He stressed to the jury foreman, William J. Moseley, that as much time as possible was needed to allow the Sheriff and prisoner safe passage to Macon.

Folsom was frustrated with the delay. He desperately wanted to get to the jail as quickly as possible in order to follow up on the story. He understood, however, the necessity of stalling for time. Once the verdict was given, the mob would certainly seek revenge against Tom Woolfolk.

The jury carefully worded its statement. "We, the jury impaneled to hold an inquest on these bodies find that the nine persons deceased, namely Richard F. Woolfolk, Mrs. Mattie Woolfolk, Richard F. Woolfolk, Jr., Pearl Woolfolk, Annie Woolfolk, Rosebud Woolfolk, Charlie Woolfolk, Mattie Woolfolk, and Mrs. Temperance West, came to their deaths from blows delivered by an ax. It is our opinion the wounds were inflicted by Thomas G. Woolfolk and that the same is murder."

While Moseley reread the statement, Folsom hurried to the buggy he borrowed minutes earlier. The reporter wanted to get off the property and well on his way to town before the verdict was read, and the ominous wave of incensed humanity began its trek to the jail for revenge.

As the reporter worked his way through the mob, the foreman emerged onto the front porch. The crowd of people rushed forward to hear the verdict.

"We, the jury impaneled,..." Moseley's words faded as the distance between Folsom and the house increased.

Turning onto Culloden Road he heard a woman scream and then a loud roar from the mob. The reporter took the buggy whip in hand and brought his horse to a gallop.

In Athens, the mood in the Crane house was somber and quiet. Dr. Whaley gave Flo and her aunt something to ease their anxiety and recommended they both stay in bed. Flo would not take it and announced she wanted to return to her home in East Macon.

"Tom needs me. I must get back home immediately," she cried.

Love Shackleford agreed and offered to accompany her.

"I've sent a telegram to your sister, Lillie, in Hawkinsville and checked the train schedule. We have enough time to make the next one for Macon," he informed her as she hurriedly packed her bag.

He wrapped his arm tightly about her shoulders, picked up her satchel, and together they walked out onto the columned veranda.

The front lawn was full of people. Love helped her down the steps. Sympathizers reached out their hands to touch her, others patted him on the back. Meekly, Flo fought back tears. The genuine sincerity of the crowd touched her deeply. As she climbed into the carriage Flo turned and tearfully waved goodbye to her aunt.

It was going to be a long, difficult trip back to Macon.

Folsom's buggy skidded on the cobblestones as he raced into Macon. He knew he was ahead of an angry mob determined to have Tom's neck in a noose. There was no time to waste.

As the shadows of the setting sun darkened the city streets, the reporter turned onto Fifth Street and immediately pulled his horse to a sudden stop. In front of him a large crowd of people almost the size of the one he left in Hazzard District filled the jailhouse yard.

Cautiously, he dismounted and slowly walked through the group to the front door. The guard recognized him as a member of the coroner's jury at the Woolfolk farm and allowed him entrance.

The front office was a madhouse as deputies, court officials, clerks, and visitors hurried about filling out paper work, examining the wood ax brought in from the house, conducting interviews, and sending telegrams. Folsom approached the agitated Sheriff.

"I'd like to get a statement from the prisoner if you don't mind," he said politely.

"Yeh sure. Nat!" Westcott yelled for the jailer. "Let Folsom, here, get a statement from Woolfolk."

Nathan Birdsong escorted the reporter up the stairs and pointed to Tom, still unshackled, standing in the corridor.

Folsom pondered the prisoner's calm appearance as periodic shouts from the gathering below echoed into the room. Tom's coat was hanging on the crook of his finger and hung loosely over his left shoulder. His right hand was on his hip.

"Folsom," he said acknowledging his guest. The two men knew each other in passing. Two years earlier, Tom ran a saloon Folsom would patronize periodically.

"Tom, don't they have a cell for you?" Folsom asked.

"Nah, I don't think they plan for me to be here long."

Folsom, uncertain if Woolfolk meant the Sheriff was planning to relocate him or expecting the mob to lynch him, was unnerved by Tom's complete lack of remorse or sorrow.

"Tom. How 'bout a statement for the paper?"

The murmur of the crowd outside intensified suddenly, indicating to Folsom that people from the Woolfolk farm were beginning to arrive. Tom ignored the noise.

"Yeh, sure. But let me think about it for a minute or two," he answered. He put his hands on his hips and stared at the floor.

Folsom readied his pencil.

"My name is Thomas G. Woolfolk. I'm twenty-seven years old. I was married about three months ago. My wife hasn't been with me for a month or more," he said calmly, pausing periodically to give the reporter time to write.

"I've been at my pa's house for a week, working in the fields for wages. Last night about two hours before light, I heard a noise in my father's room, which is back of mine. My brothers, Richard and Charlie, were sleeping in the room with me."

Folsom wrote furiously as Tom continued.

"Richard's the next oldest brother. He's twenty. Charlie's five." Tom turned and looked out the window at the growing crowd.

"I heard another noise and a groan coming from Pa's room. My brother, Dick, ran into the room, and I heard'im get hit and fall." He paused and watched the reporter write out his last statement.

"I didn't have a weapon or anything, so I jumped out the window at the head of my bed and ran down to Greene Lockett's, a colorman's house about four hundred yards from the house.

"At the gate, I heard my sisters screaming. I sent Lockett to tell the neighbors. I waited, I guess, for about half an hour for help." He began to ramble. Folsom struggled to keep up.

"In the meantime, I went back to the house and went in to see if they was all dead. They were. Ma and Pa were on their bed. Their heads were crushed in. Ma's head was touching the floor on Pa's side of the bed. I picked her up and felt of her.

"All of them had been killed with Pa's ax. On the floor were my brothers, Charlie and Richard. My sister Pearl...she's seventeen, was on the bed. I guess she was killed when she ran into the room."

Woolfolk stared out the window for a moment and then continued. "I went to the room where my Aunt Temp and the girls were sleeping. They'd all been knocked in the head. The floor was covered with blood."

"Hence, your footprints?" Folsom asked.

"That's right. Annie was lying on the floor and Rosebud was on the bed." He stopped talking. The reporter looked up from his pad and waited.

Tom looked back out the window. Folsom decided not to push him.

"I'm sick. I don't want to talk any more. Come back tomorrow," Tom mumbled and walked away.

"You got any water in there?" he asked a prisoner.

The prisoner quickly retrieved a dipper of water and handed it through the bars.

Tom took a drink and poured the rest into the palm of his hand. He washed his hands and then using the nail of his index finger on his left hand he cleaned his fingernails on the right hand. When he was through, he calmly reversed the procedure.

Noticing the prisoner's curiosity, he remarked, "Got blood on my hands when I picked up the bodies."

Folsom knew the interview was over. As he left the jail house, he noticed that the attitude of the group had calmed down. The crowd was quieter and the curious now outnumbered the angry. Folsom knew, however, that Tom was not out of danger. Sundown would bring courage to those afraid to challenge the law in broad daylight.

Love patted Flo on the hand as the train slowly pulled to a stop. It had been a horrible day for them all but for her it was especially tragic. A single telegram informed her that her family was gone and her brother was accused of murder.

"I want to go by the jail. I want to see Tom," she whispered.

"My dear, it's late. Let's get you home first. You need some rest. We'll go to the jail house tomorrow."

"Macon, Georgia," the conductor called out.

Love helped her retrieve her bag. Together they filed out.

At the top step, Flo stopped. The platform was alive with activity as passengers disembarked and baggage handlers maneuvered their loaded carts through the throng of people. Drivers shouted commands at their nervous horses. Steam belched from the engine.

Gently taking her by the elbow, Love guided her down the steps and to the waiting hack.

An incoming train whistled its approach. Folsom stood on the platform and waited. The telegram from his paper told him another reporter and an artist were coming down from Atlanta to help cover the story and for Folsom to give them every assistance.

Folsom was a Macon correspondent who spent all of his time in the Piedmont Region of the state. He knew only a few reporters who worked for the Atlanta Constitution and the telegram did not tell him whom to expect. Although he was irritated that the paper did not think he was capable of handling the story alone, he knew it was big enough for two reporters to cover.

He watched the train roll to a stop. The conductor jumped out and dropped the bottom step in place. Waiting to climb down was a short, extremely thin man. Folsom was amused at his dapper attire and small figure. The man looked around and smiled when his eyes came to Folsom.

"Folsom?"

Folsom nodded.

The boyish-faced man climbed down the steps and walked over to him.

"Call me 'Pea Jay'."

Folsom knew the name. Pascal J. Moran, better known as 'Pea Jay' was the news and telegraph editor for the Atlanta Constitution. His notoriety, however, was as the gossip columnist. The paper's managing editor, Henry Grady, made it a practice to have him cover sensational stories. When Grady sent Moran to cover a story it usually meant he intended to manipulate the public's opinion. Moran's way with words could purposefully attract or distract the public's attention depending on the political or economic agenda of the Atlanta Ring.

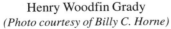
Henry Woodfin Grady
(Photo courtesy of Billy C. Horne)

Grady was a prominent member of this faction which used whatever means available for personal and political dominance in the state. The Constitution was a major tool of this alliance.

The Woolfolk murders were already sensational. Folsom shuttered to think what Pea Jay would bring into the already volatile situation, and for what purpose Grady and his cronies had in mind.

"A hell of a story," Pea Jay mumbled as he fumbled with an oversized cigar. "I hear he axed'em to death while they slept."

"I've a buggy waiting over here," Folsom said ignoring him. "I thought the telegram said there'd be an artist with you."

"There is. Over here Ramsdel," Pea Jay called out to a young man standing some distance away.

"Folsom, this is Ramsdel."

Ramsdel smiled and extended his hand. Folsom smiled weakly and then turned to Pea Jay. "It's more than twelve miles out to the house where the murders happened. You want to go on to the hotel first?"

"Hell, Folsom. Let's git on out there. We've got the murder of the century and every paper in the country's gonna send a reporter to cover it," he answered and hurried over to Folsom's buggy.

As the three men climbed aboard, a carriage with two passengers slowly rolled by. Folsom noticed one of its occupants, a woman, was crying.

"Let's git goin' Folsom. We ain't got all night." Pea Jay barked and handed him the reins.

Something told Folsom the couple was associated somehow with the murders but Pea Jay's insistence diverted his attention away from the slow moving carriage and to the task of reining his horse and buggy away from the busy train depot.

"Woolfolk," Birdsong shouted through the bars, "git up."

Tom turned over and looked at the jailer. "What time is it?" he asked.

"'Bout three a clock. Git up and git dressed."

Tom sat up slowly.

"What's goin' on?" he asked putting on his shoes.

No one answered him.

"Ready?" Westcott asked as he entered the corridor.

"Yessir. Come on Woolfolk." Birdsong opened the cell door. He held a rope in one hand and a pair of shackles in the other.

Tom stopped and stared at the rope. "What's going on? Where you taking me?"

Birdsong stepped into the cell and ordered him to stick out his hands. With the Sheriff armed and waiting behind the jailer, Tom obeyed. The shackles were heavy and tight. Roughly, Birdsong wrapped the rope tight about the prisoner's upper chest binding his arms to each side.

"Come on," he said and pulled on the rope.

Shakened and confused, Tom stumbled out of the cell.

When they entered the front office, Tom looked anxiously around. The room was empty. Westcott handed Birdsong a shotgun and was himself armed with a Colt pistol. Together they escorted their prisoner out the front door. There, they were met by two armed men.

At the door, Tom resisted, "Where you takin' me?"

"Be quiet," Westcott whispered, looking around.

Birdsong nudged him forward with the barrel of his shotgun. The five men slowly and cautiously walked down Fifth Street. The angry mob that shadowed Tom the entire day was gone. There was no one in sight.

Their two block walk to the train depot went unobserved and Westcott wanted it to stay that way. Although there was some activity at the rail station, no one seemed to notice the small group walk to the rear of the depot and into the shadows on the steps of Rubl's Ice House to wait for the train from Savannah.

Westcott waited until the platform was nearly empty before leaving the group and approaching the ticket booth. Nat Birdsong looked around nervously. The urgency at which the Sheriff removed Tom from the jail made it clear he was taking the threats against Tom seriously. Bibb County experienced lynching in the past, and there was no reason for the Sheriff to believe it would be any different in Tom's case.

Earlier, after the sun had gone down, small clusters of men gathered on nearby street corners and watched the jailhouse. Once a mysterious group rode up on horseback, slowly looked around, and then quietly rode away.

Although the family of Mattie Howard Woolfolk stayed out of the Sheriff's way at the murder scene, they were making their suspicions well known in Macon. Mattie's brother John Howard especially caused the Sheriff some alarm when it was reported the distraught man was making serious threats against Tom.

Westcott returned and instructed the group to board the train. The armed guards escorted the prisoner and his jailer to their seats in second class. Tom acted indifferent to the situation and rested his head on the back of his seat. The northbound train had few passengers and no one apparently realized who occupied the car with them.

Leaving the prisoner in Birdsong's charge, Sheriff Westcott and his deputies stood on the platform until the train disappeared into the night.

CHAPTER FOUR

"Oh, the babies...the little babies."

It was after midnight before the reporters were able to get out of Macon and on their way to Hazzard District. Folsom provided Pea Jay with the particulars of the case but did not feel obligated to elaborate. Pea Jay was known for sensationalizing his articles, taking literary license, and basically stretching the truth to the point of fiction. Using a pseudonym protected him from anyone in the general public who was negatively affected by what he wrote.

Folsom did not want to contribute to such nonsense. He was proud to put his name or his initials, "M.M.F.", to his articles. Although his writing was descriptive and to the point, it was always factual. Folsom considered himself a writer and a poet. A pseudonym was not necessary for him.

The ride to the Woolfolk house was very different from his first trip. Traffic was sparse. The night air was cool and refreshing. The full moon lighted the area and the three men could see their way clearly. Folsom was bone tired. The day had been the most tragic, intense day of his life. He rode beside the two men quietly thinking about the article he would have to write soon.

Time was running out. The paper had sent someone with more experience. Pea Jay had a reputation, a following. People loved his articles. They believed him. Altering the truth to satisfy a public starving for entertainment or to fulfill the Atlanta Ring's political objective did not seem to bother him.

Folsom, on the other hand, always felt compelled to simply write what he saw, the truth as he knew it. His copy always seemed to lack color and flare. His readers were more receptive to his Sunday columns describing picnics and socials.

He pondered on the murders, the victims, the accused man, the public outrage. Pea Jay called it the murder of the century and said that the news of the tragedy would surely be reported across the country. Folsom was on the coroner's jury and had already interviewed the suspected murderer. Thinking it all through he realized Pea Jay was no threat. He had the facts down, and, as soon as he had the time, he would have the article. His confidence returned.

"Up there's the house," he said, pointing to the light at the top of the hill.

Folsom marveled at how peaceful it looked in the near dawn light. The broad acres of the Woolfolk farm spread out before them as they turned onto the lane and continued up the hill. The canopy of oaks shrouded them in total darkness. When they emerged, they were instantly greeted with the sweet smell of flowers and dew moistened shrub.

Although there were not as many carriages, wagons, buggies, and horses as before, the number still surprised Folsom when he considered the time. The most conspicuous vehicle of all was a large black hearse adorned in silver and gold trappings with black plumes of feathers and streamers of cloth dancing in the gentle breeze.

The three men climbed down and stretched. As Folsom breathed in the fresh morning air, laughter could be heard from the front porch.

Pea Jay smiled. "People can laugh even when they're surrounded by death."

A voice from the group standing in the shadows on the porch called out to them.

"Wanna see the dead people?"

Pea Jay answered that they most certainly did and strutted up the steps.

Someone walked over to the front door and threw it open. The light from the house exploded from the structure and enveloped the three men.

They stepped into the wide hallway and stopped. To their right was the parlor where Folsom spent many grueling hours, while the Sheriff, Coroner, and Coroner's jury questioned the witnesses. Now, the lanterns in the room revealed a different scene, one for which he was not prepared. The room was full of people and opened caskets. On one side were five large black cloth covered coffins placed in a row, end to end, while on the opposite side were four more, smaller in size and draped in white.

The sheer number took Ramsdel aback. Folsom remembered the horrible scene of blood, brains, and mutilated bodies scattered about in various grotesque positions in the different rooms. Here, before them, however, was the entire family together. Nine coffins, opened for viewing.

Pea Jay walked over to the one nearest the door and looked in. Folsom followed.

"That's Temperance West. Mattie Woolfolk's great aunt," he said.

"God...how old was she?" Ramsdel whispered.

"In her eighties. She came to visit her niece."

Pea Jay shook his head. "Some visit."

The three walked over to the next coffin.

"Captain Woolfolk," Folsom said, acting as a guide to his colleagues from Atlanta.

He marveled at the undertaker's work. There was no blood. The wounds were completely clean. The Captain's hair and beard had been washed and neatly combed. With his broad shoulders and sturdy build he looked strong and definitely not as helpless as Folsom remembered.

In the next coffin was the body of the Captain's wife. Pea Jay noted her haggard, worn out look. She was not pretty. Her lips were clinched shut giving her face a harsh expression. Her large, leathery hands were folded across her hefty frame. Even in death she did not look to be at peace just angry and tired.

Next was Richard's casket and then Pearl's. Ramsdel remained at the Captain's coffin, sketching.

"Pretty girl," Pea Jay commented, looking down at Pearl's body.

She was dressed in white. Her lips were parted as if to speak.

The reporters turned to walk over to the children's coffins. McCook looked up at Folsom and mumbled, "This is a girl any man should've bin willin' to die for...any brother would be proud of." He stopped and looked at Pearl's body. "Yet, it was her no count brother's hand that killed her." Pea Jay quickly jotted his statement down.

From all Folsom had seen, he was extremely impressed with Undertaker John Clay's work. The mortician and his helpers had worked all night trying to prepare the mutilated bodies for viewing at the Woolfolk house and then burial in Macon. For all their efforts, however, there was nothing they could do for Annie. The child's wounds were so severe, so disfiguring she had to be placed on her side for viewing with her long blond hair draped over her shoulder.

Next to her was Charlie. Folsom and Pea Jay looked in and then stopped for a moment at Rosebud's small casket.

"Look's like she's smiling, don't it?" Pea Jay asked.

Folsom nodded slowly.

Finally, the reporters came to the last coffin, no larger than a carpenter's tool box. Pea Jay was able to look in before quickly walking away. Folsom stood staring down at the baby's tiny form.

"Folsom." Pea Jay called over to him, "show us where the killin' was done so Ramsdel, here, can get some sketches." Folsom had forgotten about the artist who had been quietly going about the business of quickly sketching the final portraits of the nine victims.

Folsom obliged and took them on a detailed tour of the two bedrooms. He recalled vivid memories of the bodies as they were discovered. Blood stains clearly marked where each victim died. Ramsdel drew quickly while Pea Jay jotted away in his notebook.

Reliving the gory details robbed Folsom of his remaining energy. He needed to stop. He turned, walked out onto the front porch, and dropped into the nearest rocker. Although his body ached for rest, he knew there was no time. He decided instead to relax for just a moment.

Nat Birdsong looked over at his prisoner who was still bound around the arms, his hands shackled. Tom had not moved for the first hour of the trip. His head, leaning back against the top of his seat, rocked from side to side with the movement of the train.

"You sleep?"

Tom did not answer.

"Woolfolk. You sleep?"

"Whadda ya want?"

"Didn't you get married on this train?"

Tom raised his head slightly and looked around. "No, it was on the south bound."

"That was mighty slick...gittin' a preacher to marry y'all like that. Mighty slick. Even got in the papers."

"Well, it sure didn't set well with her pa. He was fit to be tied when he found out we'd eloped." Tom chuckled lightly to himself. "I got on at Pope's Ferry and she boarded at Holton. Preacher married us right there on the train as it passed by the cemetery." He turned his head to look out the window.

"I thought it was mighty slick, mighty slick." Birdsong wanted the conversation to continue. Tom, however, did not respond. The jailer could see his prisoner's reflection in the window glass. His stare was blank.

"You murder your family?" Birdsong asked after a period of silence.

"Huh? Oh," Tom glanced over at him, "no...no, I didn't kill'em."

"I hear it was a terrible sight to see. All them dead bodies laying around...cut up like they was."

Tom shifted in his seat, leaned his head back as before, and closed his eyes. "Well," he muttered softly. "Nine of 'em are gone. The tenth will soon follow, I reckon."

The jailer stared at the prisoner sitting beside him. The train's rocking motion was relaxing him. Birdsong closed his eyes.

An hour later, Tom began shifting about in his seat. Birdsong sat up with a start realizing he had drifted off leaving his prisoner unguarded.

"These damn cuffs are cutting my wrists." Tom groaned.

Birdsong reached over and stuck his little finger between Tom's skin and the shackles. "They're fine."

"I'm telling you they're too tight."

"They stay on."

"Then...at least take this damn rope off me. My gawd man, you got it so tight I can hardly breathe," Tom growled, straining against his bindings.

His prisoner's protests and moving about in his seat caused Birdsong increased concern. The few passengers that were in the car with them began to pay closer attention. In fact, one had already recognized Tom and spoke briefly to him before the jailer discouraged further conversation.

"Sit still," he barked. "You ain't comin' outta those shackles and I ain't takin' that rope off. So calm yerself down."

"At least give me air. Open a window."

"The winder stays shut. Jeezus Woolfolk, if I didn't know better, I'd say you was gettin' nervous...'fraid of dyin'."

Tom stopped short and glared at his keeper. "I'm not afraid of dying." He dropped his head back against the seat. "My family's dead. I don't give a damn if I live or die."

Birdsong did not believe him. "Woolfolk, you're gonna hang...and you know it."

"Well...maybe so, but I'm not afraid. I can meet anything that comes my way."

Folsom woke with a start. He had no intention of falling asleep when he sat down in the porch rocker to wait for Pea Jay and Ramsdel. The sun was up and the number of people at the Woolfolk house had doubled. Ramsdel stood a short distance from the front gate drawing in his large sketch book. Pea Jay was no where to be seen.

The Macon correspondent pulled himself up and walked over to the steps.

"Ramsdel," he called out, "where's Pea Jay?"

The artist did not look up from his work but motioned that the reporter was behind the house.

Folsom hurried down the steps and disappeared around the corner. Pea Jay was standing at the well talking with a group of white men, one of whom was Sam Chambless.

Looking over at the approaching Folsom, the Atlanta reporter waved.

"Folsom, why didn't you tell me about the clothes?"

"I did tell you."

"I ain't talkin' about his dang undershirt. Why didn't you tell me about them finding his work shirt and, what was it?"

"His hat," Chambless answered.

"Yeh, his hat...in this well here. These gentlemen say that later in the day, they dropped a drag line in here and fished out a work shirt and wool hat.

Folsom realized Pea Jay had received some valuable information while he was asleep on the front porch.

"That musta been while I was at the jail interviewing the prisoner."

"Well, the way I see it, this puts the noose around his damned neck for sure."

Green Lockett approached the men.

"Mistah Chambless, suh?"

"What is it?"

"They're bringin' out d'coffins. Mistah Clay says they need help loadin'em."

The men hurried into the house. All the coffins were closed. A farmer was standing next to the Captain's nailing the lid shut. Small groups of men stood at each casket.

The undertaker looked weary, his black suit wrinkled, his hair disheveled. The old man's herculean effort to have the bodies ready to take to Macon was severely taxed by the number of victims and their disfigurements. Pressed for time, he finally had to turn to some of the Captain and Mattie's friends to help clean and dress the bodies.

Mattie's father had returned to his daughter's house and was sitting on the porch, rocking. The undertaker walked out, leaned over and spoke to the old man.

"We're ready to bring them out now."

Ben Howard nodded.

The train came to a stop. Tom had slept off and on during the hundred mile trip but was not rested. His shackles and rope bindings made his bones ache. Birdsong waited for the last passenger to leave the car before helping his prisoner to his feet.

A deputy from the Fulton County Jail met the two and escorted them to a waiting buggy. Their arrival in Atlanta had been completely secret. No one standing around the platform realized the shackled prisoner walking between the two armed men was the accused mass murderer from Macon. That early Sunday morning no one knew that the Fulton County Jail in Atlanta was to become his home for a while.

The jailer, J.J. Poole, opened the jail house door and admitted the two men. Birdsong and his prisoner were exhausted. Tom was especially tired. His eyes were swollen and red. He walked slowly, as if struggling to take the next step.

"We're gettin' a cell ready," Poole informed them as he led the way to the cell block.

Tom kept his head bowed and did not look anyone directly in the eye. His expression was unchanged, sullen and dogged.

"I'm sure you're both hungry," Poole continued. "We'll be gettin' ya somethin' to eat shortly."

Tom, in fact, was very hungry. The only meal he had in the last twenty-four hours was provided to him in the Captain's house while he was being interrogated. Chambless had offered to let his wife cook something in Mattie's kitchen, but Tom refused. He asked that his food be prepared by Emma at her house and brought to him.

Poole stopped walking and turned to speak directly to Tom. "Sheriff's gonna want to ask you a few questions when he gets in."

Tom glanced up and quickly diverted his eyes to the floor. "Spect so," he mumbled.

Poole led them into a corridor where Tom's shackles and bindings were removed. With his hands and arms finally free, he swung them about and wandered around stretching his legs. "Please give me as much freedom as ya can," he said. "Don't lock me up just yet."

His new jailer responded, "We'll do everthang we can, but 'til we git further orders we'll have to lock you up."

"Yeh, I know. But at least let me have the same freedom you're givin' the other prisoners."

"You can stay out here 'til after breakfast. But, then you'll have to be locked up in your cell."

Tom thanked him, walked over to a set of stairs and sat down.

The medicine Doc Whaley had given Flo to help her rest was working and Love Shackleford decided to let her sleep as long as possible while he went about the morning taking care of final funeral arrangements.

The night before, upon her return to her own home in East Macon, she was greeted by a group of friends and relatives as well as a member of John Clay's mortician staff. Flo discussed with him her desire to have her family buried beside her husband, Zachary, at Rose Hill Cemetery.

Early that cloudy Sunday morning, while she slept, Shackleford took the tram over to the jail where he was told that Tom had been removed to Atlanta.

The streets of Macon were unusually full of pedestrians. Small groups of people milled about on street corners. The topic of discussion did not surprise him.

Going next to the undertaker's, Shackleford was told that Clay had not returned from the Woolfolk farm. The attendant assured him the graves would be ready and that the funeral was scheduled for ten o'clock.

After sending a telegram to Forsyth for Rev. I.R. Branham, Pastor of Mount Zion Baptist Church, asking him to perform the services, he stopped to purchase the Sunday Edition of the Macon Telegraph. The street vendor was surrounded by eager patrons anxiously waiting for news of the murders.

When Love finally got a copy, he instantly became absorbed by it. On the front page was a picture of Tom and a headline written in large bold letters, "A FAMILY SLAUGHTER." Beneath it in smaller print was the subheadline, "NINE OF A HOUSEHOLD MURDERED WITH A WOOD AXE."Gradually, headings columned downward towards the article, each providing more information.

"R.F. Woolfolk of Bibb County, His Wife, Four Daughters, Two Sons, and the Wife's Aunt, Killed Early Yesterday Morning." The article stated. "Thomas Woolfolk, the Eldest Son, Charged With The Crime."

The newspaper described in graphic details the condition of the murdered bodies, witness testimonies given to the coroner's jury, and a floor plan of the Captain's home.

Shackleford was even surprised by a small article describing how Flo received the news.

"Incredible," he muttered quietly to himself.

Koscinsko C. Taylor, Clerk of Mt. Zion Baptist Church, walked through the empty sanctuary to the back office and sat down at the preacher's desk. He opened the church record and began to write.

"August 7th, 1887. No meeting today, a few to discuss the sad, brutal murders of Sister Pearl Woolfolk by her half-brother, Thomas G. Woolfolk.

"Friday night, August 5th, between 12 o'clock and day, Thomas G. Woolfolk, son of Richard F. Woolfolk by his first wife, 27 years old, did commit such an act the most horrible deed known to civilized mankind by killing: his father, Richard F. Woolfolk, age 54,

his step-mother, Mattie Woolfolk, age 41,

"   " brother, R. F. Woolfolk, age 20,

"   " brother, Charlie H. Woolfolk, age 5,

"   " sister, Pearl Woolfolk, age 17,

"   " sister, Annie Woolfolk, age 10,

"   " sister, Rosebud Woolfolk, age 7,

"   " sister, Mattie Woolfolk, 18 months,

and Mrs. Tempe West, age 84 years.

"The boddies, except Mrs. West, are to be buried today in East Macon. Mrs. West's remains will be carried to Americus.

"This, the bloodiest of Georgia, was commited in Bibb Co. about 5 miles from Mt. Zion Baptist Church. I suppose the burial and awful sadness kept the pastor and people from attending church. May God our Father grant that this may be the most blood curdling record I may ever pen."

One by one, the caskets were brought out. Pearl and Rosebud were put in the first wagon. John Howard, Mattie's brother, carried the baby's coffin and laid it beside the Captain's in the second one. Mattie was placed in the next while Richard, Jr.'s casket went in the fourth. The fifth wagon contained Mrs. West while Charlie's coffin was put in Clay's black hearse. A buggy was borrowed to carry Annie's small white casket.

When all were loaded, John Howard walked over to his father and told him it was time to go. The old man was helped to his feet. Leaning heavily on his cane he looked out at the seven hearses and then turned to look through the front door.

'The Homeplace' had been his gift to his daughter when she married Captain Woolfolk some twenty years earlier. The Captain was in serious financial trouble at the time and was on the verge of losing his home. Out of love for his only daughter, Howard purchased the plantation from his new son-in-law and then gave it to her.

"Pa," John said, gently taking his father's elbow. "They're ready to go."

The old man looked up at his son. Tears were rolling down his cheek. He was crying.

Emma Jones stood beside her husband. Together they watched the long procession file slowly by, wagon after wagon, coffin after coffin. Luanna and London Cooper, Fanny Lockett, and the James stood with them next to Lockett's shack. One by one the wagons containing the caskets rolled by. The sight of the small white coffins brought tears to Emma's eyes.

Luanna wailed, "There goes Miz Mattie. I nussed her, an' took care of her when she was sick. She was always a good woman. Lawd bless you, Miz Mattie. I'll see you in heaven, but that boy who killed you will roast in hell."

Aaron put his arm around Emma.

"Aaron," she said tearfully, "I never thought I'd see such a thang."

"Me neither, honey. Me neither."

Behind the seven hearses came the Howards and other relatives, then friends and finally the tag alongs.

Folsom was numb from exhaustion as were the two men riding with him. Bringing up the rear, the reporter noted that the funeral procession stretched at least a mile or longer and slowly wound its way through the country-side like a long, slow moving snake. Onlookers gathered at cross roads, and, with every mile, the line of vehicles grew longer.

The roadside watchers were reverent. Farmers stood with their hats to their hearts or at their sides. Children leaned anxiously into the folds of their mothers' skirts while their mothers clutched handkerchiefs to their bosoms.

The number of watchers increased as the caravan made its way into the city, and, although it had begun to rain, the drizzle did not discourage the mourners, the sympathizers, and the simply curious from turning out.

Down Columbus Road, onto Johnston Street and then College Street it went. As the death march filed pass Wesleyan College, Pearl's classmates lined the street. Some became hysterical, but the majority tenderly held each other and wept quietly.

Rose Hill Cemetery, situated on a high bluff overlooking the Ocmulgee River, rose up to meet them. The gentle rain fell harder and the umbrellas of more than two thousand mourners waiting for the funeral procession covered the cemetery grounds like a black gravecloth.

As the multitude opened the carriage way for the hearse and dead wagons to pass down Central Avenue to the Woolfolk grave plot, some two hundred yards from the river, grave-diggers went on about their business. Although a work crew large enough to handle the number of graves was employed, progress was impeded by large boulders. The pall bearers carried the nine coffins to an adjacent lot and gently placed them side by side on the ground.

The hillside was covered with mourners as the rain continued to fall. A few minutes after ten o'clock, it gradually ceased and Rev. I.R. Branham took his place between the two rows of coffins.

He stood in silence for a moment, waiting for the noise to cease. Looking up at the thousands of on-lookers, all dressed in black and standing beneath large black umbrellas, he waited. The noise slowly died away. He began to pray.

The preacher prayed not only for the souls of the victims and the surviving family members but also for Tom.

"Whatever may be his destiny, O Lord, prepare him for it."

Clerk Taylor, returned to the church to correct his error. At the bottom of the page in the church record he wrote:

"P.S. The Woolfolk family were burried in Rosehill Cemetery it was a mistake about the burial elsewhere."

Tom was finally given his breakfast which he devoured while he sat on the steps waiting for his cell to be ready. As soon as his presence in Atlanta became known, a constant stream of visitors requested entrance to the jail and audience with him.

Tom was ordered to his cell. His quiet, cooperative manner impressed his keepers and made it more difficult for them to believe he was guilty of such a vicious crime.

His first visitor was a reporter for the Macon Telegraph who found the prisoner kneeling on a blanket in the center of the cell. Tom had taken off his shirt and was simply wearing a vest.

"Tom, I'm with the Macon Telegraph," the reporter stated.

Without moving from his position, Tom stretched out his hand. "Glad to see ya."

"Tom, would you like to make a statement about the murders?"

"No. I have no statement t'make. I don't want to talk about that at all."

"Not at all?"

"It's too sad. Can't we talk 'bout something else? Anything. Just not that," he said, nervously rubbing his arms, his bottom lip quivering.

"I'm sorry, Tom. I'm here to get a statement about the murders."

"I haven't got anything to say about that. Let's talk about something else."

The reporter closed his notebook. "Sorry, Tom," he said and walked away.

As the Reverend's words filtered up through the crowd, a plea for passage through the multitude surrounding the coffins was heard.

"Oh please, please, let me by," Flo cried as she and Love anxiously worked their way through the mass of mourners. The two had started on their way to the funeral early, but the tremendous number of vehicles, equestrians, and pedestrians prevented them from arriving sooner.

Unable to gain access to the cemetery by way of carriage, they had to walk the remaining half mile in the rain.

"Please let me see them," she begged. "Please let me see my father and mother."

Dr. Branham stopped talking.

"Please, I couldn't get here sooner, please let me through."

The Reverend waited patiently.

"Oh God, can't you let me see them just once, just once."

Finally, Flo emerged from the wall of humanity; her face hidden by a black veil. Shackleford pushed through the crowd behind her and was at her side. Flo looked pleadingly at the Preacher and then at the nine boxes at his feet. Seeing for the first time the children's small white coffins, she collapsed upon her father's casket and began weeping.

"Oh, the babies...the little babies."

Love gently lifted her up, and, with her sobbing on his shoulder, he walked with her back into the crowd.

Dick, Jr. (left) as a teenager and Pearl (right).
(Photos courtesy of Mrs. Jessie Balkcom)

Mattie E. Howard Woolfolk with Little Mattie. Charlie is seated beside her. This photo is believed to have been taken only months before the murders. (Photos still missing: Temperance West, Annie and Rosebud Woolfolk)

Marble step marking the burial plot that contains the unmarked graves of the nine victims, Rosehill Cemetery, Macon, GA
(Photo courtesy of Sandy Kallas)

CHAPTER FIVE

"I want to correct a statement in the newspaper."

Sunday, August seventh, Bibb County put to rest nine members of the Woolfolk family. Only three children remained. The oldest, Floride, thirty three years old and the widow of Zachary T. Edwards, took to her bed immediately after returning from the funeral. Her thirty year old sister, Lillie, wife of Henry P. Cowan, had yet to arrived from Hawkinsville, Georgia. The third child and the Captain's first son was Thomas G. Woolfolk. He awaited his fate in Atlanta at the Fulton County Jail. The charge was murder.

Reporters from across the country hounded the survivors, distant relatives, neighbors, and officials. Pea Jay was right. It was the murder of the century.

In Macon, Folsom watched Pea Jay and Ramsdel board the north bound train and then returned to his room at the Lanier House for a desperately needed rest. The Macon correspondent had been up and involved with the tragic story for more than thirty hours.

Samuel Chambless, Ben Burnett, Robert Wright, and William Smith mutually assumed responsibility for the care of the Woolfolk farm with Chambliss acting as caretaker until the Howard family or an administrator of the Woolfolk Estate could be appointed.

Tom, meanwhile, waited in his cell. He was rapidly becoming a celebrity as Atlantans rushed to the jailhouse in hopes of seeing what manner of a man could slaughter his entire family.

A friend from Macon was allowed to see the prisoner although he did not enter the cell. State Representative James Schofield greeted Tom with genuine compassion.

Schofield had known Tom for many years. The two developed a close friendship when Tom operated the saloon and grocery on Third Street in Macon. Tom actually was no better than his father when it came to running a commercial enterprise. Citizens of the area forgot about the Captain's financial ineptness. Tom's failures, however, they seemed to remember very well.

Not wanting the nosy prisoners exercising in the corridor to overhear their conversation, Schofield leaned closer to the bars and whispered, "How you doin' Tom?"

Tom greeted his friend quietly, "Mornin' Jim."

The friends stood facing each other with the barred door between them. The only noise came from the prisoners who crowded behind Schofield to listen.

"Tom?" Schofield finally spoke up. "If there is anything I can do for you? I mean, anything at all, you just name it."

The prisoner's smile was faint. "Much obliged."

Neither man mentioned the murders. Schofield was uncomfortable. His friend's quiet, sullen demeanor did not stimulate conversation.

He again assured Tom of his desire to help make his life in the cell more comfortable. Then he said goodbye. Tom smiled, picked up the Atlanta Constitution he was reading before Schofield's visit and began to read.

As Schofield made his way down the corridor the jailer escorting a small man dressed in a three piece pinstriped suit and a brown derby, walked by him. Schofield stopped and realized the man was going to Tom's cell. Curious, he decided to see who the new visitor was.

"Woolfolk, my name is Moran. I'm with the Atlanta Constitution."

Tom was lying face down on his cell floor. His arms were folded beneath his forehead to serve as a pillow. He ignored the greeting.

Schofield called out over the reporter's shoulder. "Tom, it's me again. Jim Schofield."

Tom slowly got up and walked to the door. The cell was dark with only a faint light filtering through the small window. It was light enough, however, for Moran to see him clearly.

The prisoner was bare-chested and barefooted. He was of medium height and had a strong, compact physique. His back was straight, with shoulders square and a prominent chest. He was a fine, healthy man. His features were pleasing and quiet. Pea

Jay did not expect to find the accused mass murderer to be so handsome.

The turnkey admitted the two men into Tom's cell and then left. The prisoner put on his vest and sat down on his cot. He would not look anyone in the eye. His bottom lip was quivering.

"Mistah Woolfolk, I'd like to ask you a few questions if I may."

"I want..." Tom stopped and swallowed. Schofield looked at his friend and realized he was upset.

"I want," he began again, "to correct a statement in the newspaper." Tom muttered, looking up at the reporter and then quickly glancing away.

"What statement's that?" Moran asked, smiling.

Tom picked up his tightly rolled newspaper, walked over to the window, and began to search the front page. His trembling hands caused the paper to shake so violently he was unable to find what he was looking for. Schofield wanted to reach over and assist his friend but he remained in the background.

Moran took a step forward, still smiling. "Maybe if you would tell me what it is you're looking for, I could find it for you."

Tom said nothing. The prisoners standing around the door were silent. The two men in the cell waited for his response.

Tom turned slightly. "That statement about my sister!" He spoke slowly, his lips trembling. A muscle twitched in his neck.

His voice quivered as he continued. "I don't know who wrote that...I don't want to know. But if I ever get out of here..."

Tom stopped and walked over to the door. "It's a lie. That whole thing is a lie." He took a deep breath, held it and then let it out slowly. He had regained control. His trembling stopped. His voice returned to its original quiet tone. There was no longer a sign of emotion.

"I don't want you to print that," he said blankly.

Schofield took the paper from Tom's clinched fist and surveyed the front page. Quickly, he scanned through Folsom's lengthy article. It was factual and reported the same information as had his own hometown paper, the Macon Telegraph.

He walked over to the window for more light, and searched further. After Folsom's report, there was a second article that gave some additional facts about the coroner's investigation, the clothes in the well, and Tom's marriage months earlier.

Reading on, however, he finally came to the part that had his friend so upset. "There are facts which cannot be put in type that are going to show that for several days Tom meditated a most fiendish assault upon his sister," the article stated. "The theory founded, and it is not inconsistent with the evidence, is that Tom watched for an opportunity to enter his sister's chamber.

"The only alarm heard during the night was the scream of a woman. It was the voice of Miss Pearl as she resisted the attack of Tom Woolfolk, and breaking from his grasp, rushed to her father's room. Seeing himself thus in danger of exposure he grasped an ax..."

Stunned, Schofield stopped reading and immediately checked the end of the article for the reporter's byline.

He was dumbfounded. The author of the article was standing beside him acting so understanding of Tom's anguish. Tom apparently did not know that P.J. Moran's pseudenym was 'Pea Jay', the one and the same. Tom was conversing with the very reporter who wrote the article that had him so upset.

Pea Jay smiled politely at Schofield.

Tom regained his composure. Pea Jay appeared disappointed.

"Who killed your mother, Mistah Woolfolk?" the reporter asked.

Tom stared at the ceiling.

"I didn't kill my ma. I have no idea who did...and I have no idea who killed the others."

"Were you in the house that night?"

"I was in the house that night. I spent the night there," he said turning away. Suddenly, he jerked around and faced Schofield.

"Don't you know that a man wouldn't act like this paper says I did towards my own sister!" he said, pointing towards the paper.

"I know Tom," his friend responded quietly.

Tom took the paper from Schofield's hand and turned back to Pea Jay. "I don't know anything more about the matter, 'cept what I said to Folsom in Macon."

"Don't you think you ought to correct the false assertions made about you?" Pea Jay asked as he tapped the notebook lightly with his pencil. Schofield detected a slight smile.

"They found your shirt, you know." Pea Jay continued.

"Not mine, I reckon."

"They found it where you put it." He paused, then smiled. "...in the well."

"It must of been somebody else's shirt. It wasn't mine."

"How many shirts you got?"

"Two--one out there, and the one I have here." Tom pointed to a shirt hanging on a peg above his cot.

"Well...the one they found out there looks like that one there," Pea Jay said nonchalantly, "except it's got blood and brains on it."

"It's not mine. I don't see why you accuse me of the murder. I had no reason for killing them. Whoever did it must have put the shirt there."

"Mistah Woolfolk, a lot more points to your guilt."

"Well..." he answered flatly. "I didn't do it."

The prisoner walked over to the door and rested a hand on a bar. "I...I don't feel like talking anymore," he muttered. "I don't like to talk 'bout it. It's too, too sad."

He turned to Schofield. "You said to tell you if there's anything you could do for me."

"Yes, Tom, anything."

"Find Judge Nisbet for me. Ask him to come see me," he said softly. "Please, Jim, get the Judge for me."

Tom turned to Pea Jay and finished, "I'll talk then."

Interpreting the statement to mean Tom was ready to confess, Pea Jay jumped at the opportunity and told Schofield he knew exactly where to find the Judge.

"I'll do what I can," Schofield promised before leaving.

Judge James T. Nisbet, a member of an influential Macon family, was the private secretary to Georgia Governor John B. Gordon in Atlanta. Schofield explained to the reporter as they made their way to the Capitol that Nisbet had handled some legal matters for Tom in the past when he was a practicing lawyer in Macon.

"With the Judge now up here in Atlanta, and Tom in such a terrible spot, it makes sense that he'd ask him for help," Schofield said.

Pea Jay felt certain that his conversation convinced Tom of the futility of protesting his innocence and was planning to confess to the Judge.

Schofield shook his head in disagreement.

"You don't know Tom Woolfolk. There's a lot of things that man 'll do but killin' his whole family isn't one of them."

"So...of the thousands of people who believe he's guilty, someone speaks up in his defense."

"If Tom said he didn't do it...then I believe him."

The two men went first to the Capitol. Pea Jay told Schofield of the Governor's habit of going by his office after Sunday breakfast.

No one was there.

Their next stop was the Governor's mansion where they were told to try Nisbet's sister's on Ivy Street. He was not there either. They found him, in fact, at his own residence on Capitol Avenue. Schofield wondered why Pea Jay had not taken him there first unless the reporter wanted the extra time to get as much information as possible from him. He was, afterall, a friend of the accused.

They both climbed the steps to the veranda. The Judge was asleep in a large rocker, his feet propped on the porch railing.

"S'cuse me, sir." Pea Jay called out. Nisbet woke up. "I'm P. J. Moran with the Atlanta Constitution and you know Congressman Schofield from Macon."

"Of course. Jim, it's good to see you," the Judge greeted them.

"We have come from the cell of Tom Woolfolk," the reporter annouced proudly as he walked on to the porch.

"I was just reading about that very thing this morning. A terrible tragedy. And they think young Woolfolk did it."

"Judge," Schofield spoke up, "Tom's asking for you."

"Really?" Nisbet said, leaning forward in his chair.

"Yes, sir. He sent me to ask if you'd come by the jail as soon as possible."

"How's he doin'?"

"Alright, I guess. He's pretty upset about what the newspapers are saying."

"I can understand why." Nisbet stood and shook hands with his visitors. "I have a few matters to attend to first. If you gentlemen will call for me here at three o'clock, I'll accompany you to the jail."

As the two men walked away from the Judge's house, Pea Jay marveled at his good fortune. He had scooped Folsom again.

The telegraph messenger rapped loudly at Folsom's door. The reporter had been asleep only a few hours but woke with no problem.

The boy handed him the message and waited for his reply. Folsom fumbled through his vest pocket before retrieving a coin. Without looking, he handed it over and then absentmindedly closed the door.

Walking over to the window, the reporter used the sunlight to read the message.

"Please come see me at your earliest convenience. I have something of major importance to tell you. Signed, Mrs. John R. Crane, 774 Prince Avenue, Athens, Georgia."

Judge Nisbet walked through the crowd outside the jail. Reporters shouted questions at him. People pushed and shoved to be near him. Schofield and Pea Jay served as bodyguards and helped him get through the mob.

Once they were in the jailhouse, the Judge stopped and turned to his escorts. "Gentlemen, you are aware that if Tom has called me here for legal counseling I will have to see him in private."

"But...," Pea Jay tried to protest.

"At which time, I will immediately advise him to stop talking to the press," Nisbet finished with authority.

Pea Jay was dumbfounded. Schofield smiled. The two men agreed to wait for the Judge in the office and watched as the turnkey escorted Nisbet into the cell area.

In the corridor, the Young Men's Christian Association was conducting church services. Prayers were being said and Bible verses read. The Judge politely walked through the gathering and stopped at Tom's cell door. Tom had not joined in the religious exercise.

The turnkey admitted Nisbet into Tom's cell.

"Well, Tom. This is a serious situation you're in," he said. "What can I do for you?"

Tom greeted him with a handshake. "I want you to defend me."

Nisbet gathered his thoughts before answering. "Tom, this will be a very difficult and extremely complicated case. I would not be able to give it the attention it will require."

"Judge, my pa's estate is worth between twenty-five and thirty thousand dollars. I'll give a handsome fee to any lawyer who'll defend me."

"Tom, I need time to think this over. I can't give you an answer just yet. Let me consider your offer and get back with you Tuesday afternoon."

Pea Jay and Schofield waited in the jailer's office. Loud singing floated from the corridor. The reporter was agitated and anxious to know what Tom was telling the Judge.

The turnkey approached the two men. "Judge says y'all can come on back now."

Pea Jay leapt out of his chair and the three filed through the throng of singing prisoners.

Tom and Nisbet stood facing each other in Tom's cell. The prisoner was fully clothed, having cleaned himself up for the Judge's visit, and stood with his arms folded.

The turnkey opened the cell door and Tom greeted his guests. "Gentlemen," he said warmly, "I'll be glad to talk about anything, but you must excuse me from talking about the murders."

"That's alright, Tom," Schofield replied.

"It's too sad...too sad," Tom answered, shaking his head slowly.

"But...what else is there to talk about?" Pea Jay asked.

Tom smiled and shook his head. "I can't help it. It's too sad for me to talk about."

Pea Jay glanced over at the Judge who sat quietly on the cot. He pulled a cigar from his coat pocket. The turnkey walked over to his side and struck a match. Nisbet leaned over and lit his cigar. Pea Jay looked back at Tom and then at the smiling Schofield.

"Then...I guess there's nothing for me here," the reporter remarked. He donned his derby and asked to be excused.

"Wait, suh. I think we should both join you," Nisbet spoke up. "The prisoner needs his privacy. Turnkey, the door please."

The jailer unlocked the cell door and led the men back through the praying group.

In the outer office, Judge Nisbet explained to the reporter that the prisoner had requested his legal assistance and that he would seriously consider it.

"And what if you don't take the case?" Schofield asked.

"Tom won't have any trouble finding representation. This case will make lawyers famous."

"So, uh, Judge? Did he, uh, did he confess?" Pea Jay queried, grinning broadly.

"Gentlemen, as the prisoner's temporary legal advisor, I can not divulge the content of our discussion. I can tell you this much. He adamantly insists he is innocent and denies any knowledge or participation in the crime."

Schofield offered to take the Judge home. Pea Jay half-heartedly decided to join them.

Sarah Hardin faced the deputy. "That ain't Mistah Tom's shirt, I tell you." The Woolfolk's laundress placed her hands on her hips and stood her ground.

The deputy held the clothes Sheriff Westcott sent for her verification. Sarah was aware that Sam Chambless had pulled some clothes out of the well the day the murdered family was discovered.

"That ain't Mistah Tom's. This shirt here is Mistah Dick's. And this hat? This hat b'longs to Silas Woolfolk."

"Who's Silas Woolfolk?"

"Oh...he's just a field hand what used to work for d'Cap'n."

"Are you sure?" He questioned her again.

The white woman stared him directly in the eyes. "Look here, I'm the Woolfolk's washer woman. I know their clothes better than they do. And this here ain't Mistah Tom's stuff."

"Alright. Alright. I'll be sure to tell the Sheriff what you said. But you agree that this is his undershirt. Right?"

Sarah stared at the garment in the deputy's other hand. The shirt was dry and stained red. She nodded.

"That'uns his."

"You sure?"

"I'm sure."

Judge Nisbet considered the reporter's request for a statement and decided it would not be a breech of confidence if he gave Pea Jay some background information.

"I've known him, Thomas Woolfolk, that is...oh...'bout ten years, I guess. I've known a great many Woolfolks in my time. His grandfather, his father, uncles. I've known'em all since I was a boy."

Pea Jay eagerly jotted down the Judge's statements and allowed him to ramble along uninterrupted.

"His grandfather was a very rich man and lived at Fort Hawkins, about a stone's throw from the old frontier fort. The place was on the east side of the Ocmulgee River. His uncle, John Woolfolk, is a very respectable citizen of Houston County. His other uncles, James and Thomas Woolfolk, live near Woolfolk Station on the Macon and Augusta Railroad in Jones County."

The Judge called for some water to be brought out onto the veranda. Pea Jay continued writing.

"I'd say his other relatives across the state are of the highest respectability. Of those murdered, now...let's see...I knew his father, mother, Richard, and Miss Pearl. Mattie, Mrs. Woolfolk, was the daughter of one of my nearest neighbors. Ben Howard. Excellent man. A deacon of the Mt. Zion Baptist Church."

A servant, carrying a pitcher of water and three glasses on a silver tea tray, interrupted him. Offering some water to his guests, the Judge poured himself a glass and took a large swallow.

"Pearl," he continued, shaking his head, "I knew her when she was about fourteen years old...she had the makings of becoming a handsome, interesting woman.

"Ben Howard has a large connection in Bibb County. All of them are excellent, respectable people. Now...Tom...," Nisbet mumbled, patting his pockets as he looked for a match to light the large cigar he had clinched between his teeth. "Now...Tom..."

Pea Jay quickly pulled a match from his pocket and lit the Judge's cigar.

"Thank you. Now where was I?"

"You were telling him about Tom," Schofield said.

"Oh..yes, yes. Tom leased a plantation about two miles of my place in Bibb County, under a conditional contract of purchase from Colonel Albert Foster of Morgan County. He cultivated the land a number of years after Colonel Foster's death.

"The boy had a reputation of being a very energetic planter with some talent for handling the negroes and for making good crops. Not being able to pay for the property, though, he was obliged to surrender it. He then went to Macon and opened a store on Third Street where he sold groceries and liquor."

"Where on Third Street?" The reporter asked.

Schofield spoke up, "On Guernsey's block."

"It wasn't a success, though, and he left the business. I heard he then went to Texas with the idea of settling down there," Nisbet stated between puffs.

"How long was he out there?"

The Judge looked at Schofield for an answer.

"Oh...just a few months," Schofield responded. "When he came back, he opened a small store on the Vineville Branch between Vineville and Macon."

"I saw him in his store, oh...last September or October. Hadn't seen him since...until today that is," Nisbet elaborated.

Schofield took over the conversation. "He broke up the Vineville store in March. Some time between then and now he stayed in Athens. He then went to Hazzard District."

"He got married on the East Tennessee train," the Judge added, "as it was running between Macon and Flovilla. But...like everything else...it didn't work out for him and his wife left. He said that's how he came to be at the Captain's. He went there about a week ago and was working in the fields."

"What did the people out in Hazzard District think about him?"

"Well," Nisbet said between puffs, "his reputation in the neighborhood was that of a very, well, perverse obstinate, an eccentric. And, to use a slang expression, a 'cranky' sort of fellow. When he lived alone at the Foster Plantation, he had very few associates and no friends. I'd say his life was bare of incidents."

The three men ignored the setting sun and the coming of darkness. Pea Jay's notebook was nearly full. The Judge's cigar was almost gone.

"The boy loved money, had a great desire for it. But he lived economically...and...well, when he was away or at certain times and on certain occasions, he would spend money very freely." The Judge was tired. His comments were becoming short.

"He lived roughly. His room was no better than that of many a negro. He didn't seem to care much for such matters. But... he liked other luxuries and was fond of good horses. He usually had a fine horse and buggy."

"While he craved money," Schofield added, "he spent it recklessly and if his mind was warped at all, it was on money."

"If he's guilty," Nisbet continued, "if he's guilty of the crime alleged...a great many people who know him well will believe he was insane at the time of its commission."

"Why?" Pea Jay asked, thankful the subject of Tom's sanity finally came up.

"Well...because of their knowledge of his character and because of their conviction that no sane man would commit such an atrocious and horrible crime. It's a terrible charge against him," Judge Nisbet continued, "and yet, were you not struck with his manner of receiving you this afternoon? Do you not remember how he said he couldn't talk about it because it was too sad? How he smiled pleasantly during the conversation? Now tell me gentlemen, is this wonderful self-control...or is it an innocent conscience, free from all complicity in this terrible matter?"

The Judge's guests sat staring at him in disbelief. Nisbet cleared his throat and shifted in his chair. "I don't want to appear a partisan...for I'm not. But the sanity or the insanity of the man was mooted, and I just mentioned this little incident."

CHAPTER SIX

"He...he has no one."

The loud shrill of the locomotive's steam whistle echoed through the countryside as the single-car passenger train pulled out of Macon's Union Station on its way towards Athens.

Folsom unfolded the August 8th Edition of the Macon Telegraph and began to read. As expected, the front page was dedicated to the Woolfolk funeral.

He quickly scanned the article. Finding nothing that disagreed with his own report he turned the page.

Inside, two editorials caught his eye. The first was entitled, 'Scandalous Journalism' and commanded serious attention from the reporter.

> "It is very much to be regretted that a writer in yesterday's Constitution should have endeavored to add to the horror of the Woolfolk tragedy, by arguing that Tom Woolfolk had either outraged, or attempted to outrage, his sister Pearl, and to protect himself from discovery of that crime, the wholesale slaughter was made.
>
> The writer of the article signs himself Pea Jay. He is more or less familiar to the people of Georgia by his sensational and generally unreliable contributions over that 'nom de plume' to the Constitution."

The reporter, absorbed by the contents of the editorial, disregarded the conversations about the Woolfolk tragedy that were taking place all around him. The editorial continued.

> "There are numerous inaccuracies and misstatements in Pea Jay's two columns, but they are insignificant compared with the new horror added to the terrible crime as it happened.

There is no evidence to prove rape, or to suggest the crime; but there is every possible reason to affirm that no such assault was made. The people of Bibb County, and the Woolfolk family connections in particular, will not thank the Constitution for publishing widespread, a horror even more detestable than murder, which had no foundation in fact or justifiable inference. Such a wanton attempt to add to the horror of the most terrible murdering known, must bring its own retribution from a conservative and truth-loving public."

Folsom smiled. Finally, Pea Jay had been called to task.

The second editorial reflected the general opinion of the community. Citizens throughout the region were demanding a speedy trial.

"The Judge of this circuit is now absent from this State, and may be for some time, but the prosecuting officer desires that the case shall stand until the regular term in October. He does not think that justice will be delayed by this, but that it may be hindered by earlier action.

"If arraigned speedily Woolfolk's counsel would move for a continuance, upon the grounds of public excitement, occasioned by the crime itself, and the grounds for this are by no means weak. This trial, when it does come off, will excite this community as it has never before been moved. In the meantime, there may be important developments. At present, the case stands upon circumstantial evidence alone. While this is conclusive to all intelligent minds, there may be corroborative facts that will aid to clinch the conclusion."

Judge Nisbet picked up his stack of correspondence and examined an envelope labelled 'personal'. The writer was an old friend from Macon, Charles Howard, Mattie Woolfolk's brother. The Judge placed the remainder of his mail on his desk and, standing, he opened the letter.

Nisbet felt compassion for Mattie's family. He could only imagine the level of their grief. The Howards were close friends and he did not want to lose them. Even members of the Judge's own family were outraged when they heard he was considering Tom's request. He decided to turn him down.

Dr. William H. Felton could not hide his anger. The state representative's argument on the convict-lease system continued to lead the House in an uproar.

He jumped to his feet and shouted, "Why just the other day, gentlemen, down in Bibb County, a young man butchered his father and his father's family. I tell you evil is in our everyday life."

He pointed his finger at his chief opponent, Representative Simmons.

"And, gentlemen, I give you the 'Woolfolk' of this legislature."

It had begun. The once proud name of Woolfolk was being used in the same context of evil.

"Mrs. Crane?" Folsom addressed the woman at the door. "Mrs. Crane, I'm with the Atlanta Constitution."

"Mr. Folsom?" she asked, smiling weakly.

"Yes ma'am."

"Oh...please, do come in."

The reporter followed his hostess into the parlor where she offered him a seat.

"I must admit. I was surprised to get your telegram asking me to come see you," he said and sat down.

"Well...," she started, nervously, "...I didn't know what else to do. I knew I had to talk to someone."

"Have you talked with the Sheriff?"

"No, no one has come by here. But then what do I know?"

She looked at her guest. Her eyes were still red and swollen from days of crying. Folsom could see her pain.

"I didn't go to the funeral, you know."

"Yes ma'am."

"I just couldn't. It's all so horrible, so horrible." Her eyes began to fill with tears.

"Mrs. Crane, is there something you would like to tell me?"

"Yes...there is. I've thought about this over and over and I feel there's some things that need to be said. That's why I sent for you."

She was sitting on the sofa beside him. Her hands were folded in her lap and one held a handkerchief. She took a deep breath, and looked away.

"Thomas Woolfolk," she began in a soft, sweet voice, "is my nephew. Captain Richard Woolfolk's first wife was my own sister. Tommy's mother died a short time after his birth, so I had the care of him until he was eight years old. I was very fond of him and he said he loved me better than anybody in the world." Her voice cracked.

Folsom looked up from his notes and smiled sympathetically. "Take your time, Ma'am."

She dabbed her eyes with her handkerchief and continued. "I feel there are some things that I can say about him which may change the public feeling against him. At least, influence people...against hasty action...until Tommy can be tried or examined. He...he has no one."

She stopped and looked down at her hands. She folded and unfolded her handkerchief. Folsom waited patiently.

"You see...he has no one to speak for him. No one in the world, but me, perhaps."

"What about his sisters?"

"His sister, Flo, is prostrate with grief. His other sister, Lillie, is away...and, and although disliking publicity, I am going to tell you something which I want you to publish."

Folsom nodded.

"Of course, I don't know if Tommy did that terrible thing or not. But if he did, I am convinced he was not responsible for his acts."

Folsom tried to control the excitement her words were generating within him.

"Do you know that I have known that Tommy, that, well...," she paused and considered her words carefully, "that...he was losing his mind? His sisters and I have frequently spoken of it and we've written about it. We told Captain Woolfolk, of course, and friends outside the family have suspected it. And everytime I have seen Tommy over the years his condition has been worse and worse."

"When did you first notice this?" Folsom asked.

The woman thought for a moment. "Three years ago. My husband, John Ross, and I were visiting Macon during the fair in November. I noticed then that Tommy was...well...peculiar. At the time, he was living alone on the Foster place, near Macon. He was left much to himself, as none of his family lived near him.

"Mr. Crane, my husband, noticed that something was wrong, and commented on it. Since that time, Tom's sister, Mrs. Floride Edwards, has been convinced of Tom's...uh...aberrations and had written to me repeatedly of the strange actions of her brother.

"Mrs. Edwards has visited me here for two summers. Last year she told me, again, that she did not understand Tom at all. She knew that he did not drink. He said he tried once or twice to drink but couldn't. It made him sick every time."

Fannie Crane stood up and walked over to a small table. She poured herself a glass of water and graciously offered one to her guest. Folsom declined.

"Last December," she continued as she walked back over to the sofa, "last December I was in Macon. Tom was at his sister's. Oh, it was terrible. He was cross, irritable and suspicious. If he saw us talking together, he'd fly into a passion and say we were plotting against him.

"Tommy had said to me often that his sister was his enemy. He said he told his father the same thing. I knew this was absurd, everyone did. His sister Flo was good and kind to him. I told Floride then and there that I hated to have her live in the house with Tom. He was so...peculiar and I feared that he would harm her. But she said she could not refuse him room. He had no place else to go."

As his hostess rambled on, Folsom wrote as quickly as possible. He pressed his pencil hard against the pad that was resting on his knee and scribbled in his own crude form of shorthand. She spoke slowly and with determination. It was not difficult to keep up with her.

"Last March, he was in Athens and paid me a visit. His malady, or whatever it was, seemed to have complete possession of him. He was agitated all the time. He paced the floor the whole time he was in the house. He kept his lamp burning all night and his talk at times was, was incoherent."

"How exactly?" Folsom asked.

"Well...for instance...he would tell Mr. Crane about going into business here, then would break off into another subject...sometimes frivolous and entirely unrelated. Well...Mr. Crane said he thought Tom was losing his mind."

"Really?"

"Well, yes. And Tom said he wanted one of the boys to stay upstairs with him at night. To tell you the truth...I was afraid to trust him with a child."

She told how he convinced her one time to take a trip with him to visit her brother some distance away. "But before we got there, he wanted to turn around and come back immediately. Well...I told him we would offend the family and would have to stay for dinner. The whole time we were there he stayed out in the yard...with his hat on. It took a lot for us to convince him to even come inside for dinner.

"Tommy always carried a pistol, but I insisted before we took the trip that I wanted him to leave it home. He did, of course. Shortly after Mr. Crane's death, last June, Tom surprised me with a visit. He said he had heard about the state I was in and came right up."

"And how did he act then?"

"Oh, much stranger. He would ask me the same question over and over again. When I had company, he would call me out of the parlor repeatedly. When I would explain something to him he did not seem to remember it fifteen minutes later. Once Tommy asked me to go upstairs and talk to him but my son James would not let me go. Tommy would write letters and then go off and forget all about them."

"You say," Folsom asked, "that the Captain was told about his son's strangeness. You told him about your suspicions?"

"Oh yes. He was told last December, but he just laughed it off. He laughed at the idea of Tom being crazy. Even a week ago last Thursday, Flo told her father that Tom was crazy."

"Did he ever say anything about his father?"

"He always spoke with great respect and affection for his father. And his younger brothers and sisters were devoted to Tom.

Dick was especially so. They were very close. When Tom had the store in Macon, Dick was with him a great deal.

"Tom was always armed and seemed suspicious of everyone. He was afraid of being killed. He'd jump at the slightest noise. And then, then he ran off and married that girl from Jones County and him having no way to support her."

Tom paced his cell floor. The endless flow of reporters asking him the same questions stretched his patience to the limit. His fishbowl existence allowed him no privacy. He was under constant scrutiny. If he was not under the watchful eye of the turnkey, his neighbors in the other cells maintained their vigilance. They reported his every move to the newspapers. Tom rattled his cell door and called out for the deputy.

"What do you want?" Deputy Green barked as he stormed up to the door.

"I want you to do me a favor."

"That depends on just whaditiz."

"Keep reporters out of here. I don't want any more reporters seeing me."

"That it?"

"Uh huh. Will you do it?"

"It'll be up to the Sheriff. I'll tell'im." The deputy started to leave then turned back around. "Chief Connolly wants to see ya. He'll come back here soon's he's finished up front."

Tom nodded and stretched out on his cot.

Moments later, the Chief of the Atlanta Police Force called out to him. "Mr. Woolfolk?"

Tom jumped up and greeted his guest politely, "Chief."

The turnkey unlocked the cell door and Connolly calmly stepped inside.

The two men briefly discussed the murders. Tom spoke freely as Connolly listened attentively.

"I'm shocked," Tom remarked, "that anybody could believe me guilty. How can anyone for a moment think I'm capable of murdering my own pa? I've never heard of a man killing his own father."

"I have," Connolly answered.

Tom looked down at the floor and said nothing.

A prisoner called out from the next cell, "Tell us agin, how you found them dead folks."

Connolly shouted back, "Alright, you boys pipe down over yonder."

Tom walked over to the window and looked out. Connolly called out for the turnkey to unlock the door. Tom mumbled a quiet goodbye.

Folsom quickly climbed down from the train and hurried to a nearby hack. He asked the driver if he was for hire. The old man nodded. The reporter climbed aboard.

"I want you to take me to Holton."

"Holton, Georgia? That's a lit'l fudder than I'z plannin' t' go."

"You'll get your regular fare and, if you get me there before nightfall, I'll pay you twice that amount."

The driver needed no additional encouragement. Picking up his buggy whip, he yelled a command and brought his mare to a trot.

Folsom's early morning visit with Tom's aunt gave him reason to believe he needed to visit Woolfolk's ex-wife as soon as possible. Fannie Crane gave him directions to the home of Georgia's father, Thomas Bird, in Jones County and told him briefly about the marriage. The reporter was also aware that Tom had mailed a letter to his former wife the day before the murders. He hoped Georgia Bird would allow him to read it.

A short while later, Folsom hurried up the steps of the old farm house. Lights illuminating the interior reassured him someone was home. He knocked loudly.

Thomas Bird cautiously opened the door to the young man standing with hat in hand on his front porch.

"Mister Bird, my name is Folsom. I'm the Macon correspondent for the Atlanta Constitution."

Bird looked the reporter over closely. "Yeh, I know who you are. I told Georgia it'd be only a matter of time 'fore you boys from the papers'd be out here askin' us all kinds of questions 'bout Woolfolk."

"Well sir, I would like a few minutes of yours and your daughter's time."

"Guess we're gonna have to git used to it. Come on in."

Folsom graciously thanked him. A young woman, no more than eighteen, greeted the reporter as he walked inside. She was beautiful. Her father pointed to a chair. Folsom obediently sat down.

"Mrs. Woolfolk, I am sorry about the hour, but if you'll allow me a few minutes, I promise I will not stay long."

"That's alright, Mr. Folsom," she answered.

"Did you receive some letters from your husband recently?"

"Yes, yes I did."

"Would you mind if I see them?"

"Well...," she looked over at her father, "no, I don't mind. I have 'em in my room. I'll go get 'em."

As soon as the young girl left the room, a man dressed in dirty farm clothes entered.

"This is my brother, Pleasant Bird. Pink, this man, Folsom, is from the Constitution."

The two men shook hands. Folsom sat back down.

"You know, I never liked that Woolfolk boy. My brother, Pink, that's what we all call'im, Pink. Anyhow, Pink here introduced 'em at a picnic."

"When was that?" Folsom asked.

Pink spoke up. "Ah...back at the first of May. Tom was really taken by her. He was visitin' his Uncle Thomas at the time."

Major Thomas J. Woolfolk's home in Jones Co. where Tom met Georgia Bird during one of the Major's many parties. The design of this house is identical to that of Captain Richard F. Woolfolk's.

(Photo courtesy of Millie C. Stewart)

"I knew his pa," Georgia's father continued. "I served with the Captain in the State Militia in sixty-three. There weren't no better man than Captain Dick Woolfolk, but I wasn't gonna put up with Tom on his account."

Folsom noted the anger in Bird's voice. The man sat across from him, leaning over with his elbows resting on his knees. As he spoke, he slowly rubbed his hands back and forth.

"For his pa's sake, I treated him like a gentleman."

Georgia returned carrying a small bundle of envelopes tied with a string. "Here they are," she said and handed them over to the reporter.

"In the first place, Thomas Woolfolk fooled me," Georgia said, sitting down beside her father.

"How's that?" the reporter asked, briefly checking the postmarks on the letters. They were the ones he wanted to see.

"He said he had a place ready for me and everything to make me comfortable. Well...I thought from what I knew about the family, he was telling the truth. I went to live with his sister, Mrs. Edwards in Macon. Three days later, I found out he didn't have no place for us.

"Tom didn't do nothing during that time and I began to find out what he was really like. He told me I wouldn't like his parents."

"Did you ever meet them?"

She nodded the affirmative. "'Bout three weeks after we were married, they came to visit us. Tom was gone. They were nice folks and treated me like a daughter. The Captain even gave me some land he had in Coffee County. When Tom got back, I told him what nice people they were. He got real mad and said, 'Wait til you see more of them.' He started cussin' and said, 'The property won't do them any good. I'll burn 'em up first.' Then he said somethin' 'bout bein' kept out of his birthright. Well, by then, I stopped having anythin' to do with him. Finally, my ma came and brought me home."

"How long were you with him?"

"I stayed there only three weeks. I wasn't satisfied the next morning after I married him and would've left then had I had a way.

"I went over to see Mrs. Edwards this evening. She's still in a bad way 'bout all this. She said Tom had treated her badly and she knew he had been mean t'me. She said she'd been afraid he woulda hurt us."

Thomas Bird gently placed his hand on his daughter's and started to talk. "After Georgia came home, he came here a lot to see her. I finally refused him the house. He then met me at the field gate. He had sent Georgia a note by two coloreds and had read her answer. He said, 'PaPa, shake hands with me.' And then he said, 'I want you to shoot me through the head.'

"On Friday, a week before the murders, he came to Georgia's grandpa's house and sent for me. I told the messenger to tell Tom to come on to the house. He came and I called Georgia to talk to him, but she said she had nothing to say. I had told him if he came back here anymore, he would come in danger. He mounted his horse and rode off. I never saw him since."

"Do you think he's guilty?" Folsom asked.

The Birds were silent for a moment, then Thomas spoke up. "I don't know if he did it. But if he's guilty...I hope they make him suffer."

Folsom looked down at the bundle of letters in his hand.

"Do you mind if I read these?"

"No, go ahead," Georgia answered.

The handwriting was difficult to read. The reporter struggled to make out Woolfolk's scribbling. The letters consisted mostly of love poems. Some were written in their entirety while others were single verses.

One letter was of particular interest to Folsom. Woolfolk had expressed his undying love for Georgia, wrote of her 'angelic purity'. He then wrote, 'Two little lives are soon to go out of the world--out of the sunshine... forever.'

It was signed 'T.G.W.'.

CHAPTER SEVEN
"I believe you, honey."

The cotton was ruined, the corn crop sour. The strong smell of rot permeated throughout the river valley. Sam Chambless, walking through the Captain's flooded field, reached down and pulled an ear of corn from a collapsed stalk. He squeezed it with one hand. The cob gave way as easily as if he was squeezing a wet hankerchief.

Back at the wagon three field hands, Greene Lockett, John Jeff, and Tom Banks waited for the old man to decide what to do. They watched him tilt his hat back and scratch his head. Greene Lockett hopped down and walked over to him.

"What we gonna to, Marse Sam, suh?"

Chambless looked at him and then surveyed the area.

"We'll harvest what we can."

The widespread destruction from the flood was not limited to the rural area. The City Park of Macon near the jail was covered with a slimy silt. The race track was pock marked with deep holes. Inches of water still covered the grass not washed away by the flood.

Inspectors found the Covington and Macon Railroad Bridge bent and misaligned. The central pier had dropped four feet, and a hundred eighty feet of the west bank gone. The entire span as out of plumb.

Folsom stood in a corner at the end of the cell block and watched as the endless stream of visitors filed by Tom's cell. The spectators gawked in silence. No one spoke to the prisoner. They only whispered among themselves.

"That man ain't no more insane...than I am," someone commented to a friend.

Tom grew increasingly withdrawn. The Sheriff of Fulton County had yet to bar people from seeing him. In less than a week, he was transformed from a relaxed, cooperative prisoner, to someone sullen, depressed, and very worried.

Folsom quietly observed and wrote in his notebook, "They look at him with the same morbid interest with which they would gaze upon some physiological monstrosity. The same feeling which would prompt a man to pay fifty cents to look at Jesse James or an eight legged dog."

The reporter closed his notebook and approached the Fulton County Sheriff standing at the entrance to the cellblock.

"How many people would you say's been in to see Woolfolk?" the reporter asked.

The Sheriff thought for a moment and then answered, "I'd say about two thousand people have requested to see the prisoner."

"Two thousand?"

He nodded, surveying the crowd. "I'm going to have to put a stop to it, I guess. It's startin' to take its toll."

"How's that?"

The Sheriff folded his arms and studied the floor in front of him.

"Well," he said finally, "when he first got here he was friendly and talkative. Now he's beginnin' to brood alot. He paces the floor and, at night, he groans in his sleep. I put an extra watch on him. We can't let Woolfolk deny the people of Bibb County their right to justice by doing himself in, now can we?"

After Judge Nisbet officially notified Tom of his decision to not represent him, the process of finding a lawyer for the prisoner began. For days, the Sheriff had all persons wishing to take the case fill out a short form. The procedure was a necessary one. Thousands of curiosity seekers hounded the jail each day hoping for a glimpse of the notorious prisoner.

Tom would review each application and accept or reject an interview with the applicant.

When Frank R. Walker entered Tom's cell, the prisoner was depressed. He had been confined a week. Reporters continued to attempt interviews. Some impersonated lawyers in an effort to gain his confidence and a confession.

Tom was stunned by Nisbet's refusal to represent him. He was worried. He had no appetite and was losing sleep.

Walker, a graduate from Washington and Lee University, had been practicing law for four years. He was a good looking young man, close to Tom in age. Tom liked him instantly.

"If you're interested," the prisoner said rather despondently, "you can have my case."

"Mr. Woolfolk, I would consider it an honor to represent you."

Tom's response to his acceptance surprised Walker. He suddenly smiled broadly and thanked the lawyer. The prisoner became alert and talkative. He told his new counselor everything he could remember. Walker suggested they acquire a second lawyer, one from Macon, if possible, to assist in the case. Tom enthusiastically agreed. As his lawyer walked out of the cell, the prisoner felt assured and relieved.

The young attorney emerged from the Fulton County Jailhouse victorious. Of the volumes of applications from prominent and unknown lawyers, the accused mass murderer had selected him.

"Gentlemen," Walker said to the throng of reporters rushing up to meet him. "Gentlemen, my name is Frank R. Walker. I will be defending Thomas G. Woolfolk."

The reporters mobbed him with questions. Walker raised his hands to hush the crowd.

"Gentlemen, please."

"Is Woolfolk crazy?" a reporter shouted.

Walker cleared his throat and nodded. "I believe he is. It is my intention to defend him on the grounds of insanity."

Emma stood outside the Woolfolk house and stared at the front door. She had tried time and again to scrub away the red stains on the floors and walls in the two bedrooms and the hallway.

For three days, she and Sarah Hardin scrubbed until their fingers were raw and their knees sore. The stains would not go away.

Samuel Chambless walked up behind her. "Where's that man of yours?" he growled.

Emma turned around, startled. "Oh, Marse Chambless suh, you done put the fright of d'Lawd in me. Aaron's down at the barn lot. You wants me t'fetch 'im for ya?"

Chambless placed his hands on his hips and nodded.

Emma hiked up her threadbare skirt and hurried off. Chambless took his hat off and scratched his gray hair. He had received permission from Flo Edwards to close up her father's house to keep out vandals.

Aaron ran up breathing heavily. "Marse Sam, suh, you wants me?"

"I need you to get that lumber from under the house so we can board up the windows and doors."

"Yassuh." Aaron ran over to the edge of the house. Kneeling down he reached beneath the floor of the girls' bedroom, pulled out a wooden plank and handed it to Emma.

"Aaron, we can't use this."

Aaron looked up. "Why cain't we?"

"Look." Emma held the board out to him. Aaron ran his finger along its edge.

"Good lawd amercy. We sho cain't. Toss it over there," he said, shaking his head as he climbed further beneath the house for the remaining boards.

One by one he slid a plank out; one by one, Emma had to throw it aside.

Chambless walked over to the couple. "How ya'll doin'?" he asked.

Emma decided to let Aaron explain the problem.

"Well suh, I don't think we's gonna be able t'use these here."

The old man placed both hands on his hips. "And why not?"

Emma spoke up. "They's got blood on'em."

"Blood?"

"Yassuh," Aaron answered. "The blood from the little girl musta dripped down through the floor boards."

"Dear God," Chambless groaned, looking at the lumber. "You're right, we can't use'em. Aaron, take'em over to the trash pile and burn'em." He looked up at the house. "Only way we're gonna git the blood out of that place will be to burn it."

"Yassuh." Aaron responded. He grabbed up an arm load of wood and walked away. Emma looked at the white man standing in front of her.

"Marse Sam, suh?"

"Yes, girl, what is it?"

"Marse Sam, what's gonna happen t'us?"

"Well now...I can't rightly say. The crop's all lost and there's a problem decidin' who inherits the place."

The expression on Emma's face told him she did not understand.

"Well, you see," he continued, "if they can prove that the Captain died first then Mattie would have inherited the property."

"But...Miz Mattie...she's dead."

"But if she died after the Captain then her heirs, her blood kin, the Howards, will inherit. If she died first and the Captain after her, then his children, Flo and Lillie...and I guess Tom, will inherit. Understand?"

Emma shook her head in total disbelief. She understood. She understood that the white folk were going to argue over who of the nine dead people died first.

"What 'bout us? Aaron 'n me?"

"I guess, it'd be wise if you started looking for work elsewhere, at another farm maybe. This one's dead."

"Woolfolk!" the jailer called out.

Tom ignored him.

"Woolfolk, ya got visitors."

"Tell'em to go away. I'm tryin' t'sleep."

"Tom?" The woman's voice was barely audible.

Tom jumped up from his cot and hurried to the door.

"Flo," He whispered, "Flo...Lillie."

Tears filled his eyes as he greeted his older sisters. Frank Walker stood behind them, smiling. Lillie lightly touched his hand as he gripped the bar.

"Tom? You alright?" she asked.

"Yeh...I'm fine. It ain't too bad in here."

Flo looked around the cell block. The wet, dank smell reminded her of an outdoor privy.

"I'm glad t'see ya," Tom said softly.

"Tom...," Flo glanced nervously at the prisoner in the next cell. She leaned closer to the door and whispered, "Tom...did you kill them?"

Tom's mouth dropped open. He quickly snapped it shut. "No." He said, finally, "No, I swear it. I didn't kill them."

Tears ran down the cheeks of both women. Lillie reached up and placed her hand on top of his. They gripped the bar together.

"I believe you, Tom," she whispered tearfully.

"Flo?" He looked at his oldest sister.

Flo was six years old when her baby brother was born. She remembered he was no bigger than her doll. She and Lillie, who was three at the time, would stand on their tip toes and gaze at him.

He was a sweet child, shielded from the horror of war by his age and innocence. He, the one who never really knew their mother, seemed to miss her the most. Floride helped raise him.

When their father married Mattie Howard, Tom was the first to accept her. He was almost eight at the time. She and Lillie, who had been the women of their father's motherless household, had a more difficult time.

Flo watched Tom grow up. Over the years, she also watched the relationship between her stepmother and brother become strained.

As each additional child was born, Mattie would pressure her husband to secure for them an inheritance. Flo and Lillie were both married and were not as affected by the changing of their father's will. Tom, however, was devastated by the loss of what he considered his birthright. He became an angry, confused man desperate for recognition from the Captain.

Flo looked at her brother through the bars. She knew he had not stopped loving his father.

"Oh Tom," she cried.

Tom reached through the bars and held her hand.

With tears flowing from her eyes, she whispered, "I...believe you, honey."

Lillie Woolfolk Cowan

(Photos courtesy of Lily Norris Owen and Barbara Anchors)

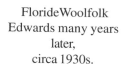

Floride Woolfolk
Edwards many years
later,
circa 1930s.

CHAPTER EIGHT
"I am not crazy."

Tom reread the letter dated August 10, 1887 and addressed to the Macon Circuit Court Judge, Thomas Jefferson Simmons. His lawyer waited patiently for him to finish.

"I thought we settled the matter of my sanity," he finally said not looking up from the letter.

"We did. It says I believe you're innocent."

"Yeh, but it also says I just might be crazy."

"We have to consider every option. Tom, I wish you would trust me. I'm not going to go into court proclaiming you, uh, well, deranged. But if it looks like we have no other choice then, in order to save your life, we may have to say you were insane and didn't know what you were doing."

"But I didn't do it...I'm not crazy!" Tom tossed the letter aside and walked over to the door. The letter landed on his cot. His neighbors were listening intently.

Walker placed his hand on Tom's shoulder and spoke softly, "A petition from Bibb County was submitted to the Governor demanding an immediate trial. One they know we are not ready for."

"Can they do that?"

"They can, and they did. Fortunately, the governor doesn't have jurisdiction. I've been told they've now resubmitted the petition to Judge Simmons. It's a good thing he's still in New York. It gave me time to compose this letter. Tom, we've got to do everything we can to delay going to trial."

Tom thought for a moment. This was not their first discussion concerning his sanity. The day after the attorney was retained, Tom read in the Atlanta Constitution that his defense would be insanity.

Their resulting argument was reported in newspapers across the state. Tom seriously considered firing the man but his friend Jim Schofield advised him to give the lawyer another chance.

"Send the letter," he finally said. "But," Tom turned and faced Walker, "I'll go to the gallows before I let you or anybody say I'm insane. You understand me?"

Walker looked deep into his client's eyes. They were dark and determined. He knew Tom was not crazy, just different. He also knew he meant what he said. He would hang before allowing the public to believe he was insane.

Walker smiled reassuringly. "I'm going to Macon soon. I need to talk to the coroner and the Sheriff." He waited for Tom's response. There was none.

"I'm also going out to Hazzard to your father's farm." He continued, "I want to talk with Chambless and the coloreds out there."

Tom put his hand on the cold block wall and stared down at the floor. "I wouldn't expect much help from them."

"I don't."

By the beginning of the third week, Tom's life as a prisoner began to settle into a routine interrupted only by visits from his attorney and selected friends. His sisters had not returned. No other relative came to see him.

His mornings began with a half hour walk alone in the corridor. Always keeping to himself, he walked in a fast pace up and down the passage way. When it was time for the other prisoners' exercise period, the turnkey would return him to his cell and serve him breakfast. During the day he would read various newspapers and his Bible, talk with his lawyer, and sleep. He never conversed with his neighbors.

He was a quiet, model prisoner always polite to his keepers. After the few arguments he had with his attorney at the beginning of their association, Tom maintained a subdued attitude. Reporters grew tired of trying to obtain entrance to see him. Fewer and fewer articles appeared in the newspapers. Citizens of Bibb County were beginning to go about their daily affairs with fewer discussions or reminders of the tragedy.

The days of relentless rain were over. River banks returned to normal levels and fields began to dry out. Stagnant pools of water brimmed with larvae. Mosquitoes swarmed in the low lying areas.

Samuel Chambless was asked to serve as administrator of the Woolfolk estate. He declined but agreed to assume temporary responsibility until one could be appointed. Henry P. Cowan, husband of the Captain's second daughter Lillie, was then selected. Cowan, however, lived in Hawkinsville, Georgia, and was not in the position to conduct on-site activities. Chambless, therefore, continued to close down the farm.

Crops were harvested and the money went to paying the six hundred dollar cost of the funeral. Equipment and stock were sold. Farm laborers were then released. The sharecroppers, including Emma and Aaron Jones, were allowed to remain on the property.

The empty farm was quiet and lonely. It had been transformed from a major ten-plow operation to a virtual ghost town. Lockett had responsibilities that required him to go to the top of the hill. He hated to go near the house. No one was allowed inside, but then, no one wanted to enter into the cold, abandoned building. Chambless had Aaron and Lockett move all the furniture into the two front rooms and lock the doors. The rooms where the murders had occurred were left unlocked.

Valuables were distributed to relatives and close friends. The nearby Midway Church received Mattie's silver tea serving set and the family bible. The Woolfolks had attended the community services there as well as Mattie's father's church, Mount Zion Baptist, located further away in Monroe County.

Just as no one would go near the house, no one would drink from the well. Although they had no proof the water was actually tainted with the blood and brains of the murdered family, the possibility repulsed everyone. Although there were several wells in the hill area, the well behind the house served as the main source of drinking water for the hilltop. Samuel Chambless decided it needed to be cleaned out and instructed Lockett to get it done immediately.

Lockett and Aaron first bailed out the standing water. Aaron then climbed down a ladder into the well to dig out the silt and mud at the bottom. It was there he found the missing socks.

Lockett immediately ran for Chambless who was on the front porch talking with some neighbors. The small group of men hurried around the house and found Aaron sitting on the side of the well holding more wet material and a brick. His pants were wet to the knees and stained from the red mud.

"Those come outta the well?" Chambless asked pointing to the rags.

"Yassur," Aaron answered, handing the bundle over to the old white man.

Chambless unfolded the two rags. Both were stained red.

Lockett shuddered. "That blood?"

Chambless nodded. "Sure looks like it, don't it. You find anything else down there?"

"Nawsur, just them socks 'n them there rags. The rags, they was still wrapped 'round this brick."

"You looked around real good down there?"

"Yassur, I looked real good."

"We need to get these thangs to the Sheriff as soon as possible," Chambless said.

Jerry Hollis, one of the neighbors, reached out and took the items from Chambless' hand.

"I'll take'em," he said. Tying the wet material up into a tight bundle and placing it under his arm, Hollis put on his hat and hurried back around the house to his horse. The sound of a horse galloping away indicated to the men at the well that he had ridden off.

Chambless looked at the two men standing before him waiting for instructions.

"You boys finish up here," the old man said and then walked away.

"Yassur boss," Lockett answered. Aaron slowly climbed back over into the well and down the ladder.

"Don't know why we's got to clean out this well." Lockett heard him muttering. "Blood be washed out by now."

Floride Edwards remained secluded at her home in East Macon. She had no desire to go out to her father's farm. Friends and relatives continued to visit. Each day, however, the visits were shorter and fewer.

Her cousin, Love Shackleford, returned to Athens to his job as clerk in the Clark County Court House. He promised he would visit as often as possible. Her Aunt Fannie begged her to return to Athens with her. She was tempted but had yet to decide what to do. For the sake of her father's affairs, she felt she needed to remain in East Macon.

The Howards, led by Charles Howard, were using their power and influence to fuel the fires of anger and suspicion against Tom. They were attempting to force the State to take her brother to trial as soon as possible.

The Woolfolk clan, led by her Uncle Thomas Jefferson Woolfolk in Jones County, tried to maintain a sense of legal propriety and calmness. Her uncle stressed that Tom could possibly be innocent and that every effort and assistance should go towards his defense.

Lillie her sister returned to Hawkinsville immediately after her visit to Atlanta. The mother of several young children, Lillie was obligated to stay out of the affair. Her letters expressed her undying love and support.

Flo kept apprised of the circumstances surrounding her brother mostly through the Macon Telegraph. She had decided not to read the Atlanta Constitution after she learned of Pea Jay's scandalous articles about her family. Of course, all the newspapers were guilty of sensationalizing the murders, Pea Jay; nonetheless, seemed to cause her the most anxiety.

She unfolded the August 28th, Sunday Edition of the Telegraph. For several days there were no new articles concerning Tom. This one appeared to be no different. She was about to close the paper and put it aside when she noticed a small article on an inside page. WOOLFOLK'S LAWYER, the headline read. The article came from the Athens Banner reporting that Frank Walker had visited her aunt in Athens. Although the newspaper did not elaborate on what Walker was able to find out, it again mentioned the subject of Tom's sanity.

The article also mentioned a curious fact. Walker had a lengthly talk with Ross, a former slave of her Uncle John Crane. She wondered what sort of helpful information he could possibly receive from the old man that would aid in the defense of her brother. There were many questions, in fact, she wished answered.

The topic of Tom's sanity was causing the Woolfolk family much concern. A newspaper reported that Frank Walker hinted he had evidence of insanity in the family line. Flo was not aware of such and wondered if Ross had something to do with it. Her Uncle Thomas promised he would get to the bottom of the matter when the young lawyer visited Macon.

Floride did not look forward to his visit. She did not like talking about the murders, about Tom. She ached for the whole 'affair', as Aunt Fannie once called it, to finally end. She wanted her life back. She wanted her family back.

Greene Lockett stood in the opening of his front door and waited patiently for the arrival of Coroner Hodnett, Sam Chambless, and Frank Walker. Chambless notified Lockett the day before that Tom's attorney from Atlanta wanted to visit the murder scene and talk to the witnesses. He was anxious about the meeting. No one seemed to believe his story that Tom had been trying to frame him for the murders. Fact was Lockett felt he was being pressured by several white men to change his story. He recently told Chambless of his fears. Chambless laughed it off and said he was imagining things. Imagination or not, Lockett was scared.

Luanna Cooper relished in retelling the story of the murders. She spoke of 'haints' and evil spirits. Lockett listened as did everyone. He believed the house was haunted. It had to be after what happened within its walls.

The morning air was hot and stuffy. It had not rained for several weeks. The water from the flood had long since receded. The red clay was dry. Deep cracks formed along the furrows in the fields. Although it had flooded just weeks earlier, farmers were now beginning to worry about drought conditions setting in.

A dust cloud signified the approach of Lockett's guests. Lockett slowly walked out into the middle of the lane and waited.

Chambless' carriage pulled up beside him.

"Lockett." Chambless acknowledged him.

"Yassur, Marse Sam, suh."

"How 'bout you meetin' us up at the house."

"Yassuh boss."

"Get word to the others that we'll be by their places shortly. I don't want us to have to go looking for nobody, you understand me, boy?"

"Yassuh boss." Lockett trotted into his shack. As he re-emerged seconds later, his wife, Fanny, hurried out the back door and over to Emma's, a short distance down the hill.

Giving the mare a slap with his buggy whip, Chambless smiled.

"Those are some scared nigguhs."

"Why would they be scared?" Walker asked.

"Oh, you know how them people git. Lockett believes someone's tryin' to make him change his story about that night."

"Are they?"

"Who knows. I had a hard time gittin' him to go inside the house and close it up. Now Aaron Jones, that's his shack down over yonder, he and his wife, Emma, have stayed right here helpin'. Never complainin'. Never scared. You can't git any better than those two."

"I am going to be able to talk to all of them, as we had planned?"

"As soon as I got your wire, I went to see each one personally and told them you were comin'. They're all here 'cept that John Owens."

"John Owens?" Coroner Hodnett seemed surprised that a key witness was not available. "Where'd he go?"

"No way of knowin' really. I ain't seen him since he testified to the coroner's jury."

"You mean, he's gone?" Walker questioned.

"Looks like it. But what can you 'pect from them people?"

Walker shook his head slowly and looked over at the farmhouse off in the distance.

"Who's place is that?" he asked.

"That's the Gilbert place."

"White?"

"Yes."

"How far would you say that house is from here?" Walker asked the coroner.

"Oh...not more than a half mile. Why?"

"And how far away is Bill Smith's?"

Chambless had to think for a moment. "He has a farm over at Lorane, near me...I'd say three...three and a half miles. But he supervised the Captain's sawmill and lived in a small house not too far from here. What are you gittin' at?"

"Why do you suppose Lockett's boy went all the way to Smith's house first?"

Hodnett looked over at the Gilbert farm adjacent to the Woolfolk property. The farmhouse was in clear view as were other outbuildings.

"Widow Gilbert's pretty old. She wouldn't have been much help had they gone there first." The coroner, knowing there was also a son still living on the farm, looked as if his answer did not convince him any more than it did the lawyer.

"Didn't somebody living on the Gilbert place testify at the coroner's inquest that he heard Tom running down the hill calling for help," Walker continued as the carriage rolled to a stop in front of the Woolfolk house.

"That was Anderson James. His shack was the one we passed on the left across the fence down at the bend in the lane." Chambless answered and slowly climbed down.

Walker looked back over his shoulder in the direction Chambless had pointed.

"Interesting" he mumbled.

Lockett stood at the gate and watched the three white men unload. He hoped they would not expect him to go inside. The quiet house bothered him.

The young lawyer stretched and looked around. The size of the Woolfolk farm impressed him. The view was panoramic. The hill was terraced and dotted with fruit trees and old slave quarters that had until recently been occupied by farm laborers and sharecroppers. Now all was quiet.

The picket fence surrounding the white house was trim and simple. The barn in the distance was large with the side stables empty of stock.

Chambless pointed to a holly bush beside the lane.

"Tom's Ma, Susan, is buried over there," he said. "She was a pretty little thang. Just a child when they married...thirteen, maybe...fourteen. The Captain and Mattie buried their second son, Charles, beside her. Little Charlie was named after him" The old man shook his head and turned towards the front door.

Walker breathed the fresh Georgia air and walked up the steps. The laughter of children filtered up from the houses at the foot of the hill. The lawyer stopped at the front door and listened. Hodnett walked passed him and entered the house.

"Ever since the murders, I've kept the place closed up," Chambless continued and then realized Walker had not followed.

"Walker?"

Walker continued listening to the children. Lockett waited at the foot of the steps.

"I hear children." the lawyer asked.

Lockett turned and looked around. "They's just some of d'chillins over at d'Gilbert's."

"Was that your house down there?"

"Yassuh."

"Did you hear anything that night?"

"Boss?"

"Before Tom Woolfolk came down to your house...did you hear anything?"

"Oh nawsuh. I didn't hear nothin' 'til Mistah Tom woke me up, bangin' on m'door."

"I see...and you heard nothing else?"

"Nawsuh."

Walker nodded and turned to enter the house when Lockett spoke up nervously.

"When...when I looked out my house that night 'n saw Mistah Tom standin' in his night clothes under a tree, lookin' white and pale like a ghost...his eyes starin' wild...if...if...he had started for me...well suh...there woulda been the loudest yellin and hollerin' ever heard in these parts."

Walker looked quizzically at him as he rambled on incoherently. The lawyer shook his head, and then walked through the door.

Inspection of the murder scene gave Walker a better understanding of the logistics of the event. Faint blood stains clearly marked the locations of the bodies. Chambless walked him through each room explaining what he found when he and Smith first entered the house. Hodnett offered additional information. The lawyer took notes, closely examining every stain, every angle, the location of windows and doorways.

At the well, Walker took off his hat and coat and wiped the sweat from his face while Chambless explained the discovery of the bloody clothes.

"Hard to imagine all the blood. Must have been a horrific sight," Walker finally said.

The two men standing with him nodded quietly.

Emma watched the three white men walk up the path to her house. "La, la, la...he's 'bout Mistah Tom's age, ain't he?" she said to Aaron standing beside her.

Her husband did not answer. She continued watching as he hurried out and greeted their guests. The men stood in a small group talking.

Emma wiped her hands on her apron, smoothed her hair, and quickly surveyed the room. When they were told of the impending visit, she spent the morning cleaning their small shack to make it ready for the lawyer from Atlanta. All was in order.

Aaron escorted the white men into the house. "This...this is my wife, Emma."

The young lawyer smiled, removed his hat, and extended his hand. Nervously, Emma looked at the other men standing before her, wiped her hands on her apron again and then lightly shook his hand.

"Emma, Mistah Walker is here to ask you a few questions about the murder. I want you to answer to the best of your ability." Chambless calmly led her to a chair.

She nodded and sat down.

"I understand you were awakened by the dogs barking up at the house, the night of the murders. Is that right?" Walker asked, pulling up a chair in front of her and also sitting down.

"Yassuh."

"What time was that?"

"Just before four in the mornin'. The dogs woke me up with their barkin' and carryin' on. I's just lyin'in bed wishin' they'd hush when I heard the screams."

She shuddered as the memory sent shivers through her.

"Are you alright?" Walker asked politely.

"Yassuh. I just hate thinkin' about it, that's all."

"I understand. Did you see any strangers hanging around before or after that terrible night?"

"Nawsuh," she answered.

Walker looked down at his notes and started to ask another question when she interrupted him.

"No...now wait. I did see somebody. I done forgot 'bout it 'til now. That Friday mornin', this man comes to my doe right at breakfast time askin' for a hand out. I tossed him a biscuit, I think."

"You say this was the morning before the night of the murders?"

"Yassuh, that Friday morning."

"Was he colored?"

Emma nodded.

"What did he look like?"

Emma looked away and thought for a moment. "He didn't have no shoes on. I 'member that. He was poorly lookin'. He had a hat and his clothes was old n' worn out. He smelled...and he was real dirty."

"Did you see him again?"

"Yassuh."

Her answer held her guests riveted to their spots. The men, including Aaron, waited for her to continue.

"I saw him right after Marse Chambless took Mistah Tom into the house to wait for the Sheriff to git here. He was standin' off to the side of the crowd by hisself."

"What was he doing?" Coroner Hodnett asked.

"Nothin' really. Just standin' there watchin'... and..." she stopped for a moment and looked away as if seeing him again. "He was eatin' chicken."

"Chicken?"

"Yassuh, he was eatin' on some fried chicken."

"Where do you suppose a beggar got fried chicken?" Walker looked around at the men with him.

"Well, there was alot of people with picnic baskets that day," Chambless offered. "From the Montepelier picnic."

"White people?" the lawyer asked.

Chambless nodded.

"I doubt he got the chicken from any of them. No, our friend got the chicken from some place else. Probably stole it."

"Miz Mattie," Emma whispered.

Walker jerked his head around and looked at her intently. "What about Mrs. Woolfolk?"

"Miz Mattie had two baskets full of fried chicken in the kitchen. I know coz I helped her fry'em up."

The lawyer looked at Chambless. "Was there any baskets of food in the house when you got there?"

Chambless shook his head. "There weren't any when I was there. In fact, when it got time to eat, we had to have food fixed over here and brought up. Emma...why didn't you tell us this before?"

The woman looked innocently at each man. "Nobody asked me 'til now. I didn't think none of it."

There was a long moment of silence. Chambless cleared his throat.

"I'd like to thank you both for your time," Walker finally said. Turning to Chambless he continued, "I'd like to talk with the washer woman, what was her name?"

"Sarah Hardin," Chambless answered.

"Right. I need to see her and then I'll be through."

Chambless drove Walker and Hodnett to Sarah Hardin's house. Hanging her newly washed clothes on the thin wire stretched between two posts, the woman stopped, raised her hand to her forehead, shaded her eyes, and watched the three men walk up to her.

"Miz Hardin, my name is Frank Walker. I'm Tom Woolfolk's attorney."

Sarah nodded, picked up a basket full of clothes and walked towards the house. The three men followed her into the kitchen and waited for her to put her clothes basket down.

Chambless cleared his throat and asked for some water. Sarah wiped her hands on her apron and then dipped him a glass full. The old farmer drank it down in one gulp.

"Tell me about the clothes found in the well. Do they all belong to Mister Thomas?" Walker asked.

"Them underdrawers, they do...that work shirt don't. That was Mistah Dick's." Sarah sat down and faced the lawyer who had taken a seat at the table.

"So...the shirt was Mister Tom's brother's shirt? And you're sure about that?"

"Yassuh. I remember Mistah Tom didn't bring no clothes with'im when he come to the house. So Miz Mattie, she told him t'put one of Mistah's Dick's on."

Walker was startled by her answer. Chambless spoke up. "You're sayin' Tom was wearing Dick's clothes?"

"Yassuh. I was there when she told him to wear Mistah Dick's clothes.

The next day Frank Walker stopped by the Bibb County Jail in Macon. It was there Folsom finally caught up with him.

When the reporter walked up to the office door, Sheriff Westcott, Coroner Hodnett, and Walker were examining the bottle found in Tom's pocket during the coroner's inquest.

Walker sniffed the bottle's contents.

"It smells to me like, probably, rye whiskey," Hodnett commented.

The lawyer took another sniff and disagreed.

"According to Tom, he was using this stuff to remove some warts. What I'm smelling now is clearly not chloroform. Just exactly what's in it I can't rightly say." Walker stopped talking when he noticed Folsom standing in the doorway.

Sheriff Westcott looked up and smiled. "Come on in Folsom. Walker, this is Folsom with the Atlanta Constitution."

Walker reached over and shook his hand.

Folsom smiled and asked the lawyer if he could ask him you a few questions.

"I think we're through here," Walker responded. "I think we have a few minutes before we leave for Mrs. Edwards, don't we?" He turned and asked Hodnett who was serving as his official escort.

The coroner reached into his vest pocket and pulled out a gold watch. "Well, actually Mrs. Edwards is already expecting us."

Walker turned back to the reporter. "If you would care to go over with us, we could talk on our way."

Folsom accepted the invitation with genuine appreciation. He wanted to stay as close to the case as possible. Two upcoming events were beginning to overshadow the story.

In the middle of October, President Grover Cleveland would be stopping in Atlanta for a visit arranged by Henry Grady. Cleveland was the first president since before the War Southerners seemed to trust. His visit would be a hallmark occasion for Atlantans, but Grady convinced him to not visit other Georgian cities, including Macon. Atlanta had, after all, been destroyed by Sherman.

A week after the President's visit in Atlanta, Macon would be hosting Jefferson Davis, the former President of the late Confederacy. One city official called it 'the last grand review.'

As the two cities made plans for the separate visits of two of the nation's leading citizens, efforts to put the morbid memory of the murders behind them, at least temporarily, were paramount. No longer did the Woolfolk name appear daily in newspapers across the state, as it had during the month of August.

The silence of the newspapers, of course, did not mean that nothing was happening in the aftermath of the murders. The defense attorney promised to reveal conspiracy and insanity. The prosecutor was determined to obtain nine murder indictments against Tom.

Since the Macon Telegraph's scathing editorial attacking Moran's 'PeaJay' articles, Folsom's counterpart remained reasonably quiet. Folsom knew, however, that when Tom's trial began in November, the reporters would reemerge and swarm around the story. In order to prevent any more attacks directed at individual reporters, the editor decided their by-lines would no longer be printed. Nonetheless, Folsom wanted to stay on top of the story. It became a near obsession with him.

"How was your visit to Hazzard District yesterday?" the reporter finally asked after the three men were well on their way to East Macon.

"I talked with Mr. Chambless, Mr. Smith and all but one of the colored witnesses. Mr. Chambless was exceedingly kind and courteous, and carried me to the house where the murder was committed, and explained how the bodies were found."

The lawyer told Folsom of meeting the witnesses at the plantation and how, as a group, they were convinced of Tom's guilt. "I may say another thing...and that is those out there want him hanged."

Folsom jotted his statement down.

"Did you find any evidence to support your insanity theory?"

"Yes, but what that was I don't care to say. I found persons out there who agreed with me as to that."

"Did you find evidence to support the other theory that the crime was committed by some one other than Tom?"

"Yes, both theories find supporters out there. I talked with the witnesses, and while all of them believe Tom did the work alone, I am satisfied in my own mind that they are wrong."

"A week back, it was reported in the newspapers that a man impersonating a house painter was nosing around Hazzard District asking a good many questions about the Woolfolk family, the murders, and Tom. Many people suspected that man was you."

"Yes, I am aware of that."

"Were you that man?"

"No."

"This was your first trip out there then?"

"Yes, it was."

"And you feel you benefitted by the trip?"

"Very much. I know now how the murder was committed, and I am satisfied that no one person committed it. I shall go home but plan to return Monday and make a more thorough investigation."

As the driver pulled up to Floride Edwards' home, the three men were greeted by Flo's uncle, Major Thomas Jefferson Woolfolk.

"Get down, gentlemen. Get down and come in," he called out from the porch.

Walker walked up the steps, followed by the coroner and Folsom. The attorney introduced himself and shook hands with the Captain's brother.

"Flo's inside. But...if you don't mind, I'd like a word with you first," his host said and guided Walker into the house.

Folsom and Hodnett remained outside.

"So...what's your opinion about Walker's trip to Hazzard District?" Folsom asked the Coroner.

"He was well-treated by the people out there. They all seemed to be willing, especially Mr. Chambless, of showing him every courtesy...though Mr. Chambless believes that the crime was committed by Tom Woolfolk alone."

"How did Walker talk as you were coming back?"

"Well, I'll tell you what I thought," Hodnett answered. The Coroner, an amputee from the Battle of Gettysburg, smiled jokingly and poked Folsom with his stump. "I thought he was a little downhearted after he got through with them witnesses."

An hour later, Walker and Flo's uncle walked out of the house emersed in conversation.

"I am convinced of Tom's innocence," the lawyer said.

Major Woolfolk smiled and placed his hand on Walker's shoulder as the two walked down the steps together.

"I am glad to hear you say that," he said. "But I must admit the report that insanity runs in my family, especially since none of us are aware of it...well that still upsets me greatly."

"I assure you, sir, I was misquoted. The strain of insanity I was referring to was on the maternal side."

The two stopped at the carriage. "Major Woolfolk, I feel assured, sir, that I can bring to light evidence that will prove Tom is innocent and convict others of the crime."

The major extended his hand. "Mr. Walker, if you can do that ,you will gain the gratitude not only of my family, but of the entire community and country at large."

This is the last known photograph of Captain Richard F. Woolfolk's brother, Major Thomas Jefferson Woolfolk, taken shortly before his death in 1892.
(Photo courtesy of Millie C. Stewart)

CHAPTER NINE

"...I wus there when it wus done."

By mid-September, the land was parched. Buildings, trees, and brush along roads were coated with red dust. Merchants had no choice but to cover their displays. Farmers rushed to harvest what remained of their cotton crop while vegetables withered in the gardens. The rich Georgia farmland had again been ravaged by the elements. The year 1887 would long be remembered.

Washington A. Kitchen closely watched the black man walking along the edge of the road ahead of him. Warned to be on the lookout for escaped prisoners from the state prison, the Sheriff of Cherokee County rode up and looked down. The drifter kept his eyes on the dirt road in front of him.

"What's your name, boy?" Kitchen finally asked.

The man ignored him and continued walking.

Turning his horse, the Sheriff blocked his way. The man stopped and looked up.

"You hear me, boy? I said, what's your name?"

"Dubose, boss. My name's Jackson Dubose," the man answered defiantly. He looked the Sheriff directly in the eyes.

"Well Jackson Dubose, what are you doin' in my county?"

"Just passin' through, boss."

"Where you headin'."

"I ain't goin' no where's particular."

Washington looked the man over from his head to his toes. His ankles had the scars of shackles.

"You know what I think, Jackson Dubose?" Washington nudged his horse towards the drifter. "I think maybe you're one of them escape convicts from A'lanta."

"Not me, boss. I ain't one a them."

Sheriff Kitchen pulled out his pistol and climbed down from his horse. Tossing a pair of handcuffs at the man, he barked, "Put'em on."

"Boss?"

"Don't give me no trouble, boy. Put'em on."

Dubose slapped a cuff on his left wrist.

"Now the other one."

The man glared as he worked the second cuff around his right wrist. Carefully, the Sheriff reached over and gave them a pull. They were locked.

"I think maybe we better make sure you ain't one of them escapees. Walk on ahead of my horse and don't try anything or I just might hafta run you down," Kitchen said calmly and climbed back into the saddle.

"You gonna make me walk all d'way t'Canton?"

"Won't be any different from what you were doing before I came up."

Frank Walker stood looking out his office window at the street below. The newspaper said he was discouraged. He was. His trip to Macon was not as successful as he had hoped. The citizens of Hazzard District were courteous and helpful enough, yet they all insisted Tom was guilty. No amount of discussion swayed their collective opinion.

The defense attorney was convinced some of the laborers were withholding information. Only Emma Jones seemed willing to give any that could be used in Tom's favor. The rest remained silent.

It was their silence that infuriated Walker. He knew there was absolutely no way they had not heard the fighting from atop the Woolfolk hill. In fact, the very day he stood on the Captain's front porch he easily heard children laughing at the houses below. Yet, each witness swore he heard absolutely nothing. The screams of the children had to be so loud and so horrible, it seemed impossible to him that no one heard anything. No one except Emma and Luanna.

A knock at his door brought Walker back to reality. His clerk handed him an envelope.

Walker thanked him, opened it and read intently.

"Frank R. Walker, Attorney At Law, Atlanta, Georgia. Have arrested one Jackson Dubose for the murder of the Woolfolk family. Need your assistance as soon as possible. W. A. Kitchen, Sheriff, Cherokee County, Canton, Georgia. September 18, 1887."

Walked grabbed his coat and hat and hurried out.

Sheriff Kitchen greeted the lawyer warmly. Walker was anxious to meet the prisoner but felt obligated to allow the Sheriff time to tell his story.

"At first, I thought he was, you know, one of them escaped prisoners from Atlanta. Just by the way he acted, I knew he was hiding something. Anyway, I brought him in, and it was while I was questioning him that he mentioned the Woolfolk name."

"I don't understand," Walker admitted.

"Well you see, I was about to throw him in jail for being on the lam when he said he couldn't have been in Atlanta during the first week of August at the time of the jailbreak because he was down at the Woolfolk's place when they all got killed."

"He actually said that?"

"That and more."

"Can I talk to him?"

"Well, actually...he asked to see you."

"Me?"

"As soon as he mentioned the Woolfolk's, he shut up. I guess he realized he was in a lot more trouble. I told him I was going to have to arrest him for the murder of the Woolfolk family, and that he was going to have to tell what he knew about the killin'. He said only if you'd defend him."

"Well I'll be damned."

Walker could hardly contain his excitement as the Sheriff escorted him back into the cellblock. In the corner of the cage, sat a black man, hunched over.

The lawyer walked over, pulled up a chair and sat down directly in front of him. The prisoner straightened up and glared back.

His hands were pressed together between his knees. He was dirty. His pants were baggy and worn. His checkered vest was torn and faded. A filthy handkerchief was tied loosely around his neck. He looked just as Emma had described him.

Jackson Dubose

"Jack, I'm Woolfolk's attorney, and I want you to tell me all about this killing."

"And then you'll hang me."

Walker leaned back in his chair and reached into his coat. "Here," he said calmly, "take a cigar."

The prisoner reached over and took the cigar from the lawyer's hand.

Walker struck a match and said, "Now, Jack, tell me."

"I didn't do it."

"Jack, do you know they will hang you for this?"

Dubose jumped up almost knocking his chair over. "No! I'll be damned if they do." The prisoner was agitated and began pacing back and forth in front of Walker.

"If...if I ever git outta this jail, " he said, leaning against the wall, "I ain't never gonna join up with no one ever agin. That's how I got in d'chain gang."

"But I thought you told me you didn't do it?"

"I didn't...but...well, I wus there when it wus done. I know all 'bout it," he said finally and walked back over to the chair. "I'll tell you if you gits me outta this."

"Well, I don't know about that," Walker said. "I'm Woolfolk's lawyer."

"You wants me to hang."

"No, no I don't. I simply want to get all the evidence I can for Tom Woolfolk's benefit. I don't want to hurt you."

Word of the arrest reached Atlanta and began to revive interest in the story. Pea Jay hurried to the Fulton County Jail but was told he could not see Tom and would have to speak to his lawyer. The reporter decided to wait.

Late in the evening, Walker finally returned from his visit to Canton and went immediately to see Tom. He could not contain his excitement and promised Pea Jay, whom he met in the front room of the jailhouse, that he would gladly talk to him after he had a chance to tell his client the good news.

Pea Jay waited.

An hour later, Walker emerged and walked over to the reporter, "Now, sir, I believe we have something to talk about."

The reporter opened his notepad. "Is it true?"

"The arrest in Cherokee County? Yes, I am glad to say. It is true. The negro was not inclined to talk at first, but finally became more communicative. He told me all about the killing..."

"What?" Pea Jay interrupted.

"Well...you see there were four of them, Jack Dubose and three others. Dubose was outside when the killing was done and when Tom Woolfolk left the house, he passed within a few feet of him."

"How's that?"

"You remember Tom left the house while the killing was going on."

"So he says."

"Jack said Tom came out after the butchery began and in escaping went very close to him."

"Who did the killing?"

"Of course, I can't give the names of the other parties until they are arrested, and I fear one of the three has left the state.

The negro in the Canton jail describes the position of the bodies and how the killing was done."

"How?"

"Well, the old man, or 'Marse Dick' as the prisoner calls him, was killed first. Then a whack was made at Mrs. Woolfolk, but, by accident, hit the baby. They did not intend to kill the baby. Then Mrs. Woolfolk was finished. The two boys ran into the room and were killed there. Miss Pearl was not killed in that room."

"Where then?"

"Out in the hall. She came to the room, and turning, started to run, when she was knocked down and killed. After that, the party went into Mrs. West's room and killed all there because they were making so much noise. Dubose describes the positions of the bodies perfectly."

"Where does he say they got the ax?"

"He doesn't say, and I neglected to ask him. But he tells about the bloody clothing in the well."

"What?"

"They were young Dick's and not Tom's. I learned that as well. You see there was to be a picnic the next day and the family had all fixed for it, even to packing baskets, and in that way Dick's clothing was lying out."

"What was Dubose doing down there?"

"He was working on a farm, and fearing that he would be suspected, left without asking for his money."

"What are you going to do with him?"

"Leave him where he is until I go to Macon and investigate. I want to see the man for whom he says he was working. I will go in the morning."

As the two men walked out of the building, Walker told the reporter how Dubose would not pose for a photograph and had to be forced to sit. Later, the Sheriff convinced the prisoner to sit for a better picture.

"I assume you've told Tom?"

"Certainly."

"How did he respond?"

"As one would expect. It has completely changed him. His spirits have been lifted. He's quite joyful."

CHAPTER TEN
"All I ask is a fair trial."

The State Fair in Macon was in full swing by mid-October. Dust from the drought which had so worried the city fathers was washed away several days earlier by a steady, gentle rain.

Jefferson Davis was in town amidst the fireworks and fanfare warranted the former President of the Confederate States. Veterans donned their old uniforms and paraded in the streets. Speeches, banquets, handshakes, salutes headlined the agenda of the day. The glory of the Old South beamed from the faces of the Old Guard once again.

A week earlier, President Grover Cleveland visited Atlanta. Industrialists and politicians flocked to see him. Henry Grady, the liberal editor of the Atlanta Constitution, showcased the affair. The progressive southerner was known for his enthusiastic speeches delivered to Northern industrialists and developers. The son of a Confederate soldier who was killed in the war, Grady was considered by many to be a leader of the New South and a prominent member of the Atlanta Ring.

"There was a South of slavery and secession–that South is dead. There is a South of union and freedom–that South, thank God, is living, breathing, growing every hour." Grady said a year earlier in a speech to The New England Society.

To the Northern powers, he painted a picture of a united South, where all southerners, white and black, former masters and former slaves, were joined together to rebuild their land. The wholesale slaughter of a prominent plantation family could have seriously compromised the state's courtship of Northern money had Tom Woolfolk not been immediately charged with the crime.

The Northern industrialists would accept a domestic problem that ended in a vicious murder. To keep the focus on Tom, therefore, Grady sent P.J. Moran, the notorious gossip columnist 'Pea Jay', as insurance. Folsom's articles would prevent anyone from accusing the paper of being one-sided.

Such a practice was a common tool for Grady and the Atlanta Ring. Anyone involved in the economic and political development of the region understood the impact of the family's murder in the larger scheme of things. It had to be at the hands of a family member.

Word that John Owens was located in South Carolina and was being brought back to Macon gave Frank Walker some cause for concern. The ex-convict had made some serious statements against Tom Woolfolk during the coroner's inquest. The man then simply disappeared. A detective arrested Owens in Camden, South Carolina, on suspicion of arson. Walker knew the state would have him testify before the Grand Jury scheduled to convene the first week of November. John Owens was the only witness at the time who clearly said he heard Tom threaten his parents.

Simon Cooper, the son of London Cooper, left Hazzard District immediately after the murders. It was the timing of his disappearance that had Folsom wondering. His name was never mentioned. His leaving was never discussed.

Jackson Dubose, still in jail in Canton, was becoming a problem. The papers reported his confession but enthusiastically dismissed its importance. His reputation as a liar and a con-man was known by lawmen state-wide. Walker decided to down play his importance and keep him out of the picture until it was time for him to testify. That is, if Tom was, indeed, indicted. Now that other possible suspects were brought to light, Walker was hoping sanity would return to the judicial system of Bibb County. He was convinced Tom was a victim of mob hysteria.

Tom's mood, of course, improved considerably after Dubose's arrest. Certain he would be freed soon, he encouraged his attorney to request bail. Walker obliged and petitioned the courts. Bail was refused.

On a rare occasion, Tom decided to see reporters. Folsom took advantage of the opportunity to interview the prisoner and arrived at the jail in time to accompany Pea Jay to Tom's cell.

"Gentlemen." Tom greeted the two men warmly as the turnkey allowed them entrance into the prisoner's cage.

"Tom," Folsom smiled and extended his hand. Tom grabbed hold and gave it a hardy shake.

"Folsom, how's it going down there in Macon?" the prisoner asked, smiling.

"Oh, fine, Tom. Just fine."

"I 'spect to be out of here soon, y'know," Tom said.

"You do?" Pea Jay asked curtly.

"Now that there's been a confession. It's only a matter of time before my lawyer gets me bail."

Pea Jay shook his head.

"I wouldn't place any hopes on that colored man up in Canton. We've already provened he's a boldfaced liar. He confesses to anything and everything in order to get free room and board at the taxpayer's expense," Pea Jay said. He casually walked over to Tom's cot and sat down.

"How's your sisters, Tom?" Folsom asked, changing the subject.

Tom put his hands in his pockets and leaned against the wall.

"Oh, they're fine, I guess. Haven't seen much of 'em. Specially Lillie. She lives so far away and got those little ones and all. Aunt Fannie came up with Flo a few weeks back...my brother-in-law, Henry, and L.A. come up whenever they can."

Pea Jay stood up, reached inside his coat pocket, and pulled out a post card.

"Ever seen one of these?" he asked and handed it over to Tom. "They're sellin'um on street corners."

Innocently, Tom took the postcard and studied it closely. Folsom watched as his hand began to shake and tears fill his eyes.

"My God," the prisoner whispered softly.

Pea Jay smiled.

Tom shoved the card against the reporter's chest and growled, "Get out of here. Both of you."

"What is it, Tom?" Folsom asked.

"Get out of here. Now."

Folsom put on his hat. The turnkey quickly unlocked the door. Folsom stepped out and turned to see Pea Jay standing face to face with the prisoner.

"Let's go, Pea Jay," he ordered.

Pea Jay smiled, put on his bowler, and walked out. The turnkey locked the cell behind him. Folsom looked at Tom standing with his back to them. His arms were stiff at his sides, his fists clinched. His back was rigid and straight. He stood looking up at the ceiling and trembling with rage.

The three men quietly walked through the cell block. Folsom waited until he and Pea Jay left the jail before pursuing the matter further.

"Let me see that," he demanded.

Pea Jay smiled and handed the card over. Folsom looked at it closely. He heard that a photographer had gotten inside the Woolfolk house and took pictures of the dead family before the Sheriff arrived. He also heard the photos were being sold in Atlanta although he, himself, had never seen one.

He looked at the picture of Annie, her arm hooked on the window sill. She was in the photo as she had been that August morning. The photographer's attempt to capture the gore surrounding her, however, was faulted by the black and white contrast. An innocent viewer was saved from the crimson horror of the slaughter. Someone who had been there, someone such as Tom or Folsom, however, was reminded of the tragedy.

"You bastard," Folsom growled, tossing the photo to the ground. He turned and walked away.

"What do you mean you let Dubose go?" Walker shouted at Sheriff Kitchen who sat quietly behind his desk. Tom's attorney continued to lean against it. "How could you just let'im go?"

"We wanted to keep'im but we had nothin' on'im. Jesus, Walker, we kept'im longer that the law even allows. Anyway, the Sheriff in Fulton County assured me this one made it a career of confessin' to crimes he ain't committed."

"He didn't confess to this crime. He tried to trade information for his freedom. For once in his sorry, miserable life he's probably tellin' the truth. Damn it."

The attorney stormed over to the window and looked out. The distant hills were blanketed by autumn leaves.

"You know where he mighta gone?" he finally asked, not turning around.

"Probably on over to Carter's Quarters. Supposedly he knows a few of the coloreds over there."

"Damn it. We needed him, George."

"I'm sorry, Frank. I had to release him."

Folsom hurried to the Bibb County Jail. Word was circulating that Tom Woolfolk was back in Macon. A small crowd waited at the front door. The reporter recognized almost everyone, except a few who were probably reporters. Tom was still a good news story. Everything he did or said continued to turn up in the papers. Reporters used other prisoners and employees of the jail as informants. Tom's erratic moods from being friendly and talkative to withdrawn and quiet kept the reporters and authorities on their toes.

Charles Howard and Solicitor-General Hardeman walked out of the jailhouse and climbed aboard a waiting hack. Tom's uncle, Major Thomas J. Woolfolk, stood to the side with Sam Chambless. Folsom walked over to them.

"Gentlemen," he said.

Chambless turned and nodded. The Captain's brother smiled and extended his hand. Folsom patted Chambless on the shoulder and shook hands with Tom's uncle.

"Waitin' to see Tom?" the reporter asked.

"Yes we are," Major Woolfolk answered.

The reporter studied the Southern gentlemen. After first moving to the Piedmont Region of the state, he heard the name Woolfolk many times. The Woolfolk brothers—Sowell, Thomas, Richard, John, and James—were extremely popular throughout the entire region. Parties at Thomas' big house in James, Georgia were social events looked forward to by everyone. Everyone knew and respected the name Woolfolk.

Before that August morning, Folsom had never heard of the man Sam Chambless. Now, his name was synonymous with the murders. The farmer became the unofficial spokesman for Hazzard District and an authority on the tragedy. Anyone wanting to visit the murder scene and talk with the laborers were referred to him. Sam Chambless had replaced the Captain as the leader of Hazzard District, and, with his newly established fame, he decided to run for the State House of Representatives.

The murders, nonetheless, occupied Chambless' mind. There were so many questions he wanted answered. He had no doubt that Tom Woolfolk committed the deed. The young man had been an embarrassment to the Captain. Richard Woolfolk was of the gentry. His first son, however, had not inherited his aristocratic blood.

When the old veteran marched along Mulberry Street during President Davis' review, he thought of how the Captain would have relished the event. Southern pride was emerging from the pain and humiliation of the defeat in sixty-five and the military occupation that followed. The newly erected Confederate monument at the intersection of Cotton, Second, and Mulberry was dedicated. Nostalgia was thick. Yet, whenever he was interviewed Chambless was rarely asked about his war experience or candidacy. Everyone wanted to know about the murders.

Sheriff Westcott walked out and nodded to the men. Major Woolfolk, Chambless, and Folsom hurried inside.

"Nat, take these gentlemen up to see the prisoner."

"Yessir," Birdsong answered and led the men through the door leading to the stairwell.

"I understand you brought Tom in last night?" Folsom asked.

"Yeh, and it went off without a hitch. No one knew 'bout it...not even Tom," the jailer chuckled.

"Surely Tom knew you were coming to get him?" Major Woolfolk asked.

"Yeh, he knew I was comin'...just didn't know exactly when. We didn't tell nobody. Had to...for security reasons, y'know. He seemed glad to see me, though. Threw his thangs t'gether and was ready t'go. I shackled him up real good 'n all...then we had t'wait for the next train. Tom was hungry so I got'im a steak. We ate right there on the platform and nobody bothered us," the jailer said proudly.

The sound of a chain rattling above their heads caused the visitors to look up. Birdsong ignored the noise.

"How's he looking?" Tom's uncle asked.

"Oh, got more weight on'im than when I last saw'im back in August. A might paler I think but heavier. I guess he's in good nuff spirits."

The four men walked into the cell block. At the far end, Tom stood waiting. His arms were hanging through the bars, a cigarette hung loose between his fingers. A chain and an ankle bracelet tethered him to the wall. The prisoner raised a hand and greeted his guests with a wave and a flick of his cigarette ashes.

"Uncle Thomas, Mistah Chambless, Folsom," he said, tossing the cigarette away and straightening up. He placed his hands on his hips and watched them approach.

"Nephew," Tom's uncle said warmly.

Chambless walked up to the door and stuck his hand through the bars to Tom. Tom gave it a light shake and then let it go.

"Well, Tom, you're lookin' better than when I saw you last," the old farmer remarked.

Tom smiled politely. "Yeh...a little fleshier, I spect. I think maybe I gotta bit of a cold, though."

"How'd it go in Atlanta?" Folsom asked.

"Oh...I had a good time. Was treated well there."

"If it's a fair question, Tom, what do you think of your approachin' trial?" the reporter continued. He readied his pencil on his notepad and waited for the prisoner's response.

Tom looked at each man. He chose his words carefully and spoke slowly. "I feel like if I get justice...I'll come out all right. All I ask is a fair trial...and I feel like the Good Lord'll be with me."

Tom's uncle tried to smile reassuringly. "That's what everybody wants, Tom, to give you justice," he said.

Tom smiled. "Yes sir, and if they do I'll come clear. I believe there're good people...as well as bad...in Macon and I hope for a fair, honest trial. Whoever says I killed my parents...tells a damned lie. I never harmed a man, woman...or child in my life, much less murdered anybody. I always tried to live right."

"But...Tom...there are some circumstances," Chambless interrupted, "that'll need to be cleared up."

"I know that," Tom snapped and then caught himself. More calmly, he continued. "But I'm not afraid of them that have power over the body. I've made peace with my Maker...I trust in Him."

Folsom marvelled at the sincerity in Tom's voice, in his expression.

"I've been wrongfully treated," Tom continued, slowly, "and I've suffered...I'm still suffering for a crime I am not guilty..."

"But, you know,...that when all the family was murdered and you were the only one that escaped...you went back there afterwards to see if they was dead," Chambless went on.

Tom interrupted. "That's true, and had I not jumped out of the house and run, I'd a been murdered, too. I didn't know they was dead until I went back."

"Tom, do you suspect anybody at all?" Folsom asked.

"No. How could I when I didn't see no one," he answered and took hold of the barred door with his right hand. "I know this much, though," he continued, "threats were made against my Pa...and Smith. I know when Pa went out to his sawmill he wouldn't go alone. He'd take somebody with him. He told me so." Tom looked at his guests closely. "Mind you, I'm not accusing anybody. I only know about the threats because Pa told me."

The prisoner began to ramble. Folsom tried to keep up. His pencil moved swiftly across the page of his tablet.

"I know that man, Birch Horn, met me on the road and asked me where Pa was. I told'im it wasn't necessary t'see Pa, that I had the notes and he could settle with me." He stopped and looked down at his feet. "...but I'm not accusing anybody."

Chambless looked around the cell block and then back at Tom. The room was quiet. The old farmer spoke up.

"I heard somethin' 'bout that. Tom, if your innocence can be established, it'd be a source of consolation to our community out there. But you know the story you told me that mornin'...all that'll have to be cleared up."

Tom glared at Chambless. His eyes flashed with anger. In a voice revealing his struggle to control his emotions he answered slowly. "I've known for some time that you're against me. I heard about what you've said on several occasions. I know no more about that killing than you do. But...," he paused and looked at his uncle, "...if they punish me, I'm man enough to stand all they put on me. I've heard that one man said he'd kill me on sight."

Tom looked down, kicked his leg out. The chain rattled loudly. He chuckled. "I reckon he'd like to see me in these chains here now...to get a chance."

"Tom," Chambless protested. "Tom, you know that I prevented them from killin' you out there. Had it not been for me they'd a hung you at once."

Tom looked away. "Well, I didn't care then. You all might have taken that same ax and knocked me in the head with it. My folks were all dead...what'd I want to live for? Then everybody pitched right in on me...because I was the only one left."

Folsom listened closely to the anger in Tom's voice. He watched the prisoner's hand tremble as he brought it back up to the bar.

He continued in a quiet tone. "If you will excuse me, we'll change the subject, now."

Chambless refused to end the conversation and continued to agitate the prisoner with his protests until Birdsong interrupted and asked the three men to leave.

As they entered the lobby, Folsom listened to the sound of Tom's chain rake back and forth across the floor of his cell above their heads.

Westcott walked out of the office accompanied by John Cobb Rutherford, the former Solicitor-General for the Southwestern court circuit. The popular forty-five year old attorney stopped and faced the Sheriff. Tom's uncle walked over to the two men. Folsom followed.

"Colonel Rutherford? I understand you're planning to join Walker in Tom's defense."

"Well, Mistah Woolfolk I am seriously considering it."

"I'd like you to know any help you can give us will be sincerely appreciated by the family. Thank you, sir. Good day, gentlemen."

Major Woolfolk put on his hat and walked away. Folsom remained near by and waited for Rutherford to finish his conversation with Westcott. The sound of Tom's chain continued to rake over their heads. Ever so often, Rutherford would look up at the ceiling. Westcott was undisturbed.

Minutes later, the two men parted. Folsom followed Rutherford out the front door.

"'Scuse me, sir," he called out.

The lawyer stopped half way down the steps; his hat still in his hand.

"Yes?"

"My name is Montgomery Morgan Folsom. I'm with the Atlanta Constitution. Would you mind if I asked you a few questions concerning Tom Woolfolk's case?"

Rutherford looked up at the sun and then pulled his watch from his vest pocket.

"I'm sorry, but I have an appointment."

"Would you mind if I accompany you. We could talk along the way?"

"No, I am sorry. Maybe we could meet at a later time...say three this afternoon at my office. I'll gladly talk with you then. If you'll excuse me."

Folsom watched Rutherford climb into his carriage and drive away. Over head, from an opened window, the reporter heard the distinct sound of Tom's chain and knew the prisoner was still pacing his cell.

That evening, Folsom waited patiently in the outer office of the firm of Bacon and Rutherford, near the Lanier House on the corner of Mulberry and Third. John C. Rutherford was a member of a wealthy and respected family from Athens. His father Williams Rutherford was a popular professor at the University of Georgia. His sister Millie was the principal at one of the state's more prominent girls school, Lucy Cobb Institute. Rutherford himself was well known as one of the state's most abled criminal attorneys. His uncle, for whom he was named, was the original partner to Augustus O. Bacon. After the elder's retirement, the younger Rutherford came to Macon, rented a room at the Lanier House, and took over the practice.

The door to Rutherford's private office opened and a young clerk stepped out.

"Mistah Folsom? Captain Rutherford will see you now," he said and walked over to his desk.

Folsom jumped from his seat and walked into the office. John Rutherford stood looking out the window to the street below. His office was in the heart of the city. Street sounds filtered through the window opened an inch at the top.

"Thank you, sir...uh, for seeing me."

Rutherford did not turn around. He was lost in his thoughts.

John Cobb Rutherford
*(Hargrett Rare Book and
Manuscript Library/University
of Georgia Libraries).*

"I wasn't here when the murders occurred," Rutherford said, still looking out the window.

"Sir?"

"I was away at the time. But I kept abreast of the case through the newspapers." He continued as he turned around and sat down behind his cluttered desk. Folsom sat down in the straight back chair strategically positioned on the other side.

"Yes, sir."

"You reporters, sir, have had quite a heyday with this murder and this man, Tom Woolfolk."

"Yes, sir."

"Now, what can I do for you?"

"Well, have you decided to take Tom's case?"

"Yes, as a matter of fact, I have."

"Can I ask why?"

"Upon the request of Frank Walker, Woolfolk's lawyer, I visited with Tom in his cell as soon as he was brought back to Macon. I was impressed with the young man's sincerity. And based on my experience as a criminal lawyer, I believe he could not have made the statements he made in the manner he made them were he not an innocent man."

"So, you believe Tom Woolfolk to be innocent?"

"Of course."

"Well, sir, there are alot of circumstantial factors that have convinced others to the contrary."

"Do you believe him guilty?"

Folsom was startled at the question. In the three months since the bodies were discovered, no one had asked him directly what he personally thought. He coughed nervously and looked down at his notepad.

"Well, I..."

"Tell me the truth, Mistah Folsom."

"No, sir, I do not believe Tom Woolfolk killed his family."

"Well then, you can understand my position. Tom was able to account for every bit of circumstantial evidence lodged against him. The prisoner is very indignant and much distressed that people believe him capable of killing his father and his family."

"Yes, sir. Did he tell you what happened?"

"The same facts I am sure you have been told by him many times before."

"Yes, sir."

"Tom believes strongly...he is convinced that if he had not gotten away he would have also been killed along with his family. Had his brother not been aroused before him and ran in ahead, he would have done so himself, and would have instead been hit as his brother was. He would not have been able to escape and sound the alarm. Of course, our interview was brief but enough to convince me of his innocence."

"Yes, sir."

"Now, sir, I am afraid this interview will also have to be brief. As you can imagine, I have a lot of work to do. The prosecution has quite a head start on this case." The lawyer stood up.

"Please, sir. A final question?" Folsom said.

"All right."

"Do you think Tom will be indicted?"

"I am afraid, sir, you reporters have made it impossible for it to be any other way. Good day."

A few days later, the Clerk of Superior Court Daniel Adams pondered the most practical and efficient way to complete the nine indictments that would be brought against Tom Woolfolk for murder. He decided to have his secretary write nine blank forms of indictments, filling out all pertinent information except the name. His instructions were to leave a space in each indictment for the name of the murdered victim. When the Grand Jury made its decision all the district attorney would have to do was simply fill in the appropriate name.

As Folsom stood on the corner of Third and Mulberry waiting for the trolley, a carriage rolled slowly by. Lost in his own thoughts, he hardly noticed it. He boarded the street car and then realized one of the occupants in the carriage was Tom's wife Georgia. Sitting beside her was her father Thomas Bird.

Bird reined onto Fourth behind the trolley and then turned left onto Cherry Street. Folsom knew the couple's destination. He pulled the signal cord over head and then hopped off before the conductor had a chance to respond.

The reporter ran down Cherry Street after them and was crossing the Central Rail tracks as they pulled into the jailhouse yard.

Thomas Bird helped Georgia down. Taking hold of her elbow he guided her towards the front steps. Folsom caught up with them as they were about to enter the jailhouse.

"Mistah Folsom?" Thomas Bird turned, startled to see the reporter run up behind them.

"Yes, sir. Are you here to see Tom?"

"As a matter of fact, we are," Bird answered and opened the front door.

"Have you had any contact with your husband, Mrs. Woolfolk?" Folsom asked as he followed the couple into the front lobby.

"Tom's written me several times."

"I'll see if they'll let us in to see'im," her father interrupted. "Wait here." Thomas Bird walked away. Folsom remained at Georgia's side.

"You've received some letters from Tom while he's been in jail?"

"Yes. I've gotten four from him." She seemed anxious.

Folsom watched as Birdsong called the turnkey over. The guard disappeared through the door to the stairs leading up to the cell block.

"Did he say anything particular? In the letters, I mean."

"Oh...no. Just what it's like in jail and his dreams."

"Dreams?"

Thomas Bird rejoined the couple. "They're goin' to see if Tom'll see us." He remarked, blankly.

The familiar sound of Tom's chain began to rattle above their heads. Folsom looked up and then back at Georgia.

"What dreams?" he asked.

Georgia was looking at the ceiling. Her father interjected for her.

"You talkin' about Woolfolk's letters?"

"Yes, sir."

"He wrote about havin' strange dreams. He said his pa was in a few of'em."

"He's dreamed about his father?"

"Yeh, he said he...how did he put it...he said he saw his 'dear old father'."

Birdsong approached the trio.

"I'm sorry, ma'am. But your husband refuses to see you."

"Oh?" she responded.

"But," the jailer continued, turning to her father, "he said he would see you, Mistah Bird."

Thomas Bird looked at his daughter. She smiled weakly.

"I won't be long," he said and followed Birdsong through the door.

A few minutes later, they both returned. Thomas Bird was not inclined to talk to the reporter. He put on his hat, took his daughter by the elbow and escorted her out of the jailhouse. Folsom walked over to Birdsong.

"What happened up there?" he asked.

Birdsong looked bewildered.

"When Tom met with his father-in-law? Did anything happen?" Folsom asked again.

"No, not really," the jailer remarked. "I mean they greeted each other pleasant enough I s'pose. Mistah Bird reached out and Tom took'is hand. They just stood there talkin' quiet like for a minute or two...still holdin' their handshake."

"Why didn't he want to see his wife, you suppose?"

"Would you want your wife to see you chained like a dog?" Birdsong asked blankly.

"No...I guess not."

CHAPTER ELEVEN
"I am not guilty, sir."

On the evening of November 11, 1887, Solicitor John L. Hardeman took the nine previously prepared indictments and filled in the name of each murder victim. Earlier, nineteen witnesses, mostly residents from Hazzard District, testified before the twenty Grand Jurors. The ten blacks and nine whites repeated their now familiar stories. No new evidence was presented. The impaneled Grand Jury had no problem rendering its decision.

The nine True Bills of Indictments against Tom were signed by Jury Foreman Ben Smith, Solicitor-General John L. Hardeman, and Prosecutor Charles W. Howard, Mattie Woolfolk's brother.

Tom Woolfolk was not informed of the indictments until Montgomery Folsom went to visit him.

"Did you know that bills had been found, Tom?" Folsom asked, referring to the indictments.

"No, I didn't."

"Well, there were nine of'em found. An indictment for murder in each case."

"No more than I expected," Tom responded softly.

Folsom watched as the prisoner turned his back to him. The interview was over.

At daybreak on the morning of December 5, 1887, people began to gather at both the jail and the courthouse. Every corner along Mulberry Street held clusters of pedestrians waiting to get a glimpse of the infamous prisoner. Sidewalks in front of and across the street from the courthouse were packed. At the intersection of Second, Mulberry, and Cotton, street car after street car stopped and unloaded countless passengers. The day of the long awaited trial had arrived, and no one wanted to miss the affair.

Emma and Aaron Jones came, along with the others from the Woolfolk farm and Hazzard District, in a wagon sent by Samuel Chambless to insure their arrival. Everyone was present although it was made clear to them by Chambless that it would be a considerable wait before they would be allowed to give their testimonies.

Reporters and photographers from across the country flocked to the courthouse. To many of the local citizens, the event overshadowed the visit by Jeff Davis a month and a half earlier.

Folsom stood with Pea Jay and Ramsdel on the steps of the Lanier House. His two colleagues from Atlanta had arrived the night before. Pea Jay was his usual self, strutting around puffing on his large cigar. Ramsdel stood off to the side, quietly sketching the scenes around them.

By 8:30 a.m., those people able to get inside were seated and waited patiently for the show to begin. Folsom looked around the room. The audience behind the bar was filled mostly by white men while a section to the side was designated for white women. In the galleries above, black, white, male and female were crowded together.

Circuit Court Judge James Simmons had been appointed to the State Supreme Court. At the bench, his replacement George W. Gustin convened his first case as judge. Originally, the senior partner of the firm, Gustin and Hall, Gustin's nomination was made by State House Representative William Felton. It was Felton who just months earlier during a speech in the House of Representatives used Tom Woolfolk's name to represent the evil lurking in Georgia.

Although Felton and the Atlanta Ring had been at odds over most every political and economic issue in the state, they all agreed the murder of a prominent Southern family could not reflect negatively on the state. Northern industrialists made it clear a year earlier to Georgia delegates visiting the New England states, of which Henry Grady was a leading member, that they did not approve of the convict lease system as well as the plight of the freed slave in the state. Until conditions improved they were not inclined to send money and industry to the South.

The murders placed the state, its convict lease program as well as the tenant farming system in the national limelight. Newspapers reported on every aspect of the Woolfolk family including the Captain leasing convicts from the state and the number of sharecroppers on his farm. All eyes were on Georgia and Judge Gustin's court.

The swearing in had already begun when the side door opened and a ragged, unshaven Tom Woolfolk walked in accompanied by his lawyer Frank Walker and Sheriff Westcott. The prisoner was shackled at the ankles and wrists. The chain forced his gait to be short and jerky.

The room was silent. No one said a word. As if choreographed, every head followed him as he shuffled across the room. From the state's table, Charles Howard watched his nephew closely.

John Rutherford hurried down the aisle and joined Walker and the defendant at the table. The three men huddled together in conference. Rutherford then left the courtroom. Judge Gustin continued with the jury call.

Forty-five minutes after nine, the case of The State of Georgia versus Thomas G. Woolfolk was called to order. William Hodnett, the coroner at the murder scene, stood and, serving as bailiff, called the names of the prosecution's witnesses.

John Hardeman stood up. "The State is ready, Your Honor."

A soft murmur floated through the room. Judge Gustin looked at the defense. Walker and Tom were in deep conversation. As he whispered to his client, the attorney would anxiously glance over his shoulder at the main door.

"Mistah Walker?" the Judge addressed him directly.

The young lawyer jumped up. Looking again at the door, he answered, "I'm sorry, Your Honor. I'm afraid..."

The door opened. John Rutherford hurried up to the table.

"What does the defense say?" the Judge asked.

"Has the state announced?" Rutherford answered.

"It was announced ready."

"Let me have the list of witnesses called," Rutherford responded.

As names of prominent and respected Georgians from across the region were called for the defense, the audience responded with whispers and murmurs. John Rutherford stepped away from his chair.

"Your Honor, I am afraid there are a number of very important witnesses who are not present to testify." He walked back over to the table and picked up a sheet of paper. "Samuel S. Pennington, Fred C. Foster, L. A. Shackleford, Alexander Bird, and Jackson Dubose."

At the mention of Dubose's name, a murmur again rose from the audience. Judge Gustin tapped his gavel.

"Go on, Captain Rutherford."

"Your Honor, subpoenas were issued to each of the witnesses. Without these men, especially Mistah Pennington, we can not continue."

Judge Gustin interrupted. "I have here a letter from Mistah Pennington stating his reason for not being in attendance."

"Your Honor, Mistah Pennington is a very important witness without whom we can not continue in our case. His testimony is important, sir, and to insure his appearance we sent him the money necessary to pay for his trip." Rutherford picked up another sheet of paper and continued.

"Our efforts to locate Jackson Dubose have been unsuccessful. However, we do have with us the Sheriff of Cherokee County, George Kitchen, to whom Jackson Dubose confessed. Sheriff Kitchen is here to testify to that fact."

The defense placed a motion to allow Kitchen's testimony. Rutherford then requested that Kitchen's affidavit be taken. The Judge agreed.

The solicitor stood and requested the motion and affidavits be recorded. The Judge agreed.

"Your Honor," Rutherford had a final request. "The defendant was not allowed the opportunity this morning to prepare himself personally for trial. As you can see, he is unshaved and in need of a bath."

The Judge looked over at Westcott who stood up. "I'm sorry, Your Honor. There wasn't time this mornin' to allow the prisoner a bath and a shave."

"While the motion and affidavits are being written," Rutherford continued, "the defendant could be allowed this time."

"Granted." Judge Gustin slammed his gavel and announced a recess.

As the noon sun warmed the cool December day, the courtroom became stuffy. Behind the defense, Flo Edwards and Fannie Crane sat quietly. Each were veiled and wore black. L. A. Shackelford and Henry Cowan sat on each side.

The large double doors opened with a loud groan. The soft murmuring response of the audience forced Folsom to turn around. Ben Howard, Mattie's father, stood at the doorway. His son John was beside him, holding his elbow. Charles Howard left the prosecution's table and hurried to his father's side. The two men assisted the old man. With tremendous effort, he slowly made his way down the aisle.

Folsom watched Howard struggle with each step. His look, though aged, his courtly manner though feeble, reminded the reporter of the many plantation owners of old, the lords and masters.

The glory that was once the plantation, however, now existed mostly in fiction and in the memories of the graying Southerners such as Howard. Their weakened land struggled to produce the same crop year after year. Efforts by agriculturalists to educate the farmers to the benefits of crop rotation were inhibited by the addiction Southerners still had for cotton.

After the defeat of the Confederacy, Howard managed to hold onto his farm. Nearly crippled by killing taxes and by the lost of his free labor, he joined the other landowners and implemented sharecropping. The tenant farmer replaced the slave and by the very nature of the agreement became indentured to the landowner.

At the front of the courtroom Tom Woolfolk entered. The much needed bath and shave had transformed him. He looked more comfortable. At the sight of her brother, Flo stood up. Tom shuffled in his chains over to her. She leaned over the railing and took his hands. Behind her, Tom's aunt dabbed her eyes. The prisoner reached out to her. The older woman grabbed a hand and squeezed it.

The opposing counsel approached the bench.

"Your Honor," Rutherford began the discussion, "every minute of the time given us was used in documenting the affidavits and additional evidence by the court stenographer. These still need to be transcribed from notes. This will take hours. I would like to suggest that the court recorder simply read his notes."

Hardeman shook his head. "Your Honor, I think it would be better if the motion be in plain English, and, as for the notes, they should be written out."

"If Your Honor will recall I was ready and willing to deliver my motion orally," Rutherford continued.

Judge Gustin looked at the two men standing before him and sighed.

"I am calling a recess until 2:30 this afternoon. The jurors and witnesses are dismissed until that time."

Tom was tired. He had been warned that the proceedings would move slowly. The details attended to in the courtroom seemed so insignificant to him, yet, his attorneys reassured him their every action and reaction was vital to his defense.

When court reconvened, Judge Gustin read the charges. Walker nudged the prisoner. Tom's chains clanked loudly as he rose from his chair.

"How do you plea?" the Judge asked.

From his position on the far side of the room, Folsom could see the muscle in Tom's jaw tighten. The defendant's eyes glistened.

"I am not guilty, sir."

Name after name was called. None of the first panel of eleven jurors were accepted. F. S. Parker, the sixth juror of the second panel was the first to qualify.

Henry Cowan leaned over and whispered to Walker.

"Your Honor," Walker called out.

"Counselor?" the Judge responded.

"Sir, I have just been given some information that I feel disqualifies this juror."

"Your Honor," Hardeman protested. "This juror was already accepted by the defense."

Walker insisted. The Judge allowed him to continue.

Henry Cowan was called to the stand.

"Would you please tell the court just exactly what you heard in the lobby during the court's recess," Walker instructed.

"Well, I heard him, Mistah Parker, say he woulda helped lynch Tom that day had he been there. Then when he heard he might be considered for the jury...he knew he'd be able to do justice then."

Pea Jay leaned over and whispered to Folsom, "At this rate they ain't never gonna get a jury."

"Not from this county," Folsom agreed.

Parker was called to the stand. Under oath, he admitted he felt Tom should be punished. The juror was dismissed.

The toll of the city clock struck four and the first juror, J. S. Lowery, an insurance salesman, was accepted.

The setting of the sun brought the soft glow of Edison lights throughout the city. In the courtroom, the selection of a jury continued without much success. After forty-four jurors were called, only four had been selected. The audience remained in their seats. Outside, groups of people stood waiting and watching the glowing windows for signs of activity, any activity.

Tom's sister and aunt rose to leave. It was late. Flo leaned over and kissed her brother good-bye. She walked away, then stopped. Suddenly, she turned back around, ran up to the prisoner and kissed him again.

CHAPTER TWELVE
"This one still has blood on it."

Pea Jay predicted a lengthy jury selection and he was right. By the end of the first day, six panels of jurors were reviewed. Of those sixty-six men, only seven jurors were accepted. Mostly bookkeepers and accountants, the seven men were sequestered together for the night.

The sixth juror Asher Ayres was engaged to be married and his wedding scheduled for the following week. Because of the possible conflict in time, the wealthy young broker regretted his selection but accepted his civic responsibility with resolve. News reporters took advantage of the situation and wrote human interest stories about the beautiful young bride Louise Conner having to postpone her wedding because of the murderer Tom Woolfolk.

The stall tactics, intentional or otherwise, exercised by the defense worked somewhat. Samuel S. Pennington finally arrived.

Tom was exhausted and appeared nervous during early evening. By nightfall, however, he regained his much recognized demeanor. Pea Jay was bored and left early. Folsom remained, scribbling notes in his notebook.

The next morning the seven selected jurors entered the courtroom and were seated in the jury box. With the roster of potential jurors exhausted the previous day, court constables had to diligently search throughout the night for individuals to complement the panels. Judge Gustin resumed the call and fifty six men were made ready.

As on the previous day, the solicitor-general announced the defense would be allowed to challenge each juror. John

167

Rutherford responded by requesting that the defense be permitted to question each potential juror about reading newspaper accounts of the murder. Tom's counsel argued that a fair and impartial jury could not be obtained in Bibb County because of the news coverage. The court denied the request.

Twelve men were considered and rejected. The thirteenth panelist was asked the standard question, "Have you from having seen the crime committed or from having heard evidence delivered under oath formed and expressed an opinion as to the guilt or innocence of the prisoner?"

"Only from readin'," he replied.

Rutherford immediately jumped to his feet and challenged.

Hardeman responded, "Your Honor, I do not doubt this man's competency to serve as a juror. The simple and innocent act of reading a newspaper should not disqualify him."

Again, Rutherford challenged. "If it pleases the court, I must protest. If a juror had prior access to the newspaper accounts of the sworn testimonies delivered that day during the coroner's inquest, said juror cannot be considered unbiased and impartial."

Judge Gustin leaned over the bench and instructed the solicitor to repeat the question to the panelist.

"Have you from having seen the crime committed or from having heard evidence delivered under oath formed and expressed an opinion as to the guilt or innocence of the prisoner?"

"If, if the prisoner could show good...uh...evidence of his innocence, I...I would be willin' t'give him justice."

Judge Gustin looked at Hardeman for a moment, then shook his head. The panelist was dismissed.

By 11:30 a.m., a total of one hundred sixty-five potential jurors had been called. Only eleven men sat in the jury box. The panel again was empty. Judge Gustin had no alternative but to call a recess so the bailiffs could search for more potential jurors.

As the city clock tolled one, the twelfth man took his seat. A photographer took pictures of the courtroom, and Judge Gustin declared a recess for dinner.

After the jury was seated and the one hundred sixty-five witnesses were sworn in, John L.Hardeman rose. Tall and distinguished, the solicitor for the state walked up to the jury box and stopped. It was three o'clock.

In a loud, sharp voice, Hardeman reminded the jury that a total of nine people had been murdered during the early morning hours of August 6–five children and four adults. He explained that although the state had charged Thomas G. Woolfolk, the defendant, for the murders, the trial in which they were participating was for the murder of just one of the victims--Richard F. Woolfolk, Tom's father. He then began a step by step review of the events that followed the discovery of the bodies.

The room was silent. Everyone listened closely to the grisly details.

Folsom looked at Tom. There was no expression, no reaction from the prisoner, yet behind him, a few feet away the black veil hid the tears streaming down the cheeks of his sister. Love Shackleford sat beside her, holding her hand.

The attorney spoke for twenty minutes. At the close of his address, he stood facing the jury, his hands resting on the railing in front of them. There was a pause. Someone coughed nervously. He pushed himself away and returned to his seat.

The room exploded in applause. The Judge tapped his gavel and instructed the defense to proceed. John Rutherford approached the jury.

In a rather quiet tone, the defense attorney calmly told Tom's story. He recreated the events following Tom's first run down the hill. He told how the mob immediately suspected the sole survivor and threatened to lynch him. He described how the Sheriff, feeling pressure from the mob, arrested Tom and rushed him to jail. He admitted that some of the clothes found in the well belonged to Tom and promised to provide a logical explanation to the circumstances surrounding them. Then, to the audience's surprise, the attorney announced he would provide witnesses who would testify under oath that there had been threats made against Captain Richard Woolfolk a few days before the murders occurred. He told about money missing from the house and the details supplied by Jackson Dubose.

As his attorney expounded the love Tom had for his family, the defendant looked down at the notepad resting on the table in front of him. His shoulders were slumped. His every action and reaction was watched and studied by members of the audience. For the first time, many saw sadness in his eyes and in his posture. His reputation for frustrating news reporters with his lack of visible emotion or expression was well established. The feelings he showed as his lawyer spoke surprised even Folsom who had grown accustomed to Tom's stoicism and granite resolve.

The reporter watched closely as the defendant, his cheek crimson, turned his head slightly and looked out a window. His moist eyes took on a distant gaze.

Rutherford paused, pointed his finger at Tom and announced in a loud, clear voice, "Tom Woolfolk did not kill his father."

Folsom checked his watch. It was four in the afternoon. Samuel Chambless, the first witness for the prosecution, was calmly describing in detail the position and condition of each body. The newspapers had done their job well. Every part of his testimony so far had been reported at various times during the four months before the trial.

The prosecutor walked over to a table and picked up a short handled axe.

"Is this the axe you found propped up against the door leading into the Captain's bedroom?" he asked.

"Yes, sir. It's the same one I saw that day."

"And what was the condition of the axe?"

"It looked like it'd been used for butcherin'."

Rutherford objected and was overruled.

Chambless cleared his throat and continued, "Uh...it was covered with blood and skin...and hair. Just like at a hog slaughter."

"Look at Woolfolk," Pea Jay whispered to Folsom.

Tom was obviously moved. At first sight of the axe, his head jerked slightly. He watched Chambless closely, but the old man would not look at him.

The prosecutor walked back over to the table. "Now then, Mistah Chambless, would you please tell the court about these." The lawyer picked up a pair of dirty, stained socks and brought them over to the witness. Chambless took them and examined them closely.

"Well, sir, we cleaned out the well a few days later, and we came up with them socks. They was covered with blood."

"And while you were in the house with the defendant after he had shown you the bodies what did he say about the tracks leading from body to body?"

"He said they was his."

"What was the defendant wearing at the time?"

"He was in his underclothes."

"What did he have on his feet?"

"Socks."

"And what were the condition of his socks?"

"They was bloody."

"No further questions."

The solicitor returned to his table. John Rutherford stood up and approached the witness. Tom leaned forward and listened closely as his attorney began his cross-examination.

"Now then, Mistah Chambless. About those tracks. You said that the defendant admitted they were his tracks, is that correct?"

"Yes, sir."

"He admitted this freely to you. Did he try to hide this fact from you?"

"No, sir."

"How was it that these tracks were made?"

"Sir?"

"How was it that there were tracks in the first place?"

"Well, there was blood ever where."

"So, anyone would have left tracks. Did you leave tracks?"

"Well, yes, but those tracks were already there when I got there."

"Did the defendant admit to going back up to the house after he sounded the alarm?"

"Yes, sir."

"Did he tell you why?"

"He said he went back to see if they was all dead."

"So he walked from body to body, checking to see if they were dead?"

"That's what he said he did."

Folsom's thought went back to the day of the murder and the tracks leading from body to body. Tom admitted the foot prints were his. By the time Folsom got there, tracks were everywhere. No one could avoid the blood. The reporter originally agreed with everyone else that a single set of bloody footprints was very incriminating evidence. It was something Chambless had just said on the stand, however, that disturbed him. It was the word butcherin'.

At a hog slaughter, the person who killed the hog rarely got blood on him. It was the one who then took the hog to the boiling shed who had to deal with the blood and would have to track through it. By then, the blood had ample time to flow into puddles.

"Now, about the well," Rutherford continued. "What else did you retrieve from it?"

"Well, I brought up some rags, a shirt, them socks, and a wool hat."

"And were all these identified to have been the property of the defendant's?"

"No, sir. The shirt belonged to young Richard Woolfolk, and the hat belonged to Silas Woolfolk."

"And...who is Silas Woolfolk?"

"He's a colored man who used to work on the farm."

"Isn't he the same Silas Woolfolk who's the brother-in-law of the colored man, George Caldwell?"

"Yes."

"Would you mind telling the court who George Caldwell is?"

"I object," the prosecutor yelled, jumping to his feet.

"I will allow it. Answer the question, Mistah Chambless."

"He used to work on the farm."

"Is he there now?"

"No, sir. He's on the chain gang. He was arrested for stealing an ox."

"From whom?"

"The Captain."

"Captain Richard Woolfolk?"
"Yes, sir."

Tom, escorted by Sheriff Westcott and his deputies, walked out into the morning light. The third day of his trial did not diminish the number of spectators milling around the jail and courthouse. The party repeated the routine of the previous two days. They boarded the buggy waiting for them at the front door. The driver's instructions were simple. He was not to stop for any reason and not to delay. The buggy raced through the streets.

In the courtroom, Lillie and Flo took their seats. Their undaunted support for their brother was praised on the street and in the newspapers. They spoke to no one. L.A. Shackleford and Henry Cowan acted as their spokesmen.

Samuel Chambless waited to be recalled. His cross-examination by the defense the day before had been interrupted by nightfall. Although John Rutherford had not drilled him, the old man felt exhausted, both physically and emotionally.

Folsom looked around the room. It was nearly empty. Pea Jay had not accompanied him to the courthouse. He chose, instead, to stay in the restaurant at the Lanier House.

Court was called to order shortly after nine o'clock, and Samuel Chambless took the stand. The defense repeated a few of the topics covered the night before. Minutes later, Rutherford turned as if finished with the witness. He walked over to the table, looked down at Tom sitting there alert but calm. Chambless shifted slightly in his seat. The court waited for Rutherford to continue.

"Mistah Chambless," he said and turned around. "What did you say was the defendant's state of mind the morning the murders were discovered?"

"Sir?"

"Tell us how he acted that morning. Was he excited? Not excited?"

"I don't rightly know."

"You testified to the coroner's jury that he was excited."

"I don't remember saying so."

Rutherford turned around, picked up the coroner's report and read Chambless' statement back to him.

"If I said that then, then it must be so...although I have no recollection of it."

The next witness to testify was William Smith who, as had Chambless, repeated his original statement given to the coroner's jury and to the papers. He told the jury about waiting with Tom and hearing the noise as if 'someone had moved a chair.' He identified the axe, now rusted but still caked with rotting tissue and strands of hair. The young farmer spoke clearly and concisely. His answers were detailed and consistent. He was on the stand fifty minutes.

Flo Edwards and Love Shackleford walked down the aisle to their seats. The fifteen minute recess afforded them time to stretch and get some fresh air. The endless testimony about the axe and the actual sight of it caused Flo so much distress that Shackleford tried to talk her into going home. She refused, insisting Tom needed her there behind him.

George Yates was called to the stand. Flo half listened as he told about arriving at the house, talking with Bill Smith, and then riding for help. His testimony was simply a repeat of the previous two.

Solicitor Hardeman handed him a bundle of clothes. The witness was repulsed by the smell but identified them as those he saw pulled out of the well.

Hardeman held the articles up to the jury. The clothing was dirty, splotched with dark stains. A veiled gasp shot through the audience, then silence. Tom's jaw stiffened. His intense expression cut a deep furrow across his brow. Flo grabbed Love's hand and held it tightly.

Yates told of examining the shirt and seeing what he determined to be brains and blood splattered over it. He spoke of the foot prints in the house and described them as 'gobs of blood'.

"Mistah Yates," Rutherford began his cross-examine. "You said you examined the clothing."

"Yes, sir."

"Who's idea was that?"

"I'm sorry. I don't know what you mean."

"Who gave you the idea to examine the clothing so closely...was it one of the coloreds helping you?"

"Uh...no, sir. When we pulled the wet clothes outta the well, we laid'em on the ground. I knelt down and took a leaf and pulled them apart. Like I said ...I used a leaf and examined the brains that was splattered on the shirt and on the drawers."

"Would you point out those spots to us, to the jury?" Rutherford asked standing next to the jury box.

"From over here?" Yates was nervous. Sweat trickled down the side of his face.

"No, sir, I'm sorry. Would you mind stepping down and coming over here and pointing out those spots to the jury?"

Yates got up and joined Rutherford at the table in front of the jury. His hands trembled as he looked the material over. He pointed to a brown spot on the shirt.

"And...what is that?" Rutherford asked.

"Uh...well...that's where the brains was."

"This small brown spot? This one here?"

"Well...uh...yes, sir."

"Mistah Yates are you saying that small brown stain was at one time brains...human brains? I thought you said you examined this shirt closely?"

"I...I did."

Rutherford took advantage of the witness's nervousness and began to pressure him. Yates stammered and contradicted himself. He became embarrassed and confused. Finally, he was dismissed.

"Your Honor, the State calls Mistah Jerry Hollis," Hardeman announced.

Hollis took the stand and identified himself as a neighbor and friend of the Captain's.

"Mistah Hollis would you mind examining this particular piece of clothing and tell the court if this is the same piece you examined that day at the Woolfolk house?"

"Yes, sir. These are the same drawers we found that day. They still have my mark, right here on the waist band. See." The witness held up the garment and pointed to an 'x' marked in pencil.

"Would you describe the drawers and what was found on them?"

"Well...they was splattered with brains. There was brains all over them...some the size of peas and some even larger. I was hopin' one large piece would've stayed but it didn't."

"Could you point out where that piece would have been?"

"Yes, sir...right here where this big brown spot is. I remember there was a large piece of brain right there."

Rutherford cross-examined but was not able to shake the man's testimony.

The final witness before dinner was William A. Davis, who had given Folsom a ride out to the farm that day. Formerly an alderman for the Fourth Ward, the local business man was known and respected by many Maconites.

"You were on the coroner's jury, were you not?"

"Yes, sir, I was."

"And were you the one who first noticed the bloody hand print on the defendant's thigh?"

"Well...I don't know if I was the first, but when I saw what looked like a palm print, I told the Sheriff."

"Would you please stand up and show the court the position of this print?"

The witness stood up and placed his hand on his leg above the knee. His thumb pointed outward. His fingers were on the inside of his thigh. He then sat down. A juryman and a neighbor of the witness, Addison Tinsley, raised his hand and asked to see the position again. Davis stood up and very carefully repeated his description of the hand print.

Flo wanted to scream. She felt as if the room had closed in on her. Over and over the same point would be made, repeated and then made again.

The Judge called recess.

Tom sat surrounded by deputies and ate quietly. He was tired of the constant fun one of the guards Fred Sparks was having at his expense. The prisoner had enough. He glared at the deputy.

"You talk mighty big for a damn coward. I ain't no match for ya all chained up like this. If we were off somewhere, out in the woods and I had a good Smith and Wesson, you wouldn't be talkin' so high n' mighty?" Tom said, the corner of his mouth turned up in a smirk.

Sparks looked surprised. Another deputy, W. A. Jones laughed.

"Ah...now Tom. Don't mind Sparks none. He's just ribbin' ya a little."

"He can go find someone else to rib. Talks pretty big when someone's chained up like this," Tom growled.

Sparks stormed passed the waiters and disappeared around the corner. Tom picked up his fork and continued eating his meal. His guards were finished. Jones leaned back in his chair and picked at his teeth.

"Mistah Jones?" one of the waiters spoke up.

"Yeh, ...what is it?" Jones answered.

"You want us t'wait for Mistah Sparks?" .

"Yeh, leave the dinner. Sparks'll be back shortly."

Minutes later, Sparks came back in. He glared down at the prisoner as he walked by. Suddenly, a loud crash at Tom's feet forced the prisoner to jump up. On the floor was a pistol. Tom dove for it. Instantly, Jones pounced upon him and Sparks grabbed the gun. Seconds later it was over. Tom leaned back in his chair and laughed.

The news of Tom's escape attempt electrified the legal proceedings. Pea Jay hurried into the room and sat beside Folsom. The room was again filled to capacity.

Court resumed at 2:30 p.m. and Henry Brown was called to the stand. Testimony for the prosecution continued to paraphrase the news reports. Pea Jay sighed. Brown's testimony seemed trivial. He told how Tom requested water, refused to drink from the dipper, and drank from a cup. He explained how the prisoner wanted breakfast and the procedure involved in procuring him food. He reviewed the events around dragging the well and stated he was the one who pulled the clothes off the hook. His testimony satisfied the prosecution. He was turned over to the defense.

Tom leaned over and spoke softly to Rutherford. The attorney then stood and asked the witness to reiterate on the events surrounding the defendant's arrest. Brown repeated Chambless' testimony. He then explained how he was responsible for convincing Tom to stay in the house for his own protection.

"While the defendant was secluded with you in the house did he say anything to you?"

Brown looked confused.

"While you were sequestered in the room with Tom Woolfolk, what did ya'll talk about?" Rutherford rephrased the question.

"Well, he...uh...Tom told me he moved his brother Dick from outta the hall. But then later on...he...he denied ever saying it. I saw a small speck of blood in his ear. I asked him about it. He said that when his pa was struck, the blood was flyin' everwhere."

Tom's head shot up. Brown was startled and shifted nervously in his seat. The defendant leaned over, whispered to Walker and then looked back at the witness. Brown tugged at his collar. Tom chuckled softly to himself.

Rutherford turned and looked at his client who immediately composed himself.

"What else did he tell you?" the attorney continued.

"Well...uh...he said that he had eaten with his family...then sat on the porch till around nine a clock. He decided to go to bed early, took a bath and shaved in his room..."

The witness became distracted. Tom was turned around and talking with Flo.

"Mistah Brown?"

"Uh...he didn't like bein' stripped and all," the witness volunteered.

Tom turned back around and listened intently.

"He...he didn't like his person being examined by the coroner's jury. Got real upset about that. When we was sittin' in the parlor waitin' for the Sheriff, I told him he was a coward to run out like that and then brave to come back and walk through all that blood. He said...he said...when he walked through the blood, it squished 'tween his toes."

"Did you participate in the dragging of the well?" Rutherford asked.

"Yes sir. I was there."

"Did the drag go to the bottom?"

"I don't know, Colonel...I wasn't down there."

"But haven't you ever dragged a well? Don't you know when it strikes bottom?"

The room exploded in laughter. Brown was humiliated.

"Who did the dragging?"

"I...I...don't remember."

"You were there, but you don't remember who did the dragging of the well?"

"No sir."

"Then...I guess I have no further questions for this witness."

Brown was excused. As the witness rose to leave he looked at the jury and then nervously sat back down. With his hands folded in his lap, he spoke softly but clearly.

"I want you to understand, gentlemen, that I am forty-two years old and this is the first time I was ever on the witness stand in my life...and if...if ever I'm caught in a similar case, I will observe more closely."

Tom's chuckle was barely audible.

The undertaker's testimony was gruesome. John Clay described in minute details each wound. He reached in his pocket, brought out a ring of keys and explained how he used a key to measure their sizes. He read from his notes and confirmed that Pearl's head wound matched exactly the size and shape of the axe.

Rutherford tried in vain to weaken his testimony, but the mortician was precise and adamant.

"About your method of measuring the wounds...do you consider a key an accurate instrument of measurement?"

"The key was used only as a tool of comparison. It was adequate and served its purpose."

"And you say it was that key. That one you specified?"

"Yes, sir. It was this key," he answered, holding the key up.

"How do you know it was that particular key? My dear sir...you have to admit your key ring is full of keys that look alike. How can you be so certain that key was the one you used?"

"Because sir...," Clay responded calmly, again holding it up, "this one still has blood on it."

Folsom rushed to the jailhouse. Tom had sent word he wanted to see him as soon as possible.

"Folsom? How ya doin'?" the prisoner greeted him warmly.

"Fine, Tom...just fine. And you?"

The prisoner smiled and walked over to his cot. The chain attached to his ankle rattled along behind him.

"Have a seat," he offered, pointing to a lone stool in the corner of the cell.

Folsom pulled the stool over and sat down.

"What was that about you gettin' a gun today?"

Tom smiled broadly. "Oh that...I was just fooling with the boys. That's all. I would have given it back to Sparks."

"Where did it come from?"

"Hell if I know. It was just there on the floor at my feet."

"Well from what I've been able to gather, Prosecutor Hardeman's pistol was taken out of his briefcase while it was in his office."

"And how in the hell would I've gotten hold of it? I don't know where it came from. It was just there."

"Is it true that you said you wished you'd a been in the woods with them boys and had a gun."

"Yeh...I was just fooling them, though. If I had been out in the field with a gun...I would have gotten away from them for sure. And they know it...but hell, Folsom that's not why I asked you here."

"Why then...?"

"You were there weren't you? At Pa's house, during the inquest?"

"Yeh, Tom, I was."

"And you wrote down everything that was said and done. Didn't ya?"

"Yeh...I did."

"You wrote down everything Henry Brown said to the coroner's jury that day?"

"Yeh...why?"

"Cause Henry Brown lied on the stand today."

CHAPTER THIRTEEN
"Her skull was split open."

The fourth day of Tom's trial began with Deputy Opry testifying on the care and treatment of the evidence. The prosecution wanted it on record that the axe and the clothing had been locked away in official custody and that no one had access to them.

Outside, the dreary December day was cloudy and unusually warm. The cold, damp Georgia winter had yet to descend upon the Piedmont region. The weather, however, did not deter the masses. The usual crowd lingered outside while the galleries and main floor contained the regulars.

After Opry's testimony, W.S. Hughes, another resident of Hazzard District, was called. As with the other witnesses, Hughes was present when the first articles were retrieved from the well. Through Hardeman's direct examination, the only new piece of information as far as Folsom was concerned was that Hughes was the one responsible for getting that evidence to the sheriff.

"Now then, Mistah Hughes," Rutherford began his cross-examination, "you've testified that the garments had brains on them."

"Yes, sir."

"Then...would you please tell the court just what do brains look like?"

"They look...like...brains, sir," Hughes answered slowly.

"Yes, but what do brains look like?"

"Well, sir, they...look like brains."

Light laughter filtered through the room. The witness looked around perplexed. He did not see any humor in the situation.

"What color are brains?" Rutherford tried again.

"The color of...brains," the witness again answered blankly.

"What is the texture of brains. Can you describe them?"

"No, sir...I only know brains when I see them."

"Then what color are they?"

The witness leaned over and rested his left forearm on his left knee and put his right hand on the other. He wrinkled his brow and continued.

"Well, sir, I have never studied colors, and can only answer that they are the color of...brains."

Laughter again rippled through the audience. Tom was unable to contain himself. Even Shackleford was smiling.

"I've no further questions for this witness."

"The state calls Silas Woolfolk."

No one responded. The bailiff called again. Again, no response. A murmur worked its way through the room. The first black witness did not show up to testify. The bailiff called the next witness Ben Hamlin, also black. There was no response. The prosecutor stood up and looked around the room. Neither witness was present.

"Call your next witness," the Judge ordered.

"The state calls Jeff Woolfolk."

A small, thin boy shyly walked up to the witness stand. Someone from the back of the room snickered.

"Your honor," Rutherford addressed the Judge, "surely this child has no concept of these proceedings and the obligation of the oath he has just taken."

Judge Gustin nodded and leaned over.

"What's your name, son?" he asked the child.

"My name's Jeff."

"Jeff what?"

"Jeff Woolfolk."

"How old are you, Jeff?"

"Pa forgot how olds I am."

"Do you know what will become of you if you don't tell the truth?"

"No, suh."

"Don't you know where you'll go if you fail to tell the truth after being sworn?"

"Satan'll git me?

The room exploded in laughter. The witness grinned nervously and swung his feet playfully. Gustin tapped his gavel and continued.

"If you fail to tell the truth now...where will you go when you die?"

"Go to the bad place?"

Frustrated, Judge Gustin straightened up and in a loud voice repeated the question.

"If you fail to tell the truth now where will you go when you die?"

The boy was terrified.

"I don't know, suh."

"This witness is not competent. Solicitor, call your next witness."

"The state calls Julia Woolfolk."

Jeff's grandmother calmly took the stand. The purpose of the prosecution's examination of the mother of Silas Woolfolk and mother-in-law of George Caldwell was to clarify the relationship of the two men with the Captain. She reassured the state that although Captain Woolfolk had fired Silas after an argument over a contract her son had failed to honor, they left the Woolfolk plantation on friendly terms. Silas then moved his family to the neighboring Gilbert farm.

"Where was Silas on the night of August 5th?"

"He was with his family 'n me. They wuz with me at church for a 'ciety meetin'. When it was over, we all come home and stayed there."

The witness remained calm throughout the state's questioning. It was obvious to Folsom she wanted her answers understood.

When it was his turn to cross-examine, Rutherford approached the witness slowly. His thumbs were hooked in his vest pockets. He stood tall.

"Who is George Caldwell?"

"My sonlaw. He's married t' my girl."

"How long has he been your son-in-law?"

"They got married back in December of eighty-five."

"How well did you know him before your daughter married him?"

"I din't know'im. She brought'im down from A'lanta, just 'fore they got married. They lived with me up 'til he stole d'Cappin's ox. He got put on the chain gang for that."

"And afterwards...did you see him again?"

"Yassuh. After he 'scape from the gang, he comes to my house. Then he left."

"He escaped from the chain gang he was put on for stealing the Captain's ox?"

"Yassur...but that was way 'fore them murders."

"Tell us again about the wool hat."

"Yassur?"

"Who's hat did you say it was?"

"Hit b'longs to my boy, Silas."

"Well, how did it get in the well?"

"He dropped it in there. I wuz there when it happened."

"That was convenient."

"Suh?"

"You're saying that on the day the hat was dropped in the well, you were there?"

"Yassuh."

"And on the night of the murders you were with your son, Silas, at a meeting?"

"Yassuh."

"Would you lie for your son?"

"I object."

"Sustained. Counselor, you are dangerously close to badgering the witness."

"I'm sorry Your Honor. Mrs. Woolfolk, I did not mean to imply anything by that question. I am just having difficulty believing you. You expect the court to believe you were there when your son lost his hat in the well–the same hat that was pulled out after the murders and covered with blood. You also expect the court to believe your son, Silas–who had a heated argument with the Captain and was thrown off the farm, just days before the murder–your son was with you the night of the murders, at church?"

"Yassuh, cause...hits the truth.".

Folsom had looked forward to hearing the black witnesses. The most damaging statements during the coroner's inquest came from them. Times being as they were, it went without saying that if a white man's life depended on the testimonies of former slaves, it was already lost. It was a rare occasion to have so many given the opportunity to testify against a white man.

The masses of freed slaves that descended on the towns and cities after the war did not diminish the large numbers who chose to stay on the plantations as sharecroppers. The centuries old feudal system had shackled them in ignorance of the world beyond the boundary markers of the land they had been tied to in bondage. It also guaranteed their dependence on their former masters.

Freedom had been obtained but was not secured. Gradually, and somewhat ignored by the northern saviors, the rights and freedoms given to the Southern black began to fade, eroded by the winds stirred from the reemerging Southern Democrat.

Two races, former masters and slaves, were forced to live together and survive. The dominate group was determined to retain its power through intimidation, segregation, and violence, if necessary. The subordinate group, having received nothing but the word 'freedom', was immersed in a struggle to rise above the scars and humiliation of slavery. They had to fight not only the ignorance, bigotry, and anger of their white neighbors but of their own as well.

It was all so incredibly ironic to Folsom. For generations, the Southern white was raised to believe the negro to be unreliable, lazy, and stupid. The reliability of a witness of color was based solely on the need of the state to convict the accused. Bigotry and racial slurs were commonplace. Yet, the state built its case on the testimonies of the very individuals it was forcing to live in the shadows of the white society.

Sarah Hardin placed her tanned calloused hand on the Bible and swore to tell the truth. Employed as the washwoman for the Woolfolks, it was her responsibility to clarify the ownership of the various garments.

Hardeman approached with two shirts. The first one he showed her, the one pulled up from the well, was brown.

"Have you ever seen this shirt before?"

"Yassuh, that's Mister Dick's shirt."

"And when was the last time you saw this shirt?"

"I was at Miz Mattie's pickin' up the laundry. That shirt was on the bed. I picked it up t'wash and Miz Mattie, she tells me t'put it back down. So I did."

"And you didn't see that shirt again?"

"No, suh, 'cept when the deputy asked me 'bout it, later."

Hardeman held up the white shirt Tom had on when he was arrested.

"Can you tell me whose shirt this is?"

Sarah looked at it closely and handed it back.

"No, suh."

"You don't recognize this shirt?"

"No, suh."

"Well then, can you tell me whose socks these are?"

"No, suh. I don't know who they b'long to either."

"What do you mean?"

"I ain't never seen'em 'fore. Mistuh Dick and Captain Woolfolk, their socks're hand knitted. These ain't."

"No further questions."

Pea Jay leaned over and whispered to Folsom, "Do you think that went the way Hardeman had expected it to?"

"Don't know? She didn't seem to give him the answers he wanted...or maybe she did. Who knows?"

"Humph!" Pea Jay responded, folding his arms across his front and settling deeper into his seat.

Folsom was confident that most of the witnesses were honest and sincere. He felt certain some had nothing to lose in telling the truth. But he was convinced, although he knew he would never be able to prove it, that some were not telling all they knew. He became more convinced after Tom Banks testified.

Banks was a laborer who lived at the foot of the hill on the Woolfolk Plantation. His closest neighbor was Greene Lockett. He testified that during the week before the murders he did not work. The days of continuous rain had made it impossible.

He stated he saw the Woolfolk men--the Captain, young Dick, and Tom--on various occasions throughout that time and had accompanied Tom on an errand of business. He said the trip wore him out, and he slept unusually hard that night and did not hear of the murders until the next morning when someone came by and told him. He stressed that the Captain had a vicious dog and no one outside the family would ever approach the house in the dark.

Rutherford tried unsuccessfully to get him to explain why, if he lived so close to the Captain's house, he did not hear the terrible noise the dogs would have made. He simply answered that he was asleep and heard nothing.

The Judge called a recess. Tom stood up and stretched. The endless examinations by the two factions battling over his life were exhausting him. He appeared withdrawn and depressed. He nodded slowly when Frank Walker informed him John Owens was to testify next.

As expected Owens' testimony caused a stir in the court although he said nothing more than what was stated at the coroner's inquest. Hearing that Tom had threatened his father, however, struck a nerve throughout the room, one that hardened the resolve of many that Tom was the killer.

The more surprising evidence came after Owens, from two white men. The first, whom Tom considered a friend, I.P. Davis, known throughout Hazzard District as 'Bone', told of a conversation he had with the defendant. Davis reiterated how, in March, Tom complained about his father's puritanical ideas on drinking. According to the witness, Tom said his father did not like him, and that he was not welcomed on the farm unless it was to work in the fields. The witness stated that it seemed appropriate for the Captain to make such a statement.

Davis continued, "Tom says, 'Well, Pa's independent n' I'm dependent. But by fire, I kin make him as dependent as I am.' I says to'im, I says, 'Tom, that won't do'...and then he says, 'I'll see'em all in hell, 'fore I stand it.'"

The room rumbled in seething response to the witness' last statement. Pea Jay was excited. Folsom watched the defendant, but there was no reaction. Tom sat quietly. His hands were folded on the table in front of him. He was looking directly at the witness.

"How long have you known the defendant?" Hardeman asked.

Davis looked at Tom and then back at the solicitor. "All m'life, I guess...since we was boys."

"And when did you first hear of the murders?"

The witness thought for a moment. "I was on m'way to m'wife's pa's house. I ran into George Yates. He told me that all da Woolfolks was dead 'cept fer one. That's when I membered what Tom said t'me so I says t' my ma, I says 'Dat one's Tom...and he kilt da rest.'"

"I object, Your Honor. The witness is offering a conclusion."

"Overruled."

During his cross-examination, Rutherford asked the witness to tell the court again exactly what Tom had said to him. Hardeman jumped to his feet.

"I object, Your Honor. The witness has already repeated that statement, several times, in fact."

"Your Honor, I believe my question to be a valid one since it seems highly unlikely someone can remember the exact words used in a conversation ten months ago."

"I would prefer to not interrupt defense's cross-examine; however, I would like for us to resist redundancy and repetition as much as possible. Continue Counselor."

"Thank you, Your Honor. Now, sir...would you again tell us exactly what the defendant said to you that day."

"Just what I said. He said he'd make his pa dependent and that he'd see'em all in hell 'fore he'd stand fer it."

When Joseph Dannenberg took the stand, Tom looked puzzled. Hardeman asked the witness his relationship to the defendant.

"In eighteen eighty-five, he rented a store that was occupied by L.J. Lippincott and Company. I was the partner. He rented it and paid me the rent."

"Do you recall a conversation you had with the defendant?"

"Yessir, I do. I was in the store, and Woolfolk asked me about the law."

"Would you mind telling us just what he said?"

"Well...he walked up to me and said something like 'Look here, Dannenberg, you know a good deal about law. You're smart. I want to ask you some questions.' Well, I told him that I really only knew commercial law, but he went on talking and told me that his step-family was living on property that really should go to him. He said he didn't have money but would be coming into some before he died. He sounded like he was planning on legally getting a hold of the property. I didn't think none about it again until I heard about the murders. Then I remembered how he had talked."

"And how was that?"

"He talked like he hated them."

Tom's shoulders dropped. The room was weighed with deadly silence.

The first person to actually see Tom the night of the murders was finally called to the stand. Greene Lockett took his seat and waited for the solicitor to begin the questions. He looked embarrassed and intimidated.

Hardeman had to coaxe information out of him. Although the witness was not hostile he was, nonetheless, uncooperative. Greene Lockett did not want to have anything to do with the trial, and his passive resistance made it obvious to the audience.

"Do you recognize this?" the solicitor asked, showing him the axe found at the murder scene.

"Yassuh."

"What is it?"

"An axe."

"And who's axe is it?"

"D'Cap'n's axe."

"When did you last see this axe...I mean before the murders were discovered."

"I seen it that Friday, 'fore d'killin."

"And where did you see it?"

"Wid Mistah Tom."

"What was he doing with it?" Hardeman continued.

"He was choppin' widdit."

"Chopping what?"

"Some post oaks."

"What for?"

"Foe some wood t'make baskets."

"Why was he doing that?"

"Cause his pa told 'im to."

"I see. And you are certain that this is the same axe he was using that day?"

"Yassuh."

After Hardeman patiently extracted the same testimony Lockett had delivered to the coroner's jury, the witness was turned over to Rutherford for cross-examination. The defense attorney was not as gentle.

"How can you be so sure that was when you saw the defendant with an axe?"

"That was d'same day that Mistah Dick went t'Marse Winn's place fer some oats."

"You're sure of that?"

"Yassuh, I 'member cuz we needed dem oats."

A chuckle floated through the gallery. Folsom had to smile. He knew that Lockett was not trying to be facetious. In fact, he was completely serious. The white audience, however, found humor in his quaint dialect, reminiscent of plantation days with the slaves' unrefined yet colorful speech patterns.

"Where was the defendant?" the attorney asked.

"In d'woods."

"Where exactly in the woods?"

"By a log."

"And where were you?"

"At d'other end of d'log."

"What sort of log was it?"

"A tree log."

"I've never heard of making baskets from postoak wood."

"I's cut many a one t'make baskets outta."

Rutherford's patience was becoming strained.

"How far is it from your house to the Captain's house?"

"I cain't rightly say."

"Take a guess."

"I dunno know how far, Boss."

"Would you say it's as far as the Lanier House?"

The witness looked confused.

"Is it as far as from here to the Lanier House, up the street?"

"I dunno where d'Lanieah House is. I dunno if I ever was in d'Lanieah House in my life."

Tom shook his head. His lips were turned up in a faint smile.

"When did you first hear the dogs up at the Captain's house?"

"When Mistah Tom come gits me."

"And you didn't hear anything before that?"

"Nawsuh."

"You didn't say to Mistah Tom 'My God! What a noise up at the house.'"

"Nawsuh."

"Why didn't you want to go up to the house?"

"Cuz I was skeered."

"What were you afraid of?"

"I guess I jest kinda woke up skeered."

Anderson James' testimony was insignificant as far as providing any new information, nor was it as entertaining as Lockett's. Rutherford asked him if he had ever been in trouble with the law. The state objected and was overruled.

"Well...yassuh," James finally answered.

"And what trouble was that?"

"I was arrested."

"What had you done?"

"Well...I whipped a girl pretty bad...but the Cap'n didn't have nuthin' t'do widdit."

Ann James, Anderson's wife, took the stand after him. Her testimony supported her husband's.

"Why did you say that?" Rutherford interrupted. "When you woke why did you say 'Oh Lord, what's the matter.'?"

"Cuz there was so much noise."

"Noise? Who was making so much noise?"

"All that carryin' on at Greene's house. It scared me coz it was still dark."

She told of going over to Lockett's. "I saw Mistah Tom. He was lyin' 'tween two trees. I says t'im, I says, Mistah Woolfolk, don't tell me that the family's all dead?' And Mistah Tom he says, 'Yes, all dead as hell.'"

Rutherford drilled the witness but could not break her testimony. Finally, he gave up and the Judge called a recess.

The day had been extremely long and trying. A total of twelve witnesses had already testified against Tom. The afternoon session continued at the same pace. S. M. Hilliard told how it was his idea to use pot hooks on the end of a line to drag the well, thus countering the defense's claim that it was part of a plot to implicate Tom.

Lockett's nephew Jim Foster told of hearing Tom say someone was killing his parents and how his uncle sent him and his cousin to spread the news.

"You worked for the Captain, didn't you?" Hardeman asked.

"Yassuh. I's the wood chopper."

"So, it was your responsibility to cut the fire wood."

"Yassuh."

"Do you recognize this axe?"

"Yassuh, that's the one from the wood pile."

"Did you cut wood that Friday?"

"Nawsuh. I was out 'til purty late. When I gits in, I goes up to the wood pile, but I can't finds the axe so...I goes on back home."

"When did you see the defendant that day?"

"I sees him 'bout noon in the barn. He was lyin' in a horse trough. He said he was sick."

"And when did you last see the Captain alive?"

"I sees him when he took little Miss Annie to the doctor t'git that needle outta her foot."

"And you didn't see him after that?"

"Nawsuh, cuz I weren't 'round after that."

"Your witness." The solicitor returned to his chair.

"You were present when the Captain and Tom Banks had their argument, were you not?" Rutherford asked from his seat.

"Yassuh. First, I hears Mistah Tom tell John Jeff he don't care no more for a white man than he does a colored. Then...I sees the Cap'n go over and cuss out Tom Banks. Then I sees Tom Banks leave."

"Tell me," Rutherford said, still seated, "did you hear anything that night?"

"Yassur."

"What exactly?"

"Well, suh, I hears them dawgs crockin' up at the house...'n then I hears Mistah Tom at the doe."

After her name was called, a middle aged woman, dressed in black, took the stand. District attorney Dupont Guerry asked her to identify herself.

"My name is Mrs. Elizabeth Black, the daughter of Mrs. Temperance West."

"And would you please tell the court who exactly was Temperance West?"

"She was the elderly woman who was murdered with the Woolfolk family that night."

Flo looked at the witness with compassion for her anguish. Theirs were similar sufferings.

In a soft, sweet voice, the woman talked about her mother's health being relatively good although she was growing deaf.

"I don't believe a train running through the house would have awakened her," she said.

When the D.A. asked her about her mother's sleeping habits, she answered that she preferred sleeping late in the morning.

He then asked her about the clothes she wore to bed.

"She'd wear a gown and a night cap...tied...under her chin."

"Did she wear one that night?"

"Yes, sir," her voiced cracked, "I know she did...the sheriff sent it to me."

The room was moved to tears. Folsom leaned over and whispered to Pea Jay.

"There is no reason for her testimony."

"Yeh there was...sympathy...and it worked," Pea Jay answered.

Following Mrs. Black's testimony, the prosecution proceeded to tie up loose ends created by Rutherford's relentless cross-examination. Hardeman produced the minutes of the Bibb County Superior Court session to show that almost a year earlier, on December 15, 1886, George Caldwell was convicted of thief and sentenced to the chain gang. Superintendent Joseph McGee then took the stand and testified that although Caldwell had, in deed, escaped on June 19, 1887, he was apprehended a week later and had been in jail since.

"Well...there goes one suspect," Pea Jay remarked.

The state called Jim Foster back to the stand in an effort to establish different ownership of the hat. Foster testified that the hat actually belonged to Jeff, Silas Woolfolk's young son, and that he was present when the boy claimed it.

Rutherford jumped to his feet. "I object, Your Honor! The State has already established the ownership of the hat to Silas Woolfolk. Now it wants to change it?"

The Judge instructed the court recorder to strike the testimony from the record.

Dr. James Holly, the first physician on the scene, testified in length about each wound. As he read from his notes, the room was deadly silent. Even Tom listened closely.

"R.F. Woolfolk, Sr., one lick over left ear, eye of axee; one over left eye, eye of axee; one over the forehead, eye of an axee. Richard F. Woolfolk, one back of head, crushing skull; one each over left and right eyes, and forehead. Charlie Woolfolk, one lick on top of head, blade of axee, and one over left temple, eye of axee."

The doctor shifted in his seat and turned the page. "Mrs. Woolfolk, back of head, eye of axe. Annie, behind left ear, in front of left ear, and slight wound in back of neck, and one in the back, which was a bruise. Mattie, one lick over right eye, eye of axe. Pearl, one lick, crushing in left ear, one, crushing in right eye, one each on right and left side of forehead, all with eye of axe."

The room was solemn. The quiet weighed heavily upon the hearts of the audience. Barely audible were quiet sobs from behind the black veils. Love Shackleford reached around Flo and pulled her head to his shoulder. Tom's shoulders were slumped forward. His eyes glued to his hands folded on top of the table.

The doctor continued, "Rosebud, one behind left ear, slight one on left shoulder. Mrs. West, one behind left ear, and one on left temple, eye of the axe."

The solicitor turned the witness over to the defense. Rutherford stood and asked the doctor to repeat his description of some of the wounds. A moan went through the room and people in the audience shifted about in their seats.

When the doctor had finished, Rutherford asked, "How could you tell if the wounds were made from the eye of an axe or the blade?"

"Because the blade will make a clean, precise cut; whereas, the eye of an axe will deliver crushing blows."

"And you are certain of your determination of which wounds were made by either the blade or the butt of the axe?"

"Yes, sir...well..."

"Yes, doctor?"

"I can't rightly say about some of the wounds. For example, the baby. Her skull was split open...it could have been made by the blade."

"Dr. Holly, you examined the blood stain on the defendant's leg, did you not?" Hardeman redirected.

"Yes, sir, I did."

"And can you tell us what you found?"

"Well...at first, I didn't think it was blood. Then I got down and looked at it closer, rubbing it with my handkerchief. It was blood. I asked Tom, ah...the defendant, about it. He said he must have done it himself before he washed the blood off his hands. Well...I pulled up his shirt and checked the band of his drawers. It had a tie string. The string wasn't bloody. I asked him how was he able to tie the string with bloody hands and it not be bloody."

"And what was his answer?"

"He didn't answer me."

Hardeman walked over to the table and picked up a shirt. "Do you recognize this shirt?"

"Yes, sir. It's the one Tom had on that morning. It's a bit dirtier, but it's the same shirt."

Rutherford chose not to re-examine, and the witness was dismissed.

"The State calls Charles W. Howard."

The prosecutor slowly pushed his chair away from the table and stood up. Picking up a large book, he approached the bailiff, placed his right hand on the Bible, and swore to tell the truth. He then took his seat and waited for the solicitor to begin.

"Please state your name."

"Charles W. Howard."

"And Mr. Howard, what is your relationship to Captain Richard Woolfolk?"

"He was my brother-in-law. He was my sister's husband."

"Would you please tell the court, the names and ages of the members of the Captain's family?"

Howard opened the large family bible and in a deep voice began to read the names and birthdates of each member of the family starting with the Captain and ending with the baby.

No one said a word. No one coughed. No one moved. Rutherford did not cross-examine. The witness was excused.

Hardeman requested time to have the blood stains on the garments examined under a microscope. The court agreed, directed the attorney to have it done, and then called court adjourned for the day.

That night, Sheriff Westcott sat in his office at the jail. The trial required not only his attendance but also that of the majority of his deputies. Work was piling up.

Tom Woolfolk was returned to his cell tired and withdrawn. No longer was he joking or smiling with his guards. The sheriff could not blame him, however; it had been a rough day.

Westcott looked up and listened. The monotonous rattle of the prisoner's chain dragging back and forth across the cell told him what he already suspected. The prisoner was worried.

CHAPTER FOURTEEN

"I was afraid I'd either have to kill'im
or be killed."

Folsom turned up his coat collar to the cold rain and hurried into the lobby of the courthouse early enough to watch the spectators and news reporters clamor for admittance into the courtroom. By the fifth day, the routine was established. The large, double doors of the courtroom would be opened at precisely 9:00 a.m., and, within minutes every available spot taken. The rumbling of feet as spectators jostled for the best seats always reminded the reporter of children exiting the school building at the end of the year.

The winter storm did not discourage even the more feeble of the audience. In some cases, old men would use their canes as weapons to ward off seat poachers. The seriousness of the affair, however, prevented the reporter from appreciating the comical scenes.

Tom's sisters and aunt took their usual seats. Folsom studied their composure and marveled at their ability to sit day after day listening to the prosecution's case against Tom and still show him their undaunted love and support. The testimonies so far had been gruesome and painful for even the unrelated to hear; yet, the three women never faltered, never weakened, and never left his side.

The first witness of the day was Dr. I. B. Clifton.

"Dr. Clifton," Hardeman began, "you are a microscopist, are you not?"

"Yes, sir. I have studied microscopic subjects for over thirty years. I am a maker of microscopes."

"And have you been allowed to examine any of the evidence in this case?"

"Yes, sir. I used a five inch objective and 150 diameter eye piece. I removed some of the dried red matter from the shirt found in the well, dissolved it in water and looked at it through the microscope. I discovered a mass of disks."

"And what sort of disks were these?"

"Well, the disks were of vertebrate animals. One can distinguish such disks from, say, mollusks. Man has the longest blood corpuscles of any animal except the elephant and sloth." The doctor shifted in his seat and continued. "I am prepared to say that these corpuscles are those of a mammalian. Uh, mammalians are animals that nurse their young."

"Dr. Clifton, were the red stains on the wool cap also tested?"

"Yes, they were. My assistant, Professor Lane, scraped some of the red matter from the cap, in my presence, and prepared the slide as before. Upon examination, there were perfect masses of the disks. The microscope showed that the wool fibers have a greater holding power than cotton fibers."

"And finally, Doctor, what of the stains on the defendant's drawers?"

"I examined them as well. They were perfect disks and, in my opinion, blood. "

"But these garments had been in water for a period of time."

"That is true, but blood is of a little heavier specific gravity than water and would readily sink to the bottom if placed in a vessel of water. Blood that had become coagulated when soaked in water, the water would come in between the particles and they would sink."

"And if it came in contact with any other woolen or cotton garments would these stains adhere to the article?"

"They would. Some of the red matter was taken from the bottom of the socks, and showed such a mass of blood disks as to almost cover the field. These had in appearance of having been pressed down into a mass, as to bring them all on a level plane."

"Again, Doctor, based on your examinations of the red stains on the garments brought up from the well, what is your opinion?"

"Blood. The red stains on the articles were that of blood...and I would go further and say mammalian blood."

"Your witness."

"Dr. Clifton, are such disks found elsewhere...in other substances other than...mammalian blood?"

"Well...yes. Such disks are found in...uh...bone, muscle, milk."

"And can you say for certain that the disks you examined were from..." Rutherford stopped and faced the audience. "Human blood?"

The doctor did not respond. Rutherford turned to him, "Doctor?"

"No...I can't say this for certain. It might be, well...hog's blood, for instance. The disks are identical in both."

"Anything else...chicken...or what did you call it...a sloth?"

"No...absolutely not a chicken and definitely not a sloth. The disks are different."

"Could these disks have been from something other than blood."

"No. Blood disks are nearly circular, with the edges slightly turned up. Identification could not be made from just one disk...but no other disks would assume the familiar grouping. The size of the disks examined were from one three-thousandths to one three-thousandths-five hundredths of an inch. I took a drop of blood from Mistah Walkah's thumb and examined it. The blood disks were identical, except the latter were fuller of coloring matter than the former. But..."

"Go ahead, doctor."

"Even though the disks are identical with human blood I can not positively identify the stains on the garments to be human blood."

"Doctor, is it not generally acknowledged among the scientific men of the world that the only trustworthy method of determining whether a stain was a blood stain is by the chemical test?"

"In my opinion...it is the most unsatisfactory method that could be used."

"Are you an expert in the chemical test?"

"No, sir, I am not."

"Dr. Clifton, as a matter of life and death, was the stain on all the garments blood?"

"To the best of my knowledge...the disks were blood disks."

Rutherford looked down at the evidence on the table, shook his head, and turned around. "I have no more questions."

"Your Honor," Hardeman jumped to his feet, "I would like to redirect."

"Go ahead, Counselor."

"Dr. Clifton, tell us alittle more about the wool hat."

"Well...in my opinion, based on my examination of the wool fibers, the blood disks had diffused the hat. The appearance was that the hat had been in a fluid in which blood had been placed. The appearance was the same...except in two places where the groups of disks were large."

"And Doctor, would you tell us your training."

"Certainly. I went to Eton and from there to Madeline College, Oxford, England and then graduated Oxford."

"I have a question," Judge Gustin interjected. The doctor turned in his seat and faced the Judge. "Would the blood disks be more likely to diffuse through an article such as a hat...when wet than dry?"

"Yes, sir. It would more readily penetrate a wet hat or other garment than dry one."

"Thank you, Doctor. If there are no further questions, you may step down."

"Your Honor," Hardeman addressed the court, "the State rests."

John Rutherford rose from his chair. "Your Honor, my colleague, Mistah Walker visited the jail this morning for the purpose of consulting with our client. He was denied the privilege of talking with the prisoner unless in the presence of the jailer. Therefore, Your Honor, we would like to now have the privilege of consulting with our client in private before we begin his defense."

Judge Gustin looked at Frank Walker who responded by standing up and concurring with Rutherford's explanation. Nathan Birdsong, the jailer in question, stepped forward.

"Your Honor, I stood far enough away to simply observe and not overhear. I allowed Mistah Walker the opportunity to talk with the prisoner; however, I could not allow him to enter the prisoner's cell."

"And why was that?" the Judge asked.

"The prisoner was not chained, and Sheriff Westcott left me strict orders to allow no one in the cell with the prisoner when he is unchained."

"Your Honor," Walker interrupted, "the prisoner was, in fact, chained. I informed the jailer of this and that I could not satisfactorily consult with my client through the cell bars."

Birdsong again stepped forward and angrily requested to be sworn in so his word would not be contested. The Judge allowed the jailer an opportunity to state his case under oath. Birdsong repeated his initial explanation and then elaborated further.

"I was afraid to allow any such visits inside the prisoner's cell, Your Honor. The prisoner had previously threatened to grab a gun and escape. I was afraid I'd either have to kill'im or be killed."

"The defense may now have the opportunity to consult with the defendant. Court is in recess for thirty minutes." The Judge stood up, tapped his gavel, and left the room.

Folsom stretched. For months he had heard the state's case. He reported the testimonies given at the coroner's inquest and had seen all of the evidence. Other than Tom declaring his innocence, arguments in his defense had not occurred. The reporter was ready to hear them now. In fact, it was clear to him that everyone in the audience was ready for the defense.

At 11:45, court reconvened. Rutherford rose to call his first witness. "The defense calls, Samuel S. Pennington." No one responded to the call.

Instantly, Hardeman jumped to his feet. "Your Honor, while Mistah Pennington is being located, I request that the jury retire."

Rutherford turned and faced his opponent in amazement.

"Retire? Why counselor?" the Judge asked.

"Your Honor, the prosecution would like to present a proposition."

After the last juryman left the courtroom, Hardeman called District Attorney Guerry to submit the proposal.

As the D.A. began his lengthy oration, Pea Jay leaned over towards Folsom. "What in the hell is going on?" he whispered.

"I think the State is trying to prevent the defense from presenting testimony about threats made against the Captain and his family by someone other than the defendant."

"Why?"

"Supposedly testimony from someone overhearing a threat is not admissible."

"But...didn't the State do just that earlier against Tom?"

Folsom shrugged and turned his attention to Rutherford's protest.

"Your Honor, the evidence of this witness will be followed up by a chain of testimony. I must also protest the removal of the jury while the State questions the character of this evidence."

Guerry jumped to his feet and retorted, "Such a procedure is quite regular."

"May we have a ruling from the court?" Rutherford turned to the bench.

Gustin ruled the testimony inadmissable. The arena exploded with legal jousting as the attorneys for the defense shouted their protestations. Walker bowed to his senior. Rutherford stormed to the bench.

"Your Honor! How can this testimony be inadmissable when the testimonies by Misters Dannenberg and Davis, as to threats made by the defendant two long years ago and the latter March last...be allowed by the court. If these are admissible, why should the Court object to evidence of threats made more recently...in fact, only a few days before the murder. The witness is willing to swear that he heard this person say he would kill Woolfolk and the last of his name. This was only a few days before the crime was committed, and shortly after this person had a personal difficulty with Captain Woolfolk."

Gustin responded loudly. "Mistah Pennington has not stated what particular Woolfolk was referred to in this threat."

Rutherford stormed across the room. "Your Honor, Mistah Pennington heard the negro who made the threats claim that he had chopped cotton for Captain Woolfolk and that Woolfolk refused to pay him and that he contemplated revenge." He stopped and continued in a calmer manner. "We intend to trace the chain of evidence link by link, until we find the man who committed the murder."

"My ruling stands," Gustin ordered. "However, the defense may call Mistah Pennington to the stand, during the jury's absence, in order to show the court exactly what it had intended to prove."

Pennington was sworn in and took the stand.

"Mister Pennington, how long had you known Captain Richard Woolfolk?"

"Twenty-eight years. I've known'im since I was a little boy."

"And would you please tell the court about the events of July 28, 1887."

Pennington shifted in his seat and addressed the Judge. "Well, sir, ya see, Yer Honor. I was passin' through Macon, transportin' this lunatic...uh...Celia Campbell...to the asylum when she went berserk. I got this niggra, Jube Thweat, he's a hack driver, t'help me get her under control. Well...after she calmed down a bit, this tall niggra...about six foot high and about a hundred and sixty pounds comes up t'me and wants me t'pay him fifty cents and he'd help me. Well, I tell him that's too much. That a quarter would be enough."

"And what happened after that?" Rutherford questioned the witness.

"Well, sir, he got real angry at me and said 'You're just like them damned Woolfolks. I've just been choppin' cotton for them...and they won't pay me. I expect t'kill the last damned one of them.'"

Gustin leaned over and asked, "Do you know the name of this particular negro?"

"No, sir."

The Judge directed the bailiffs to round up several black men to see if Pennington might be able to recognize him. Greene Lockett, Silas Woolfolk, Anderson James, and Tom Banks were brought in. Pennington looked at each man.

"No, sir...ain't none of them." He pointed to Greene Lockett. "He almost looks like'im but he ain't tall enough."

The court dismissed the men. The defendant looked at them closely as they walked by. Lockett was noticeably unnerved. Tom's faced reddened. Folsom could hear the light tapping of his foot clear across the room.

The defense requested that John Jeff be brought in. Gustin sent a bailiff to retrieve the witness. Rutherford continued by requesting that I.P. Davis' testimony as to what he said to his mother after hearing about the murders be ruled out.

The court refused.

The defense requested that due to the fact that John Owens had once been on the chain gang for having stolen from the Captain that his testimony was clearly prejudicial and should be ruled inadmissible.

The court refused.

Using the same argument the prosecution used to prevent Pennington's testimony, Rutherford requested that Dannenberg's testimony be ruled inadmissible.

The court again refused and declared a recess.

"Your Honor," John Rutherford addressed Gustin, "during the recess, Mistah Pennington identified John Jeff as the man who made the threat."

Hardeman jumped to his feet and demanded that the jury retire. Again, the twelve men were directed to leave the courtroom. Sam Pennington returned to the stand.

"Were you able to identify the man or not?" Gustin asked.

"If it was not the same man, is was his twin brother."

Gustin's jaw stiffened. "If the defense brings out any more evidence pointing to this man, I may or may not admit it."

"Your Honor," Rutherford responded, "this is where the defense intends to begin its chain of evidence."

"Then I will rule out the evidence, entirely."

Rutherford sat down dumbfounded. Walker and Tom leaned over. The three men conferred quietly.

"If it pleases the court," Rutherford again addressed the bench, "the defense would like to make a motion. And it does so reluctantly."

"And what is your motion?"

"Considering the state of public excitement is such that the prisoner can not secure a fair trial, our witness, Mistah Pennington has been threatened with mob law." A murmur filtered through the room. "Mistah Pennington came to me several times and said that he had been threatened with being mobbed. For the sake of a fair trial, the defense request that Mister Pennington be returned to the stand to testify concerning the threatened mobbing against him."

On the stand, Pennington informed the court that two men had indeed told him that threats were being made against him.

The two men, James and John Searcy, were called to the stand. Both denied making any threats. Jim Searcy admitted to joking with the witness. His brother, John, testified he did in fact relay to Pennington that he had overheard threats being directed toward him.

"Did you in anyway attempt to intimidate Mistah Pennington?" Hardeman asked.

"No sir," John Searcy answered.

"You are excused. Mistah Pennington, would you please return to the stand."

Sam Pennington returned to the witness chair. "Friends and fellow citizens," he began.

"Sit down." Gustin growled. "You are not to make a speech. Has anything been done to intimidate you?"

"No, sir, but I tell you, I am not generally considered scary. When I followed General Gordon on the field of battle, I didn't ask for any odds. I've known Jim Searcy ever since he was a boy, and he's not in the habit of joking about such things. I'm one hundred and seventy five miles from home and I confess that it made me feel mortified. I know they had lynched a man here once before."

"After your testimony today, did any one molest you?"

"Nobody. I've been treated most kindly ever since I've been here."

"You may retire." Gustin then turned to the defense and continued, "I don't think this is sufficient for a continuance."

"I stated to you what the witness told me, and he seemed to feel that he was in danger," Rutherford responded.

"Well...four or five hundred people heard Mistah Pennington's testimony this morning which shows he is evidently in no danger of being molested. Bailiff, you may return the jury to the box. Counselor, call you next witness."

"The defense calls, Mrs. Fannie L. Crane."

Tom's aunt stood up, paused and then edged her way to the aisle. Her veil covered her face, and she clutched tightly to her handkerchief. Once in the witness box, she sighed and dabbed at her eyes.

"Mrs. Crane, would you please tell the court your relationship to the defendant?"

"He is my nephew. His mother Susan was my sister."

"And are you close?"

"Oh yes. After his mother died, I took care of him up to the time his father married Mattie Howard."

"What was he like as a child?"

"Oh...he was a very lovable little boy all the while I knew him as a child. He always confided in me and spoke in the highest terms of his father."

"Then...by your observations...Tom Woolfolk loved his father?" Rutherford asked.

"Oh yes, he loved him very much," Fannie answered. Her voice was soft and polite.

"And what of his stepmother Mattie and her children?"

"He called her 'mother' and he referred to his brother Richard in the kindest terms. He seemed to think that his sister Pearl was a very lovely lady."

"Your witness."

Hardeman remained in his seat and smiled up at Mrs. Crane. "How many children did your sister, the Captain's first wife, and the Captain have?"

Fannie looked bewildered at the question. "Well, they had only three. Floride, um... Mrs. Edwards, Mrs. Cowan, and...Tommy, uh, Tom."

"Thank you, Mrs. Crane. I have no further questions."

Judge Gustin smiled, "You may step down."

"The defense calls Mrs. Henry P. Cowan."

Tom watched Lillie as she slowly walked up to the witness stand.

"Mrs. Cowan, what is your relationship to the defendant?" Rutherford asked.

"I am an older sister."

"Are you the oldest?"

"No, Flo...Mrs. Edwards is the oldest."

"What would you say was your brother's opinion of your father?"

"Well...for example...last November, I complained that I felt that our father was not helping Flo out as much as he should have. Tom got real angry at me for being so disrespectful. He always spoke highly of Father and his family." She smiled slightly and with a nervous twitter in her voice, said, "He one time told me it was a good thing I was off the carpet...you know...married, cause Pearl would lay me in the shade." She stopped at the thought of Pearl. Tears filled her eyes.

"And what did your father think of Tom?"

Another smile. "When our father heard what I had said, he said he was glad Tom had taken up for him. He said that he knew Tom would do such a thing because he had such a high opinion of him."

"Mrs. Cowan, were you ever aware of any apprehensions of danger on the part of your father?"

"I object."

"Your Honor, such questions were allowed for the state relative to the defendant's relationship with his father."

"Sustained, you may answer the question, Mrs. Cowan."

"Well...uh...it was just after father had George Caldwell put in jail. I was at his home and was dipping some water from the bucket. When I dropped the dipper back in, it made a loud noise. Father jumped up from the table and said, 'Oh daughter! How you frightened me.' I said, 'You are not usually so easily frightened.' He said, 'Yes, but since George Caldwell was put in jail, I have been very nervous.'"

On cross-examination, Lillie told the court she was not aware of her father taking any additional precautions during the night. She knew there was a gun in the house but thought it had been left in the parlor.

Tom smiled at his sisters as they traded places. Lillie walked by and gave him a reassuring smile. Flo adjusted her black dress as she nervously took her seat at the witness stand.

"Mrs. Edwards, was Tom's relationship with your family a loving one?"

"Oh yes, he always thought a great deal of Father and always seemed to think very much of our stepmother and her children. If he treated anyone better...I guess it would have been the younger ones over his own sisters."

"And what about your stepmother?"

"Well...she always seemed to think much of Tom. I remember not too long ago she spoke highly of him...that he was always good at heart."

"Your Honor, I object."

"On what grounds, counselor?"

"The testimony is hearsay."

Judge Gustin instructed the counselors to approach and spoke softly to Rutherford.

"If I allow this line of testimony I will be obligated to allow a similar line of testimony during the State's rebuttal."

"I am sorry Your Honor," Rutherford whispered back, "I am not in the position to make any such agreement and request, upon the defendant's legal right, that the court so judges the testimony in or out."

"Your Honor," Hardeman said, quickly, "I withdraw my objection."

The two lawyers returned to their places and the court, after admitting her testimony to the record, excused her.

Flo returned to her seat and L.A. Shackleford was called to the stand. She looked lovingly at her cousin as he told the court of growing up with Tom. When asked about Tom's relationship with his father, Shackleford recalled a conversation they had a year earlier when Tom had said no one had a kinder father. The prosecution objected and was overruled.

Folsom watched the prisoner as witness after witness came forward to speak for him or against those who testified for the prosecution. The defense brought forth men who contested I.P. Davis' reliability and John Owens' honesty.

Fred Foster testified that when he had to foreclose on Tom's farm, the defendant refused to turn to his father for help.

"He said his father had a large family, that he had been embarrassed financially once himself so he'd rather I not say anything to the Captain. It just seemed to me he was showing a lot of consideration for his father."

At the close of the day, the defense presented expert witnesses to refute Dr. Clifton's testimony. Professor F.J.M. Daly testified that the modern method of determining if blood is human or not is through a combination of microscopic and chemical analysis. Folsom tried to record the professor's testimony in his notebook but became confused by the clinical terminology.

Two additional physicians were called to the stand to confirm Daly's testimony and to clarify the complexity of the issue. Their testimonies only increased the air of confusion concerning the identification of the stains on Tom's clothes.

"Scientific men," Folsom wrote later, "are like lawyers. They differ very much."

CHAPTER FIFTEEN
"Oh Lord! Oh Lord!

Friday, December 10, 1887, Tom entered the courtroom accompanied by the guards. There were no lawyers with him, no relatives. With his head bowed, the prisoner hobbled over to the table, picked up a newspaper and sat down. His expression was dark and sullen. No one spoke to him.

A guard removed his chains. Tom ignored him.

Moments later, Walker and Rutherford hurried in. The prisoner ignored them choosing instead to read the newspaper. Gradually, the room filled and court was called to order.

Although Luanna Cooper and Emma Jones had both been summoned by the prosecution, Hardeman did not call them to testify. Rutherford decided their testimonies were necessary to show that the screams and fighting could be heard over some distance.

The first witness Luanna Cooper boldly took the stand and calmly recalled the night she heard the dogs barking up at the Woolfolks'.

"After while I hear a scream, a woman's scream, then, a whole lotta talkin' comin' from Greene Lockett's."

"How far away do you live from there?" Rutherford asked.

"'Bout half mile I spect."

"And you clearly heard a scream and then loud talking?"

"Yassur."

During his cross-examination, Hardeman asked her to repeat what she heard that evening. With a sigh, Luanna told her story again.

"What time was it when you heard the screams? Do you remember?"

"Yassur, I do. It wuz 2:15."

"No further questions."

"The defense calls Emma Jones."

Emma looked at her husband and then stood up. Her heart pounded in her chest as she took her seat in the witness box.

"Now, Mrs. Jones, would you tell the court exactly what you heard that night?"

Emma straightened her back and looked at the Judge.

"First, I heard the Cap'n's dogs barkin'. They woke me up. They was makin' such a fuss I 'cided I better see what was wrong. So, I got up and looked out my window. I couldn't see nothin' cause there was no light at the Cap'n's house. I hear a scream, then another one."

"The first scream...was it from a man, a woman or a child?"

"A woman..."

"And the second one?"

"It was a girl screamin' 'Oh Lord, Oh Lord.' There was a stompin' sound like she was stompin' her feet and screamin'."

To make her point, Emma suddenly stomped her foot to the floor and screamed loudly, "Oh Lord! Oh Lord!"

The audience jerked to attention. Someone laughed nervously. Tom did not look up. He remained slumped in his chair and continued to stare at the floor.

"Go on," Rutherford coaxed with a nod.

"I could hear all sorts a noise... like fightin' 'n people runnin' 'round. I could hear the chairs bein' moved and people jumpin' outta their beds. Then it got real quiet."

"How long would you say the fighting sounds lasted?"

"Can't rightly say...not long. Then I hear somebody call out for Anderson James."

"Did you hear anything else?"

"No, sir...that was all I heard."

"Was anyone else awake at the time?"

"Yassur, Aaron, my husband," Emma answered, looking at Aaron.

"Your witness," Rutherford said and sat down.

"How far do you live from the Woolfolks' house, Miz Jones?" Hardeman asked from his seat.

"Not far."

"How far in distance? A mile? A half mile? Few feet?"

"Cain't say, less than a half mile, I guess."

"A half mile?"

"Less than that I spect. I just live at the foot of the hill from Miz Mattie's house."

"I see...and you clearly heard what was going on at the Captain's house that night?"

"Yassur, I did. The dawgs woke me up then I heard the screams."

"That'll be all Miz Jones. No further questions."

Pea Jay hurried down the aisle and sat down next to Folsom.

"Miss anything?" he whispered.

"Just the two colored women. Dr. McHatten's testifying now. He's stated already that he could not make a conclusive identification of blood on the clothing," Folsom answered.

"Really? Too bad I missed the women. I know what hysterics they can be."

"Now, Dr. McHatten, let's talk about this wool hat," Rutherford said and handed it to the witness.

"Yes, sir," the doctor responded.

"If that hat was in the well...oh, let's say eight months as the prosecution would lead us to believe and had been found about the middle of August...would the microscope have detected blood on it?"

"No, sir. I do not think it would."

"Now if you would look at these garments," Rutherford continued, handing him the drawers and socks. "What if on the sixth of August some bloody clothes were thrown in a well and was there let's say for eight or nine hours. Would there still be blood on the clothes?"

"No, sir. By that time the blood would have dissolved into the water, pretty much like salt would."

"Is there anything else with cells that looks like blood cells when viewed under a microscope?"

"Yes, sir."

"And what would that be?"

"Cells from a yeast plant look very similar to blood cells."

Rutherford turned the witness over to Hardeman and sat down. The solicitor-general approached the witness and in a loud, commanding voice asked if a clot of blood had fallen on the wool hat from the bloody clothes after they were thrown in the well would the hat absorb the blood.

"No, sir. I do not think it would. The blood would simply go into the water."

"But if the hat was dry, would the blood go into it faster?"

The doctor looked bewildered. "I would think that blood would be absorbed more readily by the dry hat. You see it depends on the medium..."

Hardeman interrupted, "You don't think that blood would be soaked up by the hat faster in the well than dry?"

Exasperated the doctor leaned forward in his chair and tried to explain. "No, you see the capillary attraction is not as great in the water..."

"We will get rid of capillary attraction, and I will ask you directly if you do not think the blood would soak into a wet hat more readily than a dry one?"

"Yes, sir, it would."

Folsom shook his head in disbelief. Hardeman had succeeded in getting the doctor befuddled. He confused the issue. The point the doctor was trying to make was lost. In the end, he contradicted himself. Hardeman returned to his seat.

Dr. W. C. Bass,
President of Wesleyan College.
*(Photo courtesy of
Mrs. Jessie Balkcom)*

The next witness Dr. W. C. Bass was the President of Wesleyan Female College. Dr. Bass explained that Pearl was a student of the college and that her father had recently communicated to him by letter concerning payment of her tuition. Rutherford asked him to read the letter.

The president cleared his throat, put on a pair of glasses and began to read. In his most rapid form of shorthand, Folsom recorded what he said.

"Macon, Georgia. July 8, 1887–Rev. Bass, Macon, Ga.: Dear Sir–I received your note and have been trying to effect sale of something to meet the paper. I find it easy to effect sales at sacrifices and on long time, but as yet have met no one who seems to want to pay down ready money.

"I have effected the sale of one hundred dollars, due two weeks from tomorrow, which I will pay on your note, and will do my best to raise the balance, if it has to be done at sacrifice. I am determined you shall be paid at the earliest possible moment. Yours respectfully, R. F. Woolfolk."

The letter disappointed Folsom. Rutherford had alluded to the existence of money in the house prior to the murders and suggested the motive was burglary. The letter did not prove the money existed, but only that Tom's father was planning to have the money by that time. It did, however, suggest that the Captain was having financial difficulty prior to his death.

Hardeman remained seated. He tapped his pencil on the table a few times and then spoke up, "Dr. Bass, does this letter say that there was money in the Captain's house?"

"No, sir. I do not believe so."

"What does this letter say?"

"Well...it says that he does not have the money, but he is planning to get at least a hundred of it in two weeks."

"Was he able to get the money? Was there money in the house the night he was murdered?"

"I have no way of knowing that, sir."

"Nor do we. No further questions."

The defense called Greene Lockett's nephew Jim Foster back to the stand.

"Do you know a colored man by the name of John Jeff?" Rutherford asked.

"Yassur."

"Did he work for the Captain?"

"Yassur."

"And what did he do?"

"Chopped cotton."

Folsom looked over at Tom. The prisoner was downtrodden, distant. The reporter became so engrossed in the defendant's appearance he realized he was not listening to the testimony. Rutherford had finished, and Hardeman was cross-examining.

"Were you aware of any trouble between the Captain and John Jeff?"

"I object."

"Overruled."

"Naw, suh. He worked right on up 'til his time was up 'n then he left."

"When was this?"

"I don't know...'bout two weeks 'fore the murders."

"Did the Captain pay Jeff for his labor?"

"Cain't rightly say if he did."

"Who else did he work for?"

"Nobody else...just the Cap'n. Well.. later he worked for Mistah Chambless, but that was in the Cap'n's fields and after the Cap'n was dead."

"Now Mistah Pennington, do you recall overhearing a threat made against..."

"I object!" Hardeman shouted and jumped to his feet. "Your Honor, I object to the line of questioning the defense is about to take."

Rutherford retorted loudly, "Your Honor, I have not asked the question. How can the state object to something not said?"

"Your Honor, as you will recall the court ruled on this line of questioning yesterday," Hardeman reminded the Judge.

"Bailiff, please escort the jury from the court room."

"Your Honor, I protest!" Rutherford shouted.

Judge Gustin slammed his gavel on the bench and then pointed it at the attorney. "Captain Rutherford, I can accept an objection, but not a protest against the action of the court, and it must stop right now."

Rutherford straightened his shoulders and faced the Judge. "With all possible respect for the court, I do once again enter a most solemn protest. We cannot afford to jeopardize the life of this young man by submitting, without a protest, to having the jury sent out and not allowing them to even know what sort of evidence we want to introduce."

Tom looked up and listened as his attorney began to respectfully demand, then plead with the court to allow the jury to hear Pennington's testimony.

"Your Honor will recall yesterday Mistah Pennington was able to identify John Jeff as the individual he heard threaten to...and I quote...'kill every damned one of them.' As sure as I am a living man more than one man killed the Woolfolk family! One man could not have done it alone, and when Your Honor considers the matter carefully, this fact will come to you overwhelmingly."

"Your Honor," Hardeman interrupted, "the witness did not pick John Jeff out of a group of negroes. John Jeff was singled out...alone, then Pennington was able to recognize him. Even then his answer was deceptive by saying...and I also quote...'If that is not the man, it is his twin brother.' Your Honor, that is not a positive identification."

Judge Gustin listened to both men argue their points and then ruled that Pennington's testimony was hearsay and would not be heard by the jury.

Tom's shoulders dropped. He lowered his gaze to the floor and no longer listened. Rutherford threw his hands up in surrender.

"Then will the court permit us to clarify to the jury why it will not be presented the evidence we promised to deliver during our opening statements?"

Gustin nodded and instructed the bailiff to bring in the jury.

Rutherford waited until the twelve men were settled and then approached the jury box.

"Gentlemen of the jury, the court has permitted me to state to you that I offered Mistah Pennington as evidence, in regard to the threat of which I spoke in my opening address, and the court has ruled it inadmissible, thus depriving me of the benefit of that testimony." The attorney looked each man in the eye. He then returned to his seat.

Gustin dismissed Pennington and declared a recess. As the room emptied, no one moved from the defense table. Tom continued to stare at the floor. Walker turned and smiled weakly at Flo Edwards who had just arrived. Rutherford spoke to no one. He sat with his elbow on the table and pulled at his mustache.

"The defense calls Sheriff George Kitchen."

No one responded. Rutherford looked around the courtroom. The Sheriff was not there.

"As I understand it, Sheriff Kitchen was discharged last night," Gustin offered.

Walker stood up. Rutherford looked at him and waited for an explanation.

"Your Honor, last night Sheriff Kitchen told me that Captain Rutherford said we would not need his testimony...so I discharged him."

Rutherford was dumbfounded. He looked at Walker in disbelief and then addressed the court, "I am sorry Your Honor, there has been a grievous mistake. We need the witness' testimony, especially under the present circumstances."

"Well, if the evidence you intend to produce is admissible..." Judge Gustin offered, "I will send for the witness, and you will be allowed to enter his testimony before the close of the trial. That is IF," he raised his voice. "...his evidence is admissible, and if he is located in time."

Rutherford accepted the court's offer and walked over to the defense table.

"Your Honor, I have here two pictures taken in Sheriff Kitchen's jail of a prisoner, one Jackson Dubose," the attorney said handing the photos up to the Judge. "Here is one taken at his best, and here is the other taken when Dubose, for some reason, tried to prevent his picture being taken."

The Judge handed the photos back to Rutherford.

"He looks better at his worst," he said with a smile.

Rutherford nodded and proceeded to tell the court the events leading up to Sheriff Kitchen sending for Frank Walker. He then reiterated Dubose's testimony. Hardeman objected and reminded the court of Dubose's reputation among lawmen.

"His story was a clear case of fabrication brought about by pressure and coercion. He was turned loose because the Sheriff had nothing on him. The poor fellow was intended to be nothing more than someone's scapegoat," Hardeman stated.

"Your Honor," Frank Walker was on his feet. "Your Honor, this is an outrage. Counselor is implying I misused my position. Not in the least. I maintained my association with Dubose with the utmost discretion and propriety."

Judge Gustin interrupted, "Counselor, the jury does not need to be a part of this. Bailiff, please escort the gentlemen of the jury from the court room."

No one said another word until the door closed behind the last juror. The Judge then pointed at the attorneys. "I will not permit this court to be reduced to a shouting match. Mr. Walker, I believe you had the floor."

"Your Honor, the state has implied that I misused my position to coerce a confession from Jackson Dubose. Nothing could be further from the truth," Walker remarked.

John Rutherford stood up. "Your Honor, I would like to request that Mistah Walker be called as a witness and so sworn be allowed to tell his story."

"Your Honor, we can not allow second hand testimony. Jackson Dubose is not present to testify on his behalf. Anyone could attach any statement to his name, and there is no way to verify its validity!" Hardeman responded loudly.

"I must object to this criticism of my professional actions involving Jackson Dubose!" Walker shouted.

Judge Gustin hammered his gavel loudly. "Gentlemen!" he barked. "You will desist this arguing. I will allow Mr. Walker to testify on the stand but I will not allow any reference to Jackson Dubose."

"Your Honor!" Walker and Rutherford responded in unison.

"Do I make myself clear? Bailiff, send the jury back in. Colonel Rutherford you may call Mr. Walker to the stand."

As the jurymen returned to their seats, Frank Walker was sworn in.

"Now Mistah Walker, do you recall meeting with a colored man by the name of Jackson..."

"I object." Hardeman interrupted.

"Overruled. Colonel Rutherford I thought I made myself clear."

"You did, Your Honor," Rutherford responded and walked over to his table.

A long moment of silence preceded his next question. Folsom thought he heard the lawyer slowly exhale. Given no other choice, the lawyer changed his line of questioning.

"Mistah Walker, you examined the bloody clothes shortly after they were retrieved from the well?"

"Yes, sir. I was obtained as counsel for the defense a week after the murders . The only article I personally examined was the hat. However, I did watch the examination of the shirt. In fact, I allowed the doctor to draw some of my blood to serve as comparison. It was my understanding that no other tests were to be made on the clothing without my approval."

Unless he was allowed to give evidence about Jackson Dubose, there was no significant reason for Walker to be testifying. Rutherford turned the witness over to Hardeman who stood up and approached the stand.

"Mr. Walker, were you not invited by me to watch the examination of the evidence?"

"Yes, I was."

"Did my office prohibit you in any way from participating in the examination?"

"No sir."

"Did I or any member of my staff promise to make additional examinations?"

"No sir...but Dr. Clifton did."

"No further questions."

"I would like to redirect," Rutherford followed. "Mistah Walker, would you please clarify your position on the examination of the bloody clothes?"

"All I wanted was for no examinations, that is no chemical testing, be conducted without my knowledge and participation."

"Thank you. No further questions."

"I would like to ask a question," Judge Gustin leaned over. "Mr. Walker, would you have understood the procedure had you watched it?"

"No, sir...I just wanted to witness it."

William H. McKay, a friend of Captain Woolfolk's, was called to the stand.

"Did Captain Woolfolk ever express fear for his life?" Rutherford asked.

"I object."

"I will allow the evidence. I must remind you counselor of the conditions."

"Yes, Your Honor. I simply want this witness to recall a statement made by Captain Woolfolk to him."

"He said that he heard that George Caldwell did not get a long enough sentence and would be out sooner that he wished. He said that he was afraid Caldwell would come back and harm him."

"So, the Captain expressed fear of his life to you?"

"Yes, sir, he did."

"Your witness."

"Mr. McKay, when did Captain Woolfolk make this statement to you?"

"Right after Caldwell went to jail."

"And when was that?"

"I guess...by now...'bout a year ago."

Henry Cowan was Rutherford's final witness.

"Mr. Cowan, what was the value of the Captain's property?"

"Well, it was appraised at five thousand eight hundred and sixty dollars."

"Is that all?"

"Well...there was a debt of about eight hundred dollars. But I, personally, believe the property was worth twice that."

"Did the Captain ever talk about his financial state?"

"Yes, he did. After his business went under just after the war...he almost lost the rest of his property. The humiliation didn't stop him though...he said as soon as he got out from under, he was goin' to fix the place up."

"So...the Captain's personal estate was not...let's say...substantial?"

"I object. The witness is being asked to make an assumption."

"Overruled."

"Your witness."

"Who now claims the estate?" Hardeman asked.

"The three remaining children and the Howards, Mattie Woolfolk's relatives."

"So...the defendant claims an inheritance."

"He was given the same documents as were given his sisters."

"What documents? Mortgages on the claim?"

"The routine documents that follow probate."

"Do the three remaining children hold claim to the entire estate?"

"Yes, they do. Although...part of the estate was in joint ownership with Mattie Howard Woolfolk."

"Which means...?"

"Which means that the three survivors do not hold exclusive right to the property."

"No further questions," Hardeman announced.

"Captain Rutherford, call your next witness."

"The defense rests, Your Honor."

Folsom looked up from his notes. It had taken a day and a half for the court to seat a jury, two and a half days for the state to present its case against Tom Woolfolk but only a day and a half for the defense to argue his innocence. It all seemed unbalanced to the reporter.

Although the defense had put forth a herculean effort, the scales of admissibility seemed tilted away from the defendant and toward the state. Key witnesses were not allowed to testify. Evidence crucial to the defense's case was ruled inadmissible.

Hardeman stood and called his rebuttal witness–Benjamin F. Howard. The room was attentive and sympathetic as the old man slowly made his way to the witness chair. Even Tom watched with fondness and admiration.

"Mistah Howard, would you tell the court your relationship to the Woolfolk family?"

"Mattie Woolfolk was my daughter."

"And do you recall a conversation you had with your daughter a week before her tragic death?"

"I object, Your Honor."

"Overruled."

"Do you, Mistah Howard, recall a conversation with your daughter a week before her tragic death?"

"Yes, sir, I do."

"Would you please share that conversation with the court?"

"Mattie came to visit me. She was upset and worried. She said she was afraid for her life and wanted to know what to do. I asked her what was wrong. She said she was afraid of Tom. She said that he was bossing her around. He would sleep late in the mornin' and then demand breakfast. When she'd make it, he'd say something like 'is this all you've got?'

"She said he pushed the children around, and they were afraid of him. She said that a few days earlier, my son-in-law came in very angry and said that Tom was one step closer to the penitentiary."

A groan rumbled through the room. Judge Gustin tapped his gavel.

"Go on," Hardeman said politely.

"I told her to get her children together and for them all to come to my house...that I'd...I'd...protect them."

The room hushed to an agonizing silence. Tom looked down at his hands. Shackleford continued to console Flo. The defense did not cross-examine the witness. Benjamin Howard was excused.

"Your Honor," Rutherford said after the witness left the courtroom, "as a sur rebuttal...the defense calls Thomas G. Woolfolk."

The audience stiffened in anticipation as the defendant, holding a small Bible, took the stand .

"My name is Thomas G. Woolfolk. I am twenty-seven years old," he said in a low voice. "I am innocent of this terrible calamity." The defendant looked at a sheet of paper he had taken to the stand with him and began to read.

Folsom looked around at the spellbound room. Every eye was on the defendant. No one moved. The attention was hypnotic as Tom told of his activities the day of the murder and of bathing and turning in early.

"I slept until about two hours before day, when I was awakened by a groan and a blow...and a scream." He looked up at the audience and then turned the paper over. "I jumped up to go to my father's assistance, into the room where I heard the noise. My brother Richard was quicker than I was, and he rushed in ahead of me...and was knocked down. I could not see what happened. The light had been blown out. I could not see him..., but I heard him fall. I knew that my life was in danger. I was greatly excited. I turned around and jumped over my bed and out the window onto the front porch and ran down to Greene Lockett's house, the nearest negro house on the plantation.

"When I was going out of the front yard, I heard screams from the children. I called Greene and called him. He came after I called him several times and sat down on the steps as if he was very much disturbed. I begged him and begged him to return to the house with me...to help me protect the family. He said he was afraid to go."

He paused and looked at the jury. The room was still.

Tom then continued by describing how after he could not get help he decided to go back up to the hill. "I could hear the voices of the killers in the house and the dogs barking. I followed them to the back gate. I heard the gate slam as they ran down the hill. Then...I approached the house very cautiously."

He told how he entered the house and searched for his family. He described walking through the blood, how he checked each body for some sign of life and found them all dead. He explained how he moved his sister and picked up his mother.

"When help came, the suspicion was great against me, and I was immediately accused by the crowd and arrested," he said softly looking around at the audience.

He then defended himself against the testimonies given against him. "John Owens is a bad character my father had put on the chaingang for stealing corn in the swamp. He also cut a white man. I do not remember telling him anything about wanting to own my father's plantation some day. What I do remember is him saying that he may be painting the walls white now, but he'd paint them red before long...he hadn't forgot about the chaingang business.

"I don't remember any such conversation with Mr. Dannenberg, but if I said anything, it was not a threat towards my father, or parents, or anything of the kind."

He concluded his statement, folded his paper, and then turned towards the jury.

"Now, gentlemen, if you think I am guilty...I hope this crowd will take me and cut me all to pieces...and I won't flinch from it."

Intentional or otherwise, Tom's statement was not printed in the Atlanta Constitution.

Crowd, outside the Bibb County Courthouse, waiting for the verdict.
(Photo courtesy of the Middle Georgia Archives, Washington Memorial Library, Macon, GA)

CHAPTER SIXTEEN
"HANG HIM! HANG HIM!"

Monday morning, December 13, 1887, John C. Rutherford rose from his seat, slowly walked to the center of the court room, and faced the jury. The room was filled to capacity, and every spectator waited patiently for the lawyer famed throughout the state as a brilliant orator to plead for Tom Woolfolk's life.

"Gentlemen of the jury," he said and then pointed to Tom. "That man had only spoken to me a few moments, when I felt...as a man and a lawyer...that it was my duty to defend him..." With that statement Rutherford began his final argument.

"Oh how the papers have dwelt in graphic particularity upon this crime. It was a feast for them. Strange as it may appear, there is something in the public appetite that calls for sensation...and the papers seize every opportunity to feed it to them.

"The state...and the newspapers would like for you to believe that Tom Woolfolk and Tom Woolfolk alone...murdered nine members of his family. I say to you the theory of the State falls to the ground. The chain is broken. One man could not have perpetuated the deed alone and unaided. It is a physical impossibility that Tom Woolfolk...or any other single man...could have done it."

The lawyer looked up, his arms outstretched. In a voice as sincere as a prayer he then said, "I stand in the presence of my Creator and declare that I do not believe that one man could have committed the terrible tragedy alone."

He paused, then said, "Sheriff Westcott, would you please hand me the axe?"

The Sheriff walked over to the evidence table, picked up the axe, and carried it to him. Rutherford took the axe and raised it high over his head. The Sheriff looked startled and jumped aside as the lawyer ran about the room thrashing and slashing at the air. Over and over he delivered imaginary blows.

Flo closed her eyes and tried to block the images that were forming in her mind. Tom looked at the floor. Lillie began to cry.

He stopped and surveyed the room. "A witness in describing the blows stated that most of the death blows had been made by the back of the axe, but that one or two of them looked as if they were made by the sharp edge of the axe. On one of the bodies, testimony said there were blows inflicted both by the edge and the eye of the axe."

Turning the axe over and examining the blade, he continued in a voice so near a whisper members of the jury leaned over to hear him.

"Would a man in that bloody hour, who was dealing death blows with the back of the axe, take time to stop...turn the axe completely around and strike with the sharp edge?" He faced an imaginary victim and pantomimed the awkward action. Someone coughed nervously.

"No, gentlemen of the jury...more than one person had a hand in that bloody harvest of death." He walked across the room and returned the axe to its proper place. His back still turned he continued, "But what about the bloody handprint supposedly found on the leg of Thomas Woolfolk?"

Rutherford stormed over to the prosecutors' table. "The State," he continued loudly, "claims that the impression of the hand was made by some victim, who had grabbed Tom Woolfolk in an effort to escape death–in an effort to avoid the blows, yet, the State has not introduced a single witness or presented any evidence showing that a particle of blood was found on the hands of any of the dead. How, then, could that imprint have been made on Tom Woolfolk's leg in the manner claimed by the State?"

He looked as if he expected someone to answer him. "It got there," he continued, "in the way the prisoner said it did."

Folsom reflected back to the coroner's inquest. Tom said then that when he touched the bodies to see if anyone was alive, he got blood on his hands. He said then the print was probably his own. Could it have been? The reporter wondered.

"Ah...this bloody hand," Rutherford continued, "how the prosecution loves to dwell upon it. It is there in hoc signo vinces.

When you...as upright jurors...take into consideration that the State has not proven that blood was found on the hands of any of the dead...you must not give this bloody hand theory of the State any weight. The hand must have been smeared and reeking with blood when it rested on the drawers and soaked through onto the naked flesh."

Folsom noticed several heads in the audience nodding. The argument made sense.

"The only persons who testified to hearing the screams on the night of the tragedy were two women–Lou Cooper and Emma Jones. Yet, the State was unwilling to put them on the stand. They were sworn by the State, and yet the prosecution would not introduce them. It remained for the defense to do so.

"The State had numerable witnesses...they filled the aisles. Neither you, jurors, nor I were able to count them, there were so many...and yet the State refused to hear what these two women had to say. Why?

"When so terrible a crime has been committed, the most outrageous ever known in our country...the State declined to let the only persons who said they heard the screams testify. Does that look as if the State was seeking the truth in this matter, or does it not seem as if they were trying to suppress the truth?

"They do not wish the light to be thrown on the facts and evidence of the case. Ah, they thought that this testimony would break a link in their chain and would crush their theory to the ground. Why does the prosecution wish so earnestly to fasten this crime upon Tom Woolfolk?" He was shouting.

Rutherford walked over to the prosecutors, leaned over, placed both hands flat on the table, and faced Hardeman.

"Why do they not throw all the light in," he continued softly, "and if Tom Woolfolk is not guilty let him go free, and try to fasten the crime upon another? Do you not know that there is not a father in this broad land but who would rejoice to know that a son is not guilty of the monstrous death of his parent? They would be glad to learn that someone else was the fiend. Do you not know that every sister's heart would leap for joy to find that a brother did not slay his sister?"

The next day a violent storm raged outside. Inside, Rutherford resumed his argument. He explained to the jury that most of the defense's evidence, testimonies of threats by individuals who had recent arguments with the Captain were declared inadmissable by the court because it decided such to be hearsay. He then wondered aloud why statements the prisoner allegedly made two years ago were permitted. Why, he wondered, were threats by one individual made in the presence of another considered hearsay while another's threats were not? The more recent one came from another person and not the defendant.

The lawyer explained why Jackson Dubose's confession and all references to him by the defense were disallowed. He explained why Sam Pennington was not allowed to testify of hearing threats by John Jeff, a black man known to have had a heated argument with the Captain. Turning and facing the solicitor general, he asked why the State believed no one else wished harm on the Woolfolk family, no one else but Tom.

The audience was spellbound as Rutherford recalled point after point attempted by the defense that was seriously contested by the State and in some cases by the court.

Every shred of circumstantial evidence originally implying Tom's guilt was explained. The bloody handprint was made by Tom himself either after answering a call of nature or when he returned after checking the bodies and squatted by a tree to wait for help. Blood got on his ear when he placed his head on the chest of one of the victims to check for a heart beat.

Folsom was amazed. Rutherford was able to clarify the matter of the clothing in the well. He explained that the Thursday before the murders, Tom's brother Dick had picked up a bundle of Tom's clothes at the Southern Hotel, where Tom had been staying before moving out to the farm.

The attorney hypothesized how the clothes got in the well when someone, probably the actual murderers, threw the entire bundle in the well. He admitted he did not know why. Maybe they wanted to implicate Tom, or they grabbed the bundle lying at the foot of Tom's bed to wipe the blood from their own hands.

Rutherford then reminded the jury that expert witnesses could not positively identify without leaving a shadow of a doubt the stains on the clothing to even be human blood. He brought home a familiar note by recalling the staining effect Georgia red clay has on cloth. Again, heads nodded in agreement.

Rutherford argued that the Captain was in financial distress. Tom was aware of this, yet would-be robbers would not have known. The lawyer stood in front of the jury and asked a final question.

"What happened that night? The State wants you to believe that Tom Woolfolk in a fit of greed and super human strength alone killed nine members of his family. They were not killed in their sleep. Some of them got up from their beds and struggled for their lives. Did they stand in line and wait their turn?

"What happened that night? Was it a lone son out to get a fortune he clearly knew did not exist? Or did several persons go into that house that night? For what reason, we may never know. Was it for murder, robbery, hatred, revenge? They would not have known the Captain was broke. He lived in this nice house on a hill overlooking a thousand acres of rich farm land.

"I ask only that you give this considerable thought, gentlemen of the jury. Look at it through the eyes of the intelligent and rational men you are. A man...an innocent man's life depends on it."

Rutherford thanked the jury for its attention and returned to his seat. His argument had lasted eleven hours. He was exhausted. The court called a recess until three o'clock.

"It is not necessary to go out of the evidence to find the prisoner guilty," Hardeman said, "nor should you mistake the ingenious argument of the learned counsel for the defense in the cause."

The solicitor-general began his final argument by reviewing each incriminating piece of evidence. His powerful build and thundering voice commanded attention. Tom kept his eyes glued to the floor and would not look at the attorney as he stormed back and forth in front of the defense's table and pointed an accusatory finger at him.

The State reminded the jury of Tom's anger and threats. It repeated Ben Howard's testimony about his daughter's fear of her stepson. Hardeman then brought up the handprint.

"And I tell you this day," he said in a loud voice, "that the bloody handprint was a sign placed there by the Almighty Himself to fix the prisoner's guilt. And henceforth...I will adopt the language of prisoner's counsel in describing the scene. There was a deluge of blood in that house and I will convince you, gentlemen of the jury, that Tom Woolfolk's was the guilty hand that caused the red stream to flow."

He stopped and surveyed the room. No one moved.

"And what of the victims...least we forget them?" The solicitor talked softly and gently about each member of the murdered family. He spoke of the children's youth and vitality being stolen from them in a horror no one living could ever imagine. He touched on Pearl's maiden innocence and beauty and Dick's young manhood and potential. He reminded the jury that only someone rabid with greed would kill a helpless babe so she would not live to inherit the family fortune.

"What would a murderer gain...what would a burglar gain from killing the baby. The infant was no threat, not in a physical sense. But if you wanted to remove all claims to the estate. If you wanted to insure that no one survived to claim inheritance, then the babe would have to go."

Elizabeth Black sobbed quietly, her face buried in her hands as the solicitor reviewed the murder of Temperance West. "Just as the baby," he reminded the jury, "the old woman posed no threat and in fact heard nothing. She was murdered in her sleep.

"The defense contends that the murders were committed by more than one man. All the evidence points to the fact that five, including Richard and Charlie, were killed in the Captain's room...and not in their own bedroom. Now, if more that one was engaged in the crime...would they not have commenced the attack on Tom, Richard and Charlie simultaneously with the attack on Mr. Woolfolk?

"No. I tell you," he yelled, "the evidence points to only one man, and that one man is sitting there before you now. That one man is Thomas Woolfolk."

"HANG HIM! HANG HIM!" someone shouted. The courtroom exploded in a uproar. Bailiffs ran into the crowd standing to the side in search of the disrupter. Gustin hammered his gavel loudly and commanded order.

"The State will proceed."

Rutherford jumped to his feet.

"I object, Your Honor, and request that the room be cleared until order is regained."

"Overruled. Proceed counselor."

Hardeman turned back to the jury and continued, his finger pointing towards heaven. "The evidence points to only one man. Thomas Woolfolk killed his family."

Cicero Tharpe, a former sheriff and local businessman, jumped to his feet and shouted.

"HANG HIM!"

The room again erupted. Judge Gustin furiously hammered his gavel.

"I will clear this room. Order. Order. Sheriff remove that man!" the Judge shouted.

Hardeman leaned against the jury box, his head bowed. Tom's sisters and aunt embraced each other and wept. Tom did not move. Sheriff Westcott escorted Tharpe out. Rutherford again requested that the room be cleared.

"That is not necessary, Counselor. The State will continue."

"I hope," Hardeman announced to the audience, "I hope that I will not again be interrupted in this manner. The court is sitting, and the jury is impaneled to try the case according to the law." He shouted, "And according to the law, it will be tried."

"Solicitor, I am calling a recess. We will reconvene tomorrow morning at nine o'clock." The Judge said and tapped his gavel.

Four deputies rushed to Tom's side and quickly ushered him from the room.

The morning of December 15th was cold and dreary. The overcast sky threatened a repeat of the storm that accentuated the previous day. Tom Woolfolk was shaved and allowed to bathe. To insure against a repeat of the threatening outburst that ended court the day before, Sheriff Westcott and three of his deputies personally escorted the prisoner to his seat.

Tom's trial had lasted ten days.

Officials took their familiar places, and court was called to order at ten minutes after nine. Hardeman rose, gave a warning glare to the audience, and approached the jury box. Sheriff Westcott stood to the right of the Judge's bench and faced the audience. As children would act after a serious reprimand, the audience sat quietly and watched attentively.

Tom turned his chair towards the window and stared out. The cold, shallowness of the day did not offer warm reassurance. The distant trees were gray and naked. The prisoner, however, chose to continue looking outside at the wintery dead than at the proceedings continuing in front of him.

Hardeman cleared his throat, leaned against the jury box, and smiled at the jurors.

"Let's talk about the bloody clothing," he said. "Testimony upon testimony has clearly stated that the clothing found in the well had blood and brains on them. The defense would have you believe that grown, intelligent men, farmers, do not know what blood and brains look like. The defense would like for you to believe that the stains on the clothing, stains you yourselves saw, were caused by Georgia red clay. The expert witnesses did not make such a claim."

The solicitor asked why were the clothes put in the well, and then answered his question. "Tom Woolfolk threw the clothes, covered with the blood and brains of his family in the well. He knew the bloody clothes were there, and when he asked for a drink of water, he refused to drink the water from the well brought to him in a dipper. Instead, he insisted on drinking from a cup.

"And when questioned about the blood in his ear, the prisoner explained that blood was flying every where."

"That's a lie. I never said that," Tom muttered aloud.

Hardeman turned and looked at the prisoner. Walker turned to his client and placed his hand on his shoulder to restrain him. Tom anxiously continued.

"The witness lied, I tell you. I never said that...it's a mistake."

Gustin tapped his gavel. Rutherford placed his hand on Tom's other shoulder. The prisoner shut up and turned to look out the window.

A recess was called.

At 9:35 Hardeman resumed his argument. "A few minutes ago the prisoner stated that, and I quote, 'it's a mistake.' Well, gentlemen of the jury, I tell you that the mistake was made on the part of the prisoner in using such language."

The solicitor then recited a poem. "'The shadows are many, the sunlight is one, but in tracing the shadows...we find out the sun.'"

Walking over to the evidence table, Hardeman picked up the wool cap.

"If Silas Woolfolk, the owner of this hat, had committed that murder, do you think he would have claimed this to be his as he clearly did the day it was found? The hat fitted the negro, and the negro fitted the hat."

The large double doors in the rear of the courtroom opened with a low groan. Folsom turned and watched as Flo Edwards, Lillie Cowan, and Fannie Crane slowly walked down the aisle. All eyes fell on the three women who had won the hearts of the community for their undying love and support of the prisoner.

Hardeman began to ramble on about how history had, infact, records of killings in wells and the stones at the bottom were still covered in blood. Members of the audience became disinterested.

Pea Jay leaned over and whispered, "What's he talking about?"

"The Sopoy Rebellion, I think, where the women committed suicide by throwing themselves in a well. Rocks at the bottom still had blood on them," Folsom answered.

Judge Gustin tapped his gavel.

After reviewing every point of testimony, the expert witnesses' conclusions, and each item of evidence, the solicitor declared that fact and fact alone pointed a condemning finger at the prisoner. Hardeman concluded his argument and returned to his chair. The solicitor-general had argued for the State a total of three and a half hours. Judge Gustin declared a recess.

The courtroom filled to capacity and then overflowed as spectators crowded in to hear the Judge's challenge and the jury's verdict. Judge Gustin walked in and seated himself behind the bench. The room hushed to silence and was called to order.

He challenged the jury to consider the evidence before them and then reminded them they must decide beyond a shadow of a doubt if the defendant did or did not commit the crime of murder. In a face blank of expression he stated he sympathized with them and the task he would soon assign to them.

"I have tried this case all through the livelong night when others, including the accused, were wrapped in slumber," he admitted and sent the jury to chambers to render its verdict.

The twelve men rose from the chairs and followed the bailiff out of the room. Shoulders long stiff with the tension of the proceedings drooped. Members of the audience breathed in unison and shifted in their seats.

Twenty minutes later, the jury returned.

Folsom was shocked at the shortness of time. Pea Jay had predicted it would not take them long to make a decision. Judge Gustin asked the jury foreman Henry Harvey a preacher and manager of the I.B. English and Company Compress and Warehouse, if the jury had reached a verdict.

Harvey stood up and cleared his throat. "We have, Your Honor."

"And what say you?"

"We the jury find the defendant, Thomas G. Woolfolk, guilty."

The three women sitting behind the defendant gasped and began to weep openly.

"Will the defendant stand."

Tom pushed his chair back and stood up.

"Does the defendant have any reason why sentence should not be passed upon him?" the Judge asked.

"I have been tried by twelve honest, competent and intelligent men, Your Honor," Tom answered clearly. "I feel satisfied they have done their duty...but prejudice against me from Hazzard District is so strong, Your Honor. Witnesses lied, although...they're honest and intelligent men. The court's treated me well...,but the court and jury followed the witnesses."

Tom put up his right hand and in a voice strong and determined said, "I am an innocent man."

Judge Gustin tapped his gavel and announced, "I am declaring a recess until tomorrow morning, nine o'clock, at which time sentence will be read."

The room stood and began to empty. Folsom watched the Judge leave but noticed that the opposing counsel, the Sheriff, the jury, and court officers did not move. He decided to wait and watch. Moments later, after the room was nearly emptied, Judge Gustin returned to the bench and reconvened the proceedings.

He instructed the defendant to again stand. Tom rose to his feet as did John Rutherford and Frank Walker.

"The Jury empaneled in this case having returned a verdict finding you, Thomas G. Woolfolk, guilty of the crime of murder, and you showing no reason why the sentence of the Court should not be pronounced upon you. It is therefore considered ordered and adjudged by the Court that you, Thomas G. Woolfolk..."

Folsom half listened to the death sentence. His attention was fixed on Tom.

"...hung by the neck until you are dead, dead...dead. May the Lord have mercy on your soul."

Tom turned and faced his relatives. Flo, her faced buried in Shackleford's shoulder, was sobbing loudly. Tenderly, he spoke to his sister.

"Don't cry and take on like that, Flo. I'm as well as I ever was in my life."

Rutherford informed them the defense would appeal. Sheriff Westcott approached Tom, shackled his wrists, and led him from the courtroom.

Later that evening, juror Asher Ayres married Louise Conner.

CHAPTER SEVENTEEN

"The bastard done cut through his leg irons."

New Years Eve, 1887 Nat Birdsong made his rounds through the Bibb County cell block. The night of revelry was already increasing the number of occupants under his charge, and the young jailer was prepared to maintain total control.

Walking slowly between the rows of cells, he glanced in each cage and checked the lock before moving on. Near the middle of the block, he stopped and warmed himself next to the old potbellied stove.

After Tom's conviction, Sheriff Westcott had the jailer and a deputy secretly transport the condemned man to Atlanta. Although the court sentenced Tom to die, public outrage was so intense that Westcott felt the legal execution could still be preempted by a lynching. The Sheriff was determined to protect the community's rights and keep the convicted murderer safe until his scheduled hanging, February tenth.

Upon their arrival in Atlanta, Birdsong, the deputy, and their prisoner tried to walk nonchalantly through the busy depot towards the waiting hack. Their efforts to go unnoticed and unmolested, however, were thwarted when someone recognized Tom and drew attention to them. Immediately, the three men were surrounded by curious spectators excited to see the convicted killer.

The crowd in its enthusiasm almost overwhelmed the small group, until Birdsong took hold of Tom's arm and pushed his way through the gawkers. Their ride down the streets of Atlanta was fast and furious, but word spread and another crowd waited for them at the county jail. Birdsong remembered his prisoner seemed relieved to be there. He greeted the Atlanta jailer warmly and requested his old cell.

The cold late December night required a constant vigil of the old stove that served to warm the prisoners. Birdsong shivered. The bitter wind outside reminded him of the day he went back to Atlanta to retrieve Tom.

When word of his removal from the Bibb County Jail circulated through the community, the citizens of that county were offended. Judge James Nisbet, Tom's first choice for counsel, reflected the sentiment of the entire area when he talked to a reporter from the Atlanta Constitution.

"I was much surprised and annoyed to find that Woolfolk had been sent by the authorities to the Fulton County Jail for safekeeping," Nisbet was quoted as saying. "It seems to me to be a reflection upon the people of Bibb County, that they were so bloodthirsty they would attempt to break into a jail and hang Woolfolk before he could have the benefit of an appeal to the Supreme Court. I think Woolfolk was as safe in Macon as in Atlanta. I know that there is no more conservative and law-abiding county than that of Bibb."

The next day, Solicitor-General Hardeman instructed Westcott to have the prisoner returned to Bibb County.

Birdsong opened the stove's heavy, cast iron door and dropped in a scoop of coal. A prisoner coughed and turned over in his sleep. The jailer proceeded down the aisle.

Tom seemed genuinely surprised when Birdsong came to take him back and said that he did not expect to be taken to Macon until February. The prisoner was not happy when he reentered the Bibb County Jail. In Atlanta, he was given a large cell, was treated well, and was not shackled. In Macon, his cell was much smaller, his treatment harsher, and he was once again shackled and tethered to the wall.

Soft mumbling from the corner cell made the jailer stop and walk over to the door to investigate. There in the center of his cage was Tom Woolfolk on his knees, facing the wall.

Birdsong listened for a moment to the condemned prisoner's passionate pleas for God to relieve him of his burden. The young jailer respectfully turned around and quietly walked away.

John Hardeman looked up when his secretary tapped at his door.

"Yes?"

"Sir, Mrs. Edwards and Mrs. Cowan are here to see you."

The lawyer stood up and adjusted his vest. "Please show them in."

Hardeman had been curious for days about the scheduled appointment he had with Tom Woolfolk's sisters. The trial resulting in a death sentence for their brother had concluded only two weeks earlier. Although he did not know the sisters personally, he was, nonetheless, impressed with their devotion to the man accused and found guilty of murdering their family.

The two women dressed in long black dresses entered his office.

"Mrs. Edwards...Mrs. Cowan...please sit down. May I have my secretary get you something?"

"No...no, thank you," Flo answered and shifted nervously in her seat.

"Now, how may I help you?"

Flo looked at her sister. Lillie nodded for her to continue.

"We need your legal advice on a serious matter," Flo finally answered.

"And what matter is that?"

"As you know my sister, Lillie, our brother... Tom...and I are the heirs to our father's estate."

"Yes, I heard that the Howard family has contested your inheritance."

Flo nodded and continued with a sigh, "Charles Howard our stepmother's brother was appointed the administrator of her estate."

Hardeman nodded.

"Uncle Charles is attempting to sell Father's land and other property."

"I see but under such circumstances sales are usually required in order to cover any outstanding debts incurred by the deceased while living."

"We know. But there are no longer any such debts. Mistah Chambless sold the crops and equipment and paid off everything that was outstanding."

"Well, if that is the case, then you should be represented by counsel and have your grievance argued before a judge."

"That's why we came to you. Colonel Rutherford and Mistah Walker are busy in the appeal process and can not help us," Flo said quietly.

Hardeman looked from one woman to the next. Lillie smiled weakly and said, "We would like for you to represent us...Flo, myself, and...and Tom."

The lawyer leaned back in his chair and tapped his pencil on the note pad lying on his desk. His term as solicitor-general was up, and he had returned to his private practice. He thought the matter over before answering.

"I would be honored to present your case," he finally said. Lillie smiled tearfully and looked at Flo.

"Thank you," Flo continued. "As you can imagine, we do not want to...on top of everything else...lose 'The Homeplace'." Her voice cracked.

Hardeman smiled reassuringly. "I can understand that," he said and stacked the papers in front of him. "I believe our first course of action is to get Judge Gustin to disqualify himself. As you know, before the murders he was the Howards' attorney. I believe we can convince him there is a conflict of interest here. We'll get the case moved to another circuit court where we will then request a writ of certiorari."

"I'm sorry...I don't understand what that means," Lillie responded honestly.

"Well...basically it will say that the sale is not necessary and should not be conducted until heirship is determined. Don't worry, I'll look into the matter and get back to you."

Flo stood up and extended her gloved hand. "Thank you," she said. Lillie followed her out the door.

Hardeman watched the two women exit his office and then returned to his work. Judge Gustin had asked him to help the new solicitor-general in opposing Tom's appeal.

In Atlanta, newly elected Sam Chambless took his seat in the House of Representatives.

Tom worked furiously at the metal link connecting his ankle bracelet to his chain. He moved the case knife, its blade half gone and the remaining portion nicked, back and forth against the metal staple until finally he had cut through. No one noticed the meticulous and earnest regimen he began shortly after his return to Macon. Although he knew that his lawyers were appealing his conviction, he no longer had faith in the system.

When he saw the broken knife jutting out of the ceiling of his cell one day while he was lying on his cot, he considered it an opportunity he could not ignore. Probably left by some unfortunate prisoner previously confined to the small cell, the knife represented a glimmer of hope to the condemned man. Finally, there was something he could do to free himself. He hated the chains. And although he presented a confident front to his sisters, the authorities, and other prisoners, he did not want to die.

Tom's cell was purposefully chosen by the Sheriff because of its location directly over the office. The rattle of Tom's chain across the cell floor above their heads gave them a sense of relief. Only when the rattling stopped would they become suspicious and go up to check on him.

Tom realized this and used it to his advantage. He constantly paced the floor, dragging the chain. When he wasn't walking, he would sit and swing his crossed leg. The rattling continued during every waking hour and finally began to play on his keepers' nerves.

The prisoner inspected the severed link, congratulated himself for his achievement, and returned his tool to its hiding place. He had decided to try to free his ankle but did not know exactly what to do once he was successful. He would be patient and wait.

January 10, 1888, John Owens, whose testimony against Tom contributed greatly to his conviction, was himself convicted of simple larceny.

Emma Jones picked up the load of firewood she had just cut and turned to go back into her cabin when Greene Lockett ran up.

"Did ya hear?" he was excited.

"Hear what?"

"Tom Woolfolk's done escaped."

"He has?"

"Ya gotta be sure t'tell Aaron," he said as he ran off, "'n don't ya'll be out after dark."

Later, Emma told Aaron.

"Probably just talk," he answered dryly.

"Greene seemed purty skeered."

"That don't s'prize me none."

"He got somethin' t'be skeered of, Aaron?"

"Aw now baby, you know how Greene gits."

"I guess you're right."

"But..." Aaron paused, "...maybe it'd be best you don't go outside after dark."

Emma turned and looked at her husband.

"We ain't got nothin' to be skeered of...do we?"

Aaron got up from his chair, walked over to the door and latched it.

"Do we?" Emma asked again.

"Just do as I tell ya, woman."

The welldressed couple knocked at the jail door and was admitted by an attendant. Jailer Birdsong walked up and introduced himself.

"What can I do for you," he said politely, both impressed and curious by the presence of the obviously well to do visitors.

"We're from California," the man answered rather proudly.

"Yes?" Birdsong responded.

"We came all this way to see one of your prisoners," the woman offered.

The jailer was accustomed to relatives visiting his prisoners– wives, children, parents–but never from such a great distance. "Kinfolk?" he asked.

"Well...no," the man answered.

"No matter," Birdsong said as he began to escort the couple up the stairs leading to the cell block. "Which prisoner you want t'see?"

"The one who killed his family," the man said.

Birdsong stopped half way up the stairs and stared at the couple.

"Tom Woolfolk," the woman added, excitedly.

"You ain't kin?"

"Well...no. But we came all this way just to see him."

"Sorry," Birdsong said and started back down the stairs. "The Judge says no visitors. Only his lawyers and immediate family...them that's left...can see him."

"You don't understand, you've got to let us. We came all this way from California just to see him!" the woman cried. Birdsong turned and faced them.

"Judge's orders, ma'am. You can't see'im."

The man wrapped his arms tightly about the woman's shoulders and tried to lead her out. The woman cried bitterly in her handkerchief and resisted. Birdsong escorted them to the exit, opened the door, and closed it behind them.

"Woolfolk," the deputy called out as he entered the cell block.

"Yeh, what is it?" Tom answered from his cot.

The deputy unlocked the cell door and entered. "Git up. We're changing your bracelets." Jailer Birdsong walked in behind him, carrying a new set of shackles.

Tom hesitated a moment then rolled over, and put his feet on the floor. Birdsong kneeled down and began to unlock the bracelets. He stopped and stared. The deputy looked down. "What's the matter?" he asked.

"Well, I'll be damned. Look at this. The bastard done cut through his leg irons," Birdsong said, handed the shackles up to the deputy and then quickly secured the new ones around the prisoner's ankles.

The deputy examined the staple and realized what Tom had done. "Awlright, Woolfolk. Where's the saw?"

Tom smiled. He enjoyed aggravating his keepers. He answered innocently, "What saw? I don't know what you're talking about?"

Furious, Birdsong stood up. "I've had just about enough of you. Now tell us where you hid the saw."

Tom stood up, walked around as if checking out the new shackles. He looked over his shoulder at the two men, crossed his arms and leaned against the cell wall.

The deputy studied the chain until he was convinced it was secure and then proceeded to search the cell. Tom's cot was upturned and examined. Birdsong looked at the walls and in the cracks. Finally, while standing on the table and looking at the ceiling very closely, the deputy found the knife. Birdsong took it and stared at the prisoner.

"Where'd ya get this?" he asked.

"Found it." Tom continued to smile.

The two men left the cell and locked the door. After they were out of sight and only then Tom moved. He let out a slight sigh, walked back over to his cot and righted it. He sat down and looked at his ankles. They were sore and bruised. He picked up his chain, gave it a violent snatch, and then slammed it over and over against the floor.

Montgomery Folsom was kept busy tracking down stories about Tom. The first one developed immediately after Tom's conviction. Word got out that he had confessed to Judge Nisbet. Newspapers spread the news in the form of sensational headlines. After Folsom approached the prisoner who vehemently declared his innocence, the reporter realized the rumor mill was running at full speed. Judge Nisbet went on the record and denied any knowledge of a confession.

News of Tom's attempt to free himself from his shackles soon changed to the jailers catching him in the act of sawing through the window bars. Later, word spread that he had actually escaped. Folsom established both stories as scuttlebutt but not before the blacks in Hazzard District were terrorized by the possibility of Tom being on the loose.

What wasn't a rumor was the story that Jailer Birdsong witnessed the prisoner in passionate prayer, and that the Imminent Pastor of the First Baptist Church in Macon, Dr. E. W. Warren, was a regular visitor to Tom's cell.

Visitation was extremely restricted. Anyone wishing to see the condemned man had to request permission from Judge Gustin. Furthermore, after word leaked out about Tom praying, the Judge issued orders forbidding any information concerning the prisoner from being released.

Folsom decided to visit the jail anyway. Although he knew that the Judge's orders were being obeyed, he hoped for some news. He knocked at the door and was greeted by Nat Birdsong.

"What news?" the reporter asked.

"Nothing, not a single thing," Birdsong responded and allowed Folsom entrance.

"How is Tom Woolfolk? Does he seem to enjoy his rest?" he said looking up. The familiar sound of Tom's chains rattled loudly overhead.

Birdsong put his hands on his hips. "You need not be asking for any more news about Woolfolk. Judge Gustin has given orders not to tell anything about what's going on, or admit anyone to his cell who ain't got orders from him."

"Is that so?" Folsom was not surprised. The reporter lifted his hat, scratched his head and whistled softly to himself. Birdsong looked up at the ceiling. The aggravation on his face prompted the reporter to ask innocently, acting as if he did not recognize the noise.

"What's that?"

"Tom's takin' his regular mornin' exercise...he's been keeping it up some time now."

Folsom looked around the room hoping to continue the conversation with the jailer. The nerve racking noise overhead, however, seemed to restrict the jailer's sense of hospitality. The reporter donned his hat.

"Well...good morning," he said and walked out into the crisp, cold morning. The sound of Tom's chain coaxed Folsom to stand beneath his cell window in hopes of seeing the prisoner. Busy searching for a sign of life to go with the sound, the reporter did not hear the jailer approach from behind.

"Pretty cold day, ain't it?" Birdsong said, his breath hanging in front of his mouth.

Folsom turned with a start. The jailer had walked out into the cold without a coat. He stood facing the reporter, his hands shoved deep into his pockets. Folsom smiled his agreement, and walked away.

Tom's days were reduced to pacing his small cell. Because he had tampered with his leg irons, he was refused reading materials of all kinds. His sisters, aunt, and cousins visited whenever possible. No one else came by. Whenever reporters were allowed in the cell block to interview other prisoners, he would attempt to speak to them. He was ignored everytime, as if invisible. No one wanted to disobey the Sheriff.

His shackles remained locked at all times, making rest impossible. The overhead light was kept on by order of the Sheriff and Jailer Birdsong maintained a constant, if not fanatical, vigil.

One morning, the turnkey escorted a plumber to the cell next to him and then handed Tom a letter through the bars. The postmark was Savannah, Georgia. The envelope was addressed in a delicate script and smelled of sweet perfume. A new prisoner recently told him he was a celebrity with the young women of the area. In fact, he received several valentines from admirers so the letter came as no surprise. The content, however, did.

"Dear Mr. Woolfolk," the letter began and proceeded to tell Tom that the writer was an admirer who had overheard talk in Savannah of plans to storm the jail and lynch him within the week.

Next door, the plumber nervously hammered away on a pipe and made an extra effort to ignore the convicted killer sitting on the cot near his head on the other side of the bars. He had been ordered to say absolutely nothing to the man no matter what the prisoner said or did.

"You got some fine tools there," Tom said finally. The plumber acted as if he did not hear him. "I said you got some mighty fine tools there."

The old man could not stand the strain of ignoring someone who was simply trying to be polite. He looked around to see if anyone was watching and then thanked him.

"Make a lot of money doing that do you?"

"Naw...not much," he answered in a hushed voice.

Tom looked around and then leaned closer to the bars. "I'll give you five hundred dollars for that hammer and chisel over there."

The plumber was startled and thought he misunderstood the prisoner. He looked at the determination in Tom's dark eyes and knew he had heard correctly. He quickly gathered up his tools and called out for the turnkey. Tom turned back around and read the letter again.

The letter warning Tom of a lynching caused such an alarm that authorities considered returning him to the Atlanta jail. The motion for a retrial was being postponed time and again. Tom lived passed the execution date only because his case was in the appeal process.

News of the postponement of his execution angered many of the citizens of the area. Every day, on the hour, someone would call at the jail wanting to see the prisoner. The visitors would identify themselves as relatives, old school friends, and childhood sweethearts. The traffic in and out of the jail did not amuse Sheriff Westcott nor Nat Birdsong. No one was allowed to see Tom Woolfolk without a court order.

Sheriff Westcott considered the threat against Tom and decided he would be safe in Macon. The news stunned the prisoner who became visibly anxious when Birdsong told him of the Sheriff's decision.

Pea Jay hurried across the jailhouse yard. The hot June sun had forced him to take off his coat. He wiped the sweat from his forehead as he entered the jail. His purpose for being there had nothing to do with the Woolfolk case. In fact, Tom's motion for a retrial had been postponed so many times the reporter lost count and he had lost interest in Tom. Instead, he was there simply to interview a new prisoner. Nothing sensational. Nothing bizarre. Just an interview.

Birdsong greeted him at the door, and together the two men climbed the stairs to the second story cell block.

"You are not to say a word to Tom. You can not go near that cage. You understand," Birdsong growled the familiar command.

Pea Jay understood. It had been made clear to every reporter who entered the jail. If they wanted access to any of the inmates, ever, they were to stay absolutely clear of Tom Woolfolk. Anyone caught talking to him or having any contact with him in any way would be prohibited from entering the jailhouse ever again. To a reporter, such would be disastrous to his career.

Birdsong continued, "Woolfolk gives me so much trouble that I have to deny him everything."

Pea Jay smiled and walked into the cell block behind the jailer.

In his cell, Tom could see the reporter enter the prisoner's cell and sit down on a stool. From the distance, however, he did not recognize Pea Jay. He stood on his cot peering through the bars and watched.

"Say," Tom finally called out, "aren't you from the Constitution?"

Pea Jay looked up from his notes and ventured a response. "Uh...yeh, but only been with'em a few days," he lied.

Tom recognized the voice.

Pea Jay went back to his interview. A moment later, Tom called out again.

"Well...I'll forget what you said about me...for the present, but, a few days ago, the Macon paper said that I was the one that tried to get the cell locks out of working order, and that I told the boys how to do it. It's a lie...and I wish you'd say so."

Pea Jay ignored him.

"Say...can't you talk?" Tom called out, his face pressed against the bars. The reporter stood up to leave. "What's the matter with you?" Tom continued.

Pea Jay put on his derby and signaled for the turnkey to let him out. Tom held tightly to the bars and yelled after the reporter as he walked towards the exit. "Hey...if you've got a Constitution in your pocket, let me have it. Nat's stopped my paper, and I ain't seen one in a month of Sundays."

Pea Jay walked through the door leading to the stairs and disappeared. Tom dropped down onto his cot and continued talking to himself.

"No? That's too bad. When do you think the motion for my trial'll come up?" he turned over and shut up.

Tom missed reading the newspapers. They were his link to the world beyond his bars. He did not know that Sam Chambless died December 8, 1888 in Atlanta while serving as a State Representative. Until his sister Flo told him he was not aware that John Hardeman was successful in convincing Judge Gustin to disqualify himself from the case of the Howard family versus the Woolfolk heirs and to have a restraining order placed on the estate until the courts decided heirship.

CHAPTER EIGHTEEN
"We start all over again."

More than a year after Tom's conviction, Judge Gustin finally heard the argument for a retrial and overruled the motion. On January 30, 1889, John Rutherford appealed to the Georgia Supreme Court.

The attorneys for the defense negotiated their way through the throng of people standing on the courthouse steps in Atlanta. Reporters called out questions. People pushed and shoved for a better look at the men. Pea Jay perched himself next to the main entrance and waited for an opportunity to slip inside.

It was not necessary for Tom to attend the proceedings, and so he remained in the Bibb County Jail. His sisters also chose to stay home--Flo in East Macon and Lillie in Hawkinsville. Only Henry Cowan and L.A. Shackleford made the trip to Atlanta. On the train, Folsom entered into polite conversation with the two men and was invited to join them in the courtroom.

The reading of the three hundred thousand word compendium of the trial consumed the morning. It was eleven o'clock when Rutherford rose to plead his case. The justices had given both sides seven hours each for argument and the defense attorney intended to use up every second of his allotted time.

Although John Hardeman was no longer the solicitor-general of the Macon Circuit, he represented the state along with the new solicitor, Dr. William H. Felton, the same state representative who used the name 'Woolfolk' as a term for evil. His co-counsel before the State Supreme Court was Attorney General Clifford Anderson.

Folsom watched Rutherford walk up to the podium and open his brief book. The audience shifted in anticipation. In a voice clear and crisp, the attorney addressed the Court and proceeded to set the stage by describing the murder scene, giving exquisite detail of the positions of each body and the nature of the wounds.

"Your honors, it is our belief that one man could not have done this bloody work, and that several murderers were involved. The positions in which the bodies were found, the fact that the victims occupied different rooms, the nature and number of the wounds inflicted with the axe, all go to show that no one man could have butchered these people.

"Captain Woolfolk and Mrs. Woolfolk were murdered while sleeping and did not know what killed them. All of the testimony tends to prove this. In Captain Woolfolk's room, six bodies were found. The theory of the prosecution is that the defendant killed all of these in this room.

"The character of the wounds inflicted upon Captain Woolfolk, Richard, Charlie, and Pearl, and the positions of the bodies are all opposed to the idea of one man doing the work. These wounds were made both with the blade and head of the axe.

"Our theory is that at least two persons commenced the attack, that they were negroes, that they killed Captain Woolfolk first, then Mrs. Woolfolk, that as Richard ran in, both attacked him. He had two wounds, one on the back of the head made with the edge of an axe, the other on the forehead, made with the head of an axe. The wounds upon Mrs. West, Pearl, and Annie were made both with the edge and head of an axe.

"These are great physical facts inconsistent with the theory that one man dealt the blows. If one man dealt it, he would have had to turn the handle of the axe. He would have paused...amid that scene of slaughter to do it. It is also unreasonable that Tom Woolfolk would have left his two brothers behind if, according to the prosecution, he had planned the murder of the family. He would have known that they would rush out of the house and sound the alarm.

"As to the motive of the negroes to commit the crime, Captain Woolfolk was unpopular with them. He had several put in the chain gang. He had argued with Tom Banks and John Jeff. He cursed them and they cursed him back. He ran Silas Woolfolk off his property. This man lived only a mile distant. Jeff had threatened to kill Captain Woolfolk. The theory is that at least two of these negroes killed Captain Woolfolk and then killed the others to prevent detection."

Listening to the lawyer explain the defense's theory of the murders, Folsom had to admit the argument was sound. Several factors of the prosecution's case bothered him. He and Tom Woolfolk were about the same size, and he knew that he would not have been able to kill every single one of the nine people as savagely as the murder had been committed and prevent any of them from escaping.

There had also been witnesses willing to testify at the trial, had the Judge allowed them, that they heard serious threats made against the Captain, and that those individuals who made threats had recent altercations with him and were on the property or near the property just before the murders.

If the Supreme Court was to be convinced to grant Tom a new trial, however, the reporter knew that more than theories would have to be presented. Folsom refocused his attention on Rutherford's voice as the attorney proceeded to argue the defense's case on legal points.

"...the applause in the courtroom during the trial at Macon, when a man jumped up and yelled, 'HANG HIM! HANG HIM!' and the crowd arose in an excited manner. This tended to have a tremendous effect on the jury. Counsel for the defense appealed to the Court to have the room cleared. The Court refused to do so, which was an error.

"The Court erred in refusing to grant a continuance, which was asked for two weeks after Woolfolk was indicted, because of the excited state of the public mind, because of the absence of a material witness, because the prisoner was in jail and had no opportunity to prepare for trial, because his friends had abandoned him, and witnesses and counsel refused to talk with him. Taken in connection with public excitement, there were sufficient reasons for a continuance."

For a day and a half, Rutherford stood at the podium and argued the same points he had presented to Judge Gustin during his motion for a retrial.

He argued that it was impossible for his client to have received a fair trial in a community so inflamed with outrage. He elaborated that the integrity and honesty of the jury was sound and true but that the jurors still had to have been prejudiced by the newspapers and by the outburst of the audience during the trial.

"They feared to acquit Tom. For such a verdict would have imperilled their own lives by mob violence," he said.

The attorney compared the admissability of Benjamin Howard's testimony to the same level of hearsay as that of the defense's witnesses whose testimonies had been disallowed. He argued against I.P. Davis' conclusion that Tom had killed his family.

He stated that the hat found in the well also had blood on it and was the property of another person indicating that the evidence against Tom could not be used. If blood on the defendant's clothes fished from the well was an indication of guilt, then the blood found on the hat also fished from the well should indicate similar guilt. He argued that the Court had been prejudiced in its decision.

In all, the defense presented twenty-three points. Rutherford returned to his seat and the State began its argument.

Solicitor William H. Felton, only a few months Tom's junior, slowly rose from his seat and approached the podium. Weeks after the murders, Felton nominated George W. Gustin to replace Judge James Simmons as Macon's Circuit Court Judge. He was now representing the State on Gustin's case.

He calmly opened his notebook, surveyed the judges and proceeded to review the trial proceedings and the State's position. He pointed out that Tom was obsessed with property, had seriously resented his stepfamily and voiced his anger and hatred many times. He stressed that Mattie Howard was afraid of Tom and witnesses heard him threaten his family.

The defendant tried to conceal damaging evidence by throwing his bloody clothes in the well and had a bloody handprint on his leg. The solicitor argued that it was conceivable that someone out to kill the Captain would kill the other adults and children to prevent them from sounding the alarm, but only someone insane with greed would slaughter the helpless baby. There had to be no survivors. The baby's death insured Tom's inheritance.

Instead of defending Tom against the charges, the State argued, the defense attempted to cloud the evidence and testimonies by introducing hearsay and rumors, and by pointing an accusatory finger at individuals not present to defend themselves.

In rendering their decision, the judges focused their attention to several points and agreed with the defense that the Court had erred in allowing I.P. Davis' and Benjamin Howard's testimonies. The Higher Court felt the ownership of the wool hat should have been determined by the State and not presented as hearsay. Nonetheless, such points did not constitute grounds for a new trial.

At the jail, Rutherford showed Tom the Supreme Court's decision written by Justice James T. Simmons. Tom took the report.

"We grant a new trial in this case," Judge Simmons had written. The prisoner looked at his lawyer. Rutherford was smiling.

"Go ahead, read it," he said.

Tom sat down on his cot and began to read slowly. Rutherford watched him closely. The slight movement of his lips as he studied each page indicated to the defense attorney that he was completely absorbed. Not wanting to disturb him, Rutherford shoved his hands into his pockets, turned his back to him and waited patiently.

Tom read it through once to himself and then scanning each page he turned back to the first. He cleared his throat and pondered the meaning of the words. He began to read the document again. This time he read it aloud.

"At the conclusion of the opening argument for the State, the crowd in the court room applauded. The Judge took no notice of this applause except to rap with his gavel. And when counsel for the State was making the concluding argument, from the rear of the court room came, in an excited and angry tone, the cry 'HANG HIM! HANG HIM!' and some of the crowd arose to their feet. The Court rapped with his gavel and ordered the persons removed, but states that he does not know whether his order was carried into effect by the Sheriff or not.

"Shortly after, another person sitting within the bar and near the Judge cried, 'HANG HIM.' The Court ordered him removed, and he was carried down the back stairs. It is not known whether the jury knew that this person was taken out or not. All the jurors make affidavit that these things had no influence upon their minds; and from my own knowledge of the character of those gentlemen, I have no doubt that they believe this to be true.

"But can any man say with certainty that such things have no influence upon him? Can any of us know how far our minds are influenced by applause or excitement of a crowd which surrounds us? Can any of us say, even in this court, that this or that piece of testimony, or this or that argument of counsel, has not influenced our minds? Can any of us say that, on the trial of one of the most heinous crimes ever committed in the State or any other, the applause of the crowd, the fierce cries of 'Hang Him! Hang Him!' from members of the crowd followed later on by a repetition of the same cry from the lips of one of the most highly respected and esteemed citizens of the community, would have no influence upon our minds?

"Our minds are so constituted that it is impossible to say what impression scenes of this kind would make upon us, unless we had determined beforehand that the prisoner was guilty or innocent. The question here is not what effect these things did have upon the minds of the jury, but what effect they were calculated to produce. We cannot determine what effect they did have, but it is apparent what effect they were calculated to have.

"But counsel for the State argued before us that the defendant had no right to complain of these things. Whether this be so or not, we think the Court below should have put the seal of its condemnation upon this conduct. We think the Judge should have stopped the argument of the State's counsel then and there and ascertained the guilty parties, and should have punished them to the extent of the law.

"He should have taught them that the law was supreme; that the trial of a man for his life, however heinous the crime charged against him might be, was a serious and solemn thing, and that the law would not permit a mob to interfere, either by applause or by threatening and exciting cries.

"By so doing he would have upheld the supremacy of the law, and would have shown to the jury that whatever verdict they might find, the law would protect them. It would also have shown them that the Court was uninfluenced by the feelings of demonstrations of the crowd; that it was still able to administer justice and to give the accused a fair and impartial trial. It would have given them a moral support, and would have tended to impress upon them the necessity of resisting such influence.

"We cannot say that this jury was influenced by any of these things, but will say that in all trials, either civil or criminal, the trial is not to be affected or influenced by the clamor of the crowd, the pressure of public sentiment, or the thousand or more rumors that almost invariably attend every case of notoriety.

"There is no nobler spectacle than that of a judge and jury who quietly but firmly, in the face it may be of public sentiment and popular clamor, go forward and do their duty and their whole duty.

"Judgement reversed."

Tom looked up at Rutherford.

"What's next?" he asked.

"We start all over again," Rutherford answered. "The first thing we are going to do is request a change of venue. There's no way you'll ever get a fair trial in this county."

CHAPTER NINETEEN
"I am fully capable of trying this case."

Folsom sat in the lobby of the Lanier House reading the Atlanta Constitution. During the months between Tom's conviction and the higher court's decision, the newspapers were filled with stories of the Whitechapel murders in London. A vicious serial killer was savagely slaughtering prostitutes. The grisly murders vividly reported by the news industry seemed to keep satisfied the public's need for the grotesque and tragic. News of Tom's new trial, nevertheless, exploded back into the limelight overshadowing even the recent exploits of the murderer in England nicknamed 'Jack The Ripper'.

The reporter watched as guest after guest registered with the hotel. Already the city was mobbed with people, and everyone talked about Tom's new trial.

As ordered by the higher court, Judge Gustin convened the trial March 4, 1889. Rutherford immediately petitioned for a continuance.

He argued that several of his key witnesses, especially Jackson Dubose and Sam Pennington, could not be located. He also argued that public outrage from the Supreme Court's decision made it impossible to guarantee his client a fair and impartial trial.

The defense attorney presented a number of prominent citizens from the area who testified that newspapers were so thorough in their coverage public sentiment was greatly influenced. In addition, Rutherford informed the court that Frank Walker was ill and could no longer assist him in Tom's defense.

Solicitor Felton opposed each point. Judge Gustin listened to both arguments and then refused a continuance. The trial would not be delayed.

By the second day, it was obvious to Folsom that the court officials would have to address the problem of crowd control. The day before, the over packed auditorium and constant traffic in and out of the courtroom continuously disrupted the proceedings. The number was higher than during Tom's previous trial.

L. A. Shackleford stood up in the buggy and looked around. The wall of people standing in front of him took him aback. Dumb-founded, he dropped back into his seat. Beside him, Flo Edwards gripped his arm tightly. Her eyes were wide with fear. Folsom pushed his way through the noisy crowd and up to the buggy.

"Shackleford, need some help?" he shouted.

"Please," Shackleford called back and climbed down.

The two men helped Flo from the carriage and positioned themselves on each side of her. The crowd of people closed in around them. Folsom and Shackleford, with Flo in the middle, pushed their way through the mob until they made it to the front door. A guard opened the door and the force behind them literally propelled the three through the doorway.

The auditorium filled to capacity. Judge Gustin ordered the doors locked. No one but individuals with a legitimate need to be there would be allowed to enter after the trial started.

Daniel Adams, Clerk of Superior Court, stepped forward to begin the call of jurors. Rutherford interrupted and requested permission to read a letter.

"Colonel Rutherford, does this have anything to do with this case?" the Judge asked.

"I believe it does, Your Honor."

"Then you may present the letter."

"Your Honor, I have here a letter from Judge Robert Trippe from Forsyth, Georgia. He states that the negro, Augustus Trippe, told him that Anderson James, a witness for the state, recently talked about the murders in great detail. He went on to say that James described how Miss Annie almost escaped by hiding under a bed." Rutherford handed the letter up to the Judge who perused it briefly and then handed it down to Solicitor Felton.

"The defense would like to have Judge Trippe summoned to this court to testify."

"Denied."

"Your Honor?" Rutherford was stunned.

"I will not have this trial delayed any longer. I will remind you that we will not allow hearsay as evidence, Colonel Rutherford."

Rutherford turned to walk back to his seat. He looked at Tom, the audience and then paused.

"Then if it would please the court," he said, "the defense would like to question each potential juror as to the meaning of the words 'bias' and 'prejudice'."

"And exactly how would this question be worded?"

"The defense would like to ask each juror the definitions of the words, what they mean to the juror, personally, and also what is the juror's understanding of the term 'perfectly impartial'."

"Denied."

"May I approach the bench, Your Honor?"

"Counselor may approach."

Rutherford, joined by Felton, walked up to the bench. The Judge leaned over.

"Your Honor," Rutherford said quietly, "under the present circumstances, the defense respectfully requests that Your Honor disqualifies himself from this case."

"Denied, Colonel Rutherford," Gustin growled. "I am fully capable of trying this case."

"I have no doubt of Your Honor's capability, but maybe a judge more removed from the tragedy would..."

"Denied," the Judge interrupted.

The two attorneys returned to their seats. Rutherford decided to try one more time.

"Your Honor," he said, standing up. "The defense respectfully requests a change of venue."

"Denied," Judge Gustin tapped his gavel and continued. "If the defense has no more motions, the Clerk of Court may proceed with the call of jurors."

Just as Daniel Adams again rose to read the list of jurors, the large double doors exploded open, and a young man stormed into the court room.

"You cannot keep me from this room!" he shouted over his shoulder to the guard who had tried to prevent him from entering.

Deputy Hodnett grabbed his arm as he walked by. The man snatched away. The deputy grabbed him again. The man broke free and hit Hodnett several times before another bailiff intervened. The young man's right cross knocked the deputy down.

The room was in a total uproar. Judge Gustin, on his feet, angrily hammered for order, all the while yelling for the bailiffs to restrain the man.

Judge George W. Gustin
(Photo from private collection)

The attorneys behind the bar watched in total disbelief as Sheriff Westcott and his deputies wrestled the man to the floor.

"Sheriff, I want that man jailed!" the Judge shouted as the man struggled against the group of deputies who were trying to remove him from the courtroom.

Shackleford looked at Folsom. "I wonder who that was?" he asked.

"I think it was Tim O'Connell," Folsom answered as he wrote furiously in his notebook. "He's pretty well known around these parts. He's a law. student. Guess he's interested in the case."

The courtroom finally settled down, and the call for jurors continued. By the end of the day, ninety-six potential jurors had been called but only one man, J. C. Bannon, was accepted.

The second day, after the Sheriff doubled the guard, Tom was able to attend his trial. The prisoner appeared reserved and intense and as before, his sisters, aunt, and cousin sat near him.

Rutherford relentlessly attempted to question each juror about the words 'bias' and 'prejudice' and was repeatedly over-ruled by the Judge.

"Colonel Rutherford, I assure you that these men coming before us are competent and understand fully the meanings of those words as used in a court of law," the Judge promised.

The second juror to be seated was W.E. Hill. Folsom was surprised that Rutherford accepted him even after Solicitor Felton informed the court Hill was a distant cousin of Charles Howard. The examination of jurors continued until six were seated, two hundred thirty-four excused, and no more were available.

At the close of the day, Solicitor Felton informed the defense attorney by note that Charles Howard had overheard Juror Hill say he would cause a mistrial before allowing the defendant to be found innocent. The information greatly alarmed Rutherford and Gustin. The Judge immediately called a recess, during which time the solicitor gave his reason for revealing the information.

Felton explained that as the statement had been made in public it would have been a matter of time before Rutherford learned about it and used it in his appeal to the Supreme Court. The State simply wanted to save taxpayers' money. The solicitor offered the defense two options, the disqualification of Juror Hill or an investigation. Rutherford chose the investigation.

The morning of March 8th started with the defense informing the court that another individual had come forward saying he also heard Juror Hill say the accused should hang. Judge Gustin, Solicitor Felton, and Rutherford immediately went into the Judge's chambers. Hours later, the group returned to the courtroom where the defense formally requested a mistrial.

Pandemonium broke out. Judge Gustin rapped his gavel and dismissed Hill. Tom smiled. His attorney's gamble worked. The juror's prejudice finally revealed itself thus, supporting the defense's contention that an impartial jury could not be acquired in Bibb County.

At three o'clock, a mistrial was declared sending the public into an uproar. Folsom sat in the lobby of his hotel quietly writing in his notebook while the atmosphere around him approached near hysteria.

"It does not seem possible that a jury can now be obtained," Folsom wrote. "A change of venue seems probable."

The reporter looked away from his writing and watched Pea Jay scamper from group to group. The anger from the Judge's decision had inflamed the city and filtered over into the lobby of the Lanier House. Folsom returned to his notebook.

"Woolfolk says but little about the new developments in his case today. He says but little at any time. He stated this afternoon, however, that he is thankful for every ray of hope given him, and he thinks his mistrial today means a change of venue. Said he: 'If I can get a hearing outside of Bibb, I will never be convicted.'"

Monday, March 11, 1889 marked the State's third attempt to try Tom Woolfolk. The old and familiar routine began again.

Folsom found his seat in the courtroom and, with the other reporters, watched Flo and Love Shackleford, Lillie and Henry Cowan, and Fannie Crane quietly enter and sit down behind the defense's table. As if choreographed by some unknown master of ceremonies, Charles and John Howard then escorted their elderly father Benjamin down the aisle to his seat.

The circus-like atmosphere Folsom observed the very first day while at the murder scene, later outside the jail after Tom's arrest, and then during his confinement and previous trials, seemed to have a life of its own. Sheriff Westcott posted additional deputies in front of the courthouse to make it possible for the official and related to enter the building without being mobbed. The crowd, however, would be drawn towards the person, usually a lawyer or family member, with such force, the deputies could do nothing but help the individuals push through the mob.

To those already sitting in the courtroom, the roar of the crowd outside indicated the appearance of the entourage escorting the prisoner. When Tom was finally seated, Fannie Crane leaned over and pinned a small bouquet of flowers to his coat. Tom thanked her warmly.

As soon as Daniel Adams rose to read the list of jurors, Rutherford interrupted. The defense attorney's efforts to save his client's life, though brilliant and adamantly sincere, were by now also routine.

"Your Honor."

"Colonel Rutherford?" Gustin responded dryly.

"Your Honor, is this to be considered a new trial or a continuation of the previous one that ended in a mistrial?" Rutherford asked.

"The Court is holding a continuation of last week's trial...except, of course, for the jurors who were sworn in and then discharged, as well as the motions as to venue, continuance, and such."

Rutherford proceeded to place a motion for a change of venue and was denied. He then requested a continuance on the usual grounds of missing witnesses vital to the case. He informed the court that witnesses for the defense were being intimidated and harassed.

"One witness," he elaborated, "was intimidated by an officer of the court."

Hardeman stood up. "Your Honor, we would like the name of this officer and an investigation of this charge."

"Your Honor, we have already given this name to the court," Rutherford responded.

"And an investigation will be conducted at the proper time," Judge Gustin answered. "Now if we may proceed..."

"Your Honor," Rutherford interrupted again.

"Counselor."

"If it pleases the court, the defense would like to give you the names of our witnesses in private and not be given to the State publicly. We would also like to request that the State not give these names to anyone. This is not intended to place a negative reflection on the counsel for the State. They are honorable men, and I would not for a moment cast any imputation upon them. I do not consider them responsible for the interest the public takes in this case."

Felton jumped from his seat. His face was flushed with anger.

"Your Honor, I take exception to this!" he shouted. "I don't think the statement of Brother Rutherford, so far as the state's counsel is concerned, improves the statement he proposes to make a record of in this court. The charge in his motion, boiled down, is that the state's counsel has been guilty of subordination of perjury of witnesses summoned on the part of the defense. I hope the stenographer will take it down that it will be made a part of the record in this case, the state's counsel denies and pronounces that statement as willingly and knowingly false.

"And I respectfully submit, in any motion for a continuance I have ever heard of in any court, this is certainly the most extraordinary, and I stand and deny it as absolutely false until the gentlemen takes it out of his motion." Felton slammed his fist on the State's table. "I want it to go down upon the record as denied by me as utterly false."

From the back of the room a cheer and applause erupted. Felton turned, astonished at the crowd's response. Gustin rapped his gavel, and Sheriff Westcott rushed towards the disturbance.

Rutherford faced the audience and shouted, "If it pleases the court, I would like to know who were the parties that cheered, and what they propose to do."

Everyone stopped. Westcott worked his way around the room but found no one willing to admit their guilt or to turn in anyone.

Rutherford waited. The courtroom waited.

Finally, he turned back around and once again in a calm manner tried to explain his original motion. "Your Honor, I intended no reflection whatever on the State's counsel. It is a matter of fact that the defendant's witnesses have been intimidated. If the names of these new witnesses are revealed, they may be intimidated and frightened off. Not by the State's attorneys...but by others interested.

"It is for that reason I desire the court to communicate the names of the witnesses privately to the state's attorneys and enjoin upon them not to reveal the names of the same. By my willingness to thus reveal the names of our witnesses to the State's attorneys shows my confidence in their honor and that it is outsiders I fear.

Surely it seems that this statement should satisfy the State's attorneys that I intended no reflection on them."

The State's attorneys, however, were not satisfied by Rutherford's explanation. Dupont Guerry, hired by the Howard family to assist the State, responded.

"I wish, as one of the counsel representing the prosecution in this case, to say in this connection that so far as myself and my Brother Hall are concerned, we won't accept any information from any source with the understanding, expressed or implied, that we would withhold it from our client, Mr. Charles Howard."

Hardeman stood up and said, "I join you in that."

"We would consider it extremely unprofessional and dishonorable," Guerry continued, "to accept it upon any such terms. I wish to say in reference to the prosecutor in reply to any insinuation that may be cast upon him by the essence and substance of this motion, from the beginning of the prosecution down to the present time, he has been guilty of no act that any man could say was improper on his part. And judging from his record in the past, there is no more honorable, more honest, more conscientious and more law abiding citizen in this country.

"The only point that has been made on his conduct, so far as I know, here or in connection with the case, witnesses or jurors, is he has been too conscientious instead of otherwise, and for these reasons...and for the general reason arising from the relationship which we bear to him as prosecutors in this case we would decline to accept it, even from Your Honor, any information that we would not be permitted to impart to him."

Pea Jay leaned over and whispered to Folsom, "What are they talking about?"

"The defense has insinuated that Prosecutor Howard has intimidated witnesses. Rutherford wants names of witnesses kept secret," Folsom answered and returned his attention to Felton who was speaking.

"I still maintain, Your Honor, that Captain Rutherford should strike from his motion the words that the state's counsel deemed as reflecting upon them."

Rutherford rose from his table. "Your Honor, I have here a written amendment to my motion to certify that nothing in my motion was intended in any manner as a reflection on the State's counsel."

Gustin took the statement, read over it, and then handed it to Felton.

"I think this statement ought to be satisfactory to all parties concerned," the Judge said. Felton agreed.

"Now, Mr. Adams will you please call the jurors so we can proceed with this case," Gustin said with a sigh.

Rutherford asked to challenge the jurors on their understanding of certain legal terms and was refused. By the end of the day, nine jurors were seated.

"Looks like we might get a trial after all," Pea Jay said as he and Folsom walked out of the courtroom.

The next evening, Folsom sat at his usual place in the lobby of the hotel and headed his article, "A FRUITLESS DAY." He reviewed his notes carefully and recalled how the day began with nine jurors in the box but not enough in the panel of prospects. During the wait for jurors, Rutherford challenged the conduct of one of the bailiffs whose responsibility it was to summon jurors.

A witness was presented who stated that the deputy told him he had better be certain of the truth before he testified for the defense; otherwise, the solicitor would have to charge him with perjury.

The deputy was called to the stand and denied knowing the witness as well as making the statement. The witness was recalled and reiterated his statement. He then added that he had been given the impression that if he had been a witness for the prosecution he would not have been so warned.

Judge Gustin overruled the defense's charges.

Juror after juror was then called and rejected by either the defense or the State. By the end of the day, the defense had used its last strike but the panel was empty. No additional jurors had been seated, and there were no more from which to draw.

Pea Jay dropped into the seat next to Folsom. "Hear about Woolfolk at the jail today?"

"You mean about him getting mad because he had to have his lunch there instead of the courthouse?"

"Yeh, they say he got into an argument with the Sheriff. Wish I could've seen it."

"Me, too. I hear Tom really cussed him out." Folsom chuckled and returned to his work.

The frustration was beginning to show on the faces of the court officials. The deputies had scoured the county during the night to complete a panel of potential jurors. Eighteen responded to the call.

By midday, the court again adjourned to allow time for another panel to be compiled.

At four o'clock, court reconvened with a panel of twelve jurors to review. The defense immediately used up its entitled strikes, and a tenth juror was accepted.

The room quieted to an embarrassing hush as the eleventh juror Frank Disroon took the stand. A local business man, Disroon was well known for his political activism. He was not the first black to be summoned for jury duty. Previously, an ex-congressman, several preachers, and merchants had all been called but were subsequently disqualified.

Felton accepted Disroon, and the defense had no more strikes.

Rutherford hurried to the bench and entered into intense discussion with the Judge. Gustin called for Felton to join them, and the three men conversed quietly before the Solicitor returned to the State's table and talked with his associates.

"I understand this juror has been put upon us. Do you insist, gentlemen, that he go on the jury?" Rutherford asked adamantly.

"The juror is on you," Felton answered.

"We submit to this court that we are entitled to be tried by a jury of our peers and that the jury that tries us has the right to have no one in the box but their peers, and that this juror ought not to be put upon us or this jury."

Felton looked at his colleagues sitting at the State's table. "The responsibility of determining this question is upon me. After the objection has been made and I say on the part of the State, inasmuch as the matter is to be determined by myself, that this juror go off for cause. I take the responsibility upon myself, and I do it over the objections of my associates."

Throughout the courtroom heads nodded in agreement with the solicitor's decision. Disroon was dismissed. The panel again emptied; court was adjourned.

That evening Folsom stopped Judge Nisbet and asked him about the Disroon matter.

"Even if the other two jurors are not obtained," Nisbet answered, "Felton will not be condemned by the populace for letting Disroon off for cause. His action is in accord with public sentiment. As for Rutherford, he is sacrificing everything in the interest of his client. He cares not what effect it may have on any future political aspirations. It required nerve for him to take this stand. He deserves the praise of the people he is receiving for thus expressing himself on the color line."

Later, the reporter located a very angry Frank Disroon.

"I think my rejection, after being pronounced competent...is an outrage," he growled. "It clearly draws the line between the white man and the negro. I should not have been refused because of my color. I have acted as a juror as many as twenty-five times. This country will be destroyed if white men only try white men and negroes try negroes."

In another attempt to complete the jury, bailiffs were instructed to search the city and countryside. Thirty six prospects appeared before the Judge the next morning, March 14th.

No one qualified.

"I think this investigation, gentlemen, has gone to the extent the law requires," Judge Gustin began.

Tom straightened up in his seat as the Judge continued.

"I regret very much on account of the expense to the county this case should have to be carried to another county...but I think the examination of the jury box has been thorough. I trust that the effect...or rather...the result to be met here in connection with this case, may have the effect of impressing upon the people of this county and, especially upon the members of the legislature, the impropriety of a very large number of exemptions that have been granted under our law." The disgust was evident in his voice.

"I am satisfied," he continued, "if it hadn't been for these exemptions, a jury could have been obtained and that the expense could have been saved to the people of this county. One feature, however, about this, is that those gentlemen who have availed them-selves of these exemptions will have a very large amount of the extra tax to pay on account of this case having to be transferred."

The Judge gathered the stack of papers lying before him and then addressed Rutherford. "Do you see any reason why this panel should not be discharged?"

"No, sir."

Addressing Felton, the Judge continued, "You can take your order, Mr. Solicitor, discharge the jury."

Felton rose to his feet. "Shall I wait until we agree what county it shall be changed to?"

"I think the first point," Rutherford responded, "ought to be settled now."

"I think it would be better to have it all included in one order," the Judge answered.

"Will Your Honor give us until three o'clock?" the defense attorney asked.

"I would prefer to have a settlement of this question now," the solicitor stated adamantly. "The section of the code provides how it shall be done, and I would rather have it settled now."

Judge Gustin sent the two lawyers to his chamber with the instructions to decide on a location. In seclusion, Felton refused to consider any county other than Houston. Rutherford argued for Twiggs but offered a compromise with Crawford. They were un-able to render a mutual decision and turned the matter over to the court.

Back in the courtroom, Rutherford asked for the opportunity to explain why he did not want either of the choices. Gustin gave him permission to continue.

"As Your Honor is aware, Houston and Crawford are neighboring counties and situated so near the scene of the murder the people of those counties are more liable to have partaken of the prejudice and bias entertained by the people of Bibb towards the defendant. For this reason, it might be impossible to obtain unprejudiced jurors, jurors whose minds are not perfectly impartial.

"Wouldn't it be much better to transfer the case to Chatham, Richmond, or Fulton counties, where there are large cities and where the probability of obtaining an impartial jury is much better than in counties near Bibb? I understand the court is partial to Houston and had expressed an opinion that the case would be transferred there if a jury could not be obtained."

Rutherford's last statement caused the Judge to lean over and glare at the attorney. "I have never expressed my opinion on the subject to any man. I have purposefully refused to talk on the matter."

"I can bear the court out," Felton interjected, "as recent as the present trial, I had addressed the Court on this subject. Judge Gustin firmly refused to talk on the matter at all."

"I think I got it from some publication that Your Honor would move it to Houston," Rutherford explained.

"I thought you said the newspapers didn't tell the truth," Hardeman remarked sarcastically from his seat.

Rutherford turned and faced the former solicitor. "No, sir, I did not say that. I'm a great admirer of the press and stand by it. It's got a right to speak out what it desires, being only responsible under the law."

"I don't think I have the right," Gustin began, "to go into another circuit in this state and preside, nor do I think I have the right to shift the burden of the trial of this case upon one of the other judges in this state.

"My misfortune comes from residing in this circuit, and it devolves upon me, from my standpoint, the duty of trying this case. So far as the feeling being affected in any of the adjoining counties, I can hardly think it would be true as you suggested. In the first, place a large number of disqualifications in this case have been on account of men who come to the courthouse to listen to the testimony, some from curiosity, some no doubt for the distinct purpose, as I have heard a number avow, of listening to the evidence and expressing an opinion, so that they would be disqualified, and would not be competent jurors in case the case should ever be tried a second time.

"That will not operate in other counties than Bibb. So far as transferring the case to larger cities, I apprehend there would be more difficulty there than there would be in the counties even adjoining here, which do not get the daily newspapers. It is a well-known fact that the press of Atlanta and Augusta, and, perhaps, Savannah, to some extent, published daily the accounts of this trial before giving the evidence, and so far as any affect is concerned, it was discussed there much more than it was in any of the other counties that do not have the daily papers.

"You can take your order, Mr. Solicitor, changing the venue of this case to Houston County. That is the most convenient for witnesses and has the largest jury list."

As Felton proceeded to draw up the order, Rutherford requested that his prisoner be removed immediately to the Perry jail. Felton stopped and looked at the Judge. Judge Gustin pointed his gavel at the defense attorney.

"The custody and confinement of the prisoner is something with which you, sir, have nothing whatever to do with, and I do not care to hear from you on the subject."

CHAPTER TWENTY
"I just hope God's on my side."

The wind howled through the city streets, ripping a sign from its anchor and rattling windows. At the jailhouse, Nat Birdsong propped his feet on his desk and leaned back in his chair. He took a swallow of hot coffee, paused and then realized the familiar rattle of Tom Woolfolk's chains overhead had been silent far too long. Putting his cup aside and jumping up from his chair, he ran out of his office, up the stairs and quietly entered the cell block. Slowly and cautiously, he walked towards Tom's cell.

It was only seven in the evening. The prisoner was not likely to be asleep. The light from the single bulb illuminated the room enough for him to see Tom standing in his cage, his back to the door. The jailer crept closer and looked in. On the floor at the prisoner's feet were his shackles and chain. Tom had freed himself again.

The jailer quietly backed out of the cell block and rushed down stairs, taking two steps at a time. Adrenaline igniting his system, he ran outside and looked up and down the street for an officer. There were none. Back inside, he rushed to the wall telephone and called City Hall urging them to send an officer to the jail as soon as possible.

Two policemen responded in a matter of minutes. Birdsong told them the situation, and the three men cautiously went to Tom's cell. The prisoner was as he had been described, standing free in the semi-darkness, his chains at his feet. Birdsong pulled out a match and struck it. Tom Woolfolk whirled around, mortified.

The jailer unlocked the cell door and the officers, guns drawn, rushed in. Tom was removed to another cage while they searched his. A pocket knife was recovered. The prisoner refused to answer any questions.

Birdsong put new shackles around his ankles and secured them with rivets instead of a lock. Tom was then returned to his cell and the door bolted shut.

On his way back to his desk, L.A. Shackleford, a clerk at the Clark County Court House, paused a moment to read an article in the Houston Home Journal someone left lying on a bench.

> "Perry will doubtless be full of visitors during the trial, and ample accommodations will be made for all who come. The hotels and regular boarding houses cannot furnish accommodations for all who are expected, but none need stay away on this account. There will be a regular lunch room under the management of the Baptist ladies, and several of our best citizens will take boarders during the trial. All who come will be comfortably accommodated at moderate rates."

Shackleford rolled the paper up, tossed it in the trash can, and walked away.

Georgia Bird Woolfolk stepped from the train and was greeted unexpectedly by Folsom.

"Mrs. Woolfolk, how are you doing? Here, let me carry your bag?" he offered politely. "Would you like for me to hail you a hack?"

"No, that won't be necessary. My father will be here soon. Thank you."

The two quietly walked across the platform, through the terminal, and out onto the steps before Folsom spoke again.

"I understand there's been a postponement of Tom's trial. Rutherford collapsed from exhaustion." His companion did not respond. The reporter tried again. "Hardeman's been elected to fill

Ole Man Chambless' House seat...but that shouldn't hurt Tom's case none."

The young woman seemed to be ignoring him as she looked around for her father. Folsom put her bag down between them and faced her. Georgia stopped and looked at him. Finally, he had her attention.

"Have you seen Tom?" He asked.

"Tom? No...no. I have nothing to do with him."

"I hope you don't think I'm intruding...are you intending to get a divorce?"

"No. The way I see it...if Tom hangs, then a divorce won't be necessary...will it?"

"How 'bout it Tom?" Folsom asked. "You ready for Perry?"

"To be honest, I'm pretty anxious for trial. I'm tired of staying in jail."

"What if Rutherford gets you a postponement?"

"I don't want one."

"Tom...don't you want Rutherford to do everything he can to keep you from being convicted?"

"I'm prepared to accept the verdict, whatever it is. But...I don't believe the jury's going to hang me."

The day of Tom's fourth trial was drawing near. John Rutherford, still seriously ill, instructed his new associate, Winter Mimberly, to procure the assistance of a reputable attorney in Perry, the former State Representative Alexander Lawton Miller.

A total of a hundred twenty-five witnesses were summoned. The prosecution had lost a valuable witness a year earlier when Sam Chambless died in Atlanta. John Owens was behind bars for simple larceny. The State had not decided, yet, if his testimony would help more than his reputation would harm the case.

When Joseph Dannenberg booked a voyage to Europe, per his doctor's orders, Judge Gustin placed the State's witness under bond and threatened him with contempt of court if he decided to sail June 5th.

Houston County citizens, expecting to be summoned for jury duty, arranged their schedules to be in Perry for the trial. The roster for prospective jurors was lengthy. The towns of Fort Valley and Perry prepared themselves for the onslaught of people. Hotels and boarding houses increased their orders for meat. The Central Railroad scheduled a special run for Sunday night, June 2, from Macon to Perry.

"Tom! Tom!" the voice called out, jerking him from his sleep. The prisoner turned over, mumbled a response, and opened his eyes. Sheriff Westcott and Jailer Birdsong were standing at the door.

"Get up and dress yourself," Westcott barked. "I'm taking you to Perry tonight."

Tom jumped out of bed.

"Sure enough," he said smiling. "Well...I'm glad of that. I'm ready to get out of this jail and get a whiff of fresh air again."

The walk to the depot reminded the Sheriff of a similar walk he had taken with the prisoner more than a year and a half earlier. This time, however, just being free enough to walk outside seemed to put a spring in Woolfolk's step and a smile on his face.

On the train, Birdsong sat beside the handcuffed prisoner. Westcott placed his newspaper on Tom's lap to cover his handcuffs and then dropped into the seat opposite him. No one knew who he was.

Tom asked for a window to be opened. Westcott willingly obliged. The prisoner put his face up against the opening and enjoyed the breeze.

"I've been locked up in jail so long, this ride does me good," he laughed. "And the cool, fresh air blowing on my face is the sweetest and most refreshing thing I ever felt."

Houston County Sheriff Melton L. Cooper greeted them at Fort Valley and hurried Tom into a carriage. The transfer to Perry was to be in total secrecy, thus Cooper decided it best to go the final twelve miles by road instead of train.

Official papers were exchanged. Tom's shackles were removed at Cooper's request. As the Perry Sheriff climbed aboard the carriage, he ordered the driver to go at full gallop. Birdsong and Westcott stood together watching the group race away.

A black man approached somewhat apprehensively. "Boss?" he asked Westcott, "that a prisoner with Sheriff Cooper?"

Westcott looked at the man and then back in the direction of the carriage. "Yeh, ...that was Tom Woolfolk," the Sheriff answered, then turned and boarded the train for his return trip to Macon.

"Great God," the man whispered and ran back to his group of friends. By day break, May 29th, the citizens of Houston knew of Tom's arrival.

Folsom paid for his ticket to Perry and turned around to retrieve his bag when he noticed a detective hurrying across the platform toward two men waiting in the shadows. He studied the couple and realized one was obviously a lawman and the other his prisoner. Folsom immediately recognized the man in handcuffs from his picture in the newspaper.

The reporter watched as the detective greeted the lawman with a handshake. Together the three men walked to a waiting hack. Folsom ran up to the buggy and startled the lawmen.

"Can I help you?" the detective said sharply.

"I know that man. You see, I'm with the Atlanta..."

"I know who you are," the detective interrupted. "Wait here," he said to the other men, took Folsom by the elbow and pulled him aside. "What do you want?"

"That's Jackson Dubose over there, is it not?"

"Maybe."

"Look, that man over there looks just like the pictures of Dubose in the newspaper."

"Okay, okay. You're right. It's Dubose."

Folsom felt as if his heart jumped into his throat. He quickly pulled out his tablet and pencil. The detective looked around nervously and then placed his hand on Folsom's notebook.

"I'm sorry, but you can't write nothin' about this."

"But I...," Folsom hesitated. "Okay...I'll make you a deal. You tell me what you can about this, and I won't print a word of it until Woolfolk's trial begins. Deal?"

The detective looked over at the two men waiting for him in the buggy. He lifted his hat and scratched his head. "Oh...alright. But you gotta promise...not a word...it could jeopardize everything. Understand?"

Folsom nodded.

"That's Sheriff Hudgins from Pickens County, over in Alabama. Colonel Rutherford had sent out his picture to all the jails in Northern Georgia and Alabama. The day Hudgins got one, he already had Dubose in jail for vagrancy. Hudgins compared the picture to the face and asked a few questions. After a while, Dubose told him who he was and admitted he was there the night of the murders. Hudgins notified Rutherford who asked him to bring the prisoner here to Macon. I'm supposed to hold him until I'm told to let him go or take him on to Perry."

"What else do you know about him?"

"He was released from the convict camp just a few weeks before the murders and says he passed through the Woolfolk settlement. He claims to have been about the place on the night of the murder. Afterwards, he wandered into Cherokee County, Georgia where he was arrested by Sheriff Kitchen. You know the rest."

"Where are ya'll going to hold him? Jail?"

"I can't tell you that. No one is supposed know he's here or where he's staying, you understand me." The detective made his point clear with a cold stare. Folsom nodded.

Immediately after Judge Gustin convened court to hear Tom's case for the fourth time, Rutherford challenged and requested a disqualification. Gustin responded by asking the grounds.

"Your Honor was a law partner to J. H. Hall under the firm of Gustin and Hall at the time of the murders. It was also at this time that Charles Howard consulted with this firm concerning his dead sister's estate. J. H. Hall now sits with the State under the firm of Guerry and Hall, representing Charles Howard," Rutherford argued.

Hall rose from his seat. "Judge Gustin was not involved in the consultation with the Howard family. When Mistah Howard came to see me, the Judge was sick at home. He was unaware of the meeting."

Rutherford looked at the lawyer and then back at the Judge. "But...Your Honor accepted the judgeship at that very same time," Rutherford answered.

"Yes, I did," Gustin responded. "The partnership of Gustin and Hall was then dissolved."

Folsom leaned over and whispered to Pea Jay, "How then, if he was so sick to not know about the meeting, could the firm be dissolved with his knowledge?"

"How could he be sick and well at the same time? He was too sick to know anything about the Howard meeting, but well enough to dissolve the firm and accept the judgeship," Pea Jay added.

"I would be glad if I was disqualified in this case," Gustin said with a sigh. "But I've thought about it and can not say that I am not qualified."

Rutherford then requested a change of venue arguing that Houston County was not far enough away from the murder scene. Gustin overruled him and ordered the call for witnesses. A total of fifty witnesses were called for the defense. Only twelve responded. The defense requested a recess until after the arrival of the morning train.

Judge Gustin instructed the list of jurors to be called. A hundred prospective jurors answered, and court was adjourned for lunch.

Folsom walked into the small cell block. Although it was not as large as the one in Macon, it was, nonetheless, clean and well lighted. Tom was in his cell and greeted the reporter with a broad smile.

"Hello, Tom. Just thought I'd come by and see how you're doing."

"Oh...doing fine. Cooper's a good sheriff...he lets me have visitors, and he keeps a good jail. He treats me well." Tom looked at the bars in front of his face and continued, "...of course, jail's a little hell. There ain't no comfort in one."

"Are you nervous about your trial?"

"No, not really. I'm not uneasy any, if that's what you're meaning. I'm never nervous. I'm in God's hands now...no man oughta be afraid when he's in God's hands," the prisoner said with a convincing smile. "I just hope God's on my side."

"So you're ready to go to trial?"

"I just want the uncertainty to be over, y'know. Of course...I'm hoping for an acquittal. I'm innocent."

"You say you've had a lot of visitors?"

"Mostly reporters." He shook his head in disgust. "The Macon Telegraph was so against me. It fed the prejudice of the people...but I guess I like the other reporters well enough."

The second day of the trial in Perry was consumed with the task of obtaining twelve qualified men to serve on the jury. Rutherford used every possible legal tool available to him to delay the proceedings and to challenge the jury on pretrial prejudice.

His request to have Judge Gustin disqualify himself was denied. Although the general consensus of the trial watchers was that he would protest, Rutherford did not, giving Folsom the opinion he was saving it for the appeal, should Tom be convicted a second time.

Juror after juror was presented. Rutherford would challenge, and Gustin would overrule. By mid-day, five were seated.

A murmur filled the room as a 'John Howard' was called.

"Strike him!" Tom barked and Rutherford instantly rejected Tom's uncle.

At day's end, eleven men were accepted. Houston County had a total of six hundred fifty names of potential jurors from which to draw. Two hundred twenty-seven were already disqualified. Although it was rumored that a mistrial could happen, Folsom did not see it possible with so many jurors remaining from which to pull the twelfth man.

Judge Gustin's declaration of a mistrial Wednesday evening reverberated throughout the countryside, and, for once, Folsom felt Rutherford was correct. Houston County was not the location for a fair trial for Tom.

As before, the mistrial was as a result of jurors being overheard stating an opinion on the case. In this case, however, the opinion was that Tom was not guilty.

Several witnesses reported that Juror David Knight admitted he had read a great deal about the case and felt it was immoral to convict someone on circumstantial evidence.

The second juror J. B. Parker was also reported to have expressed his doubt about some of the evidence.

Rutherford took advantage of the situation and immediately moved for a mistrial. The jurors were separated from the remaining panel and by noon were discharged.

The State did not object to Rutherford's motion. Gustin ordered a new trial.

At the beginning of the fifth trial, Rutherford presented the same motions as before. He asked for the Judge to disqualify himself and was denied. He asked for a change of venue and was denied. He asked to question the remaining potential jurors on their understanding of the terms 'prejudice and bias'. He was denied.

By Saturday, June the 8th, and in less than an hour after court convened, J.M. Frederick took the last seat in the jury box. The room sighed. Suddenly, Tom jerked his head up. His gasp was loud enough for Folsom to hear several yards away. The prisoner appeared startled that the trial was actually going to proceed. A recess was called, and Tom was escorted from the room.

An hour before noon, everyone but the prisoner returned to their places. Representing the State was Judge W.D. Nottingham, Solicitor William Felton, the firm of Guerry and Hall, as well as Representative Hardeman.

Nottingham's opening statement lasted a half hour. It was brief and to the point. He described the murder scene, listed the evidence, and told the jury the State expected a guilty verdict.

The defense was represented by Rutherford, as the lead counsel, Winter Wimberly, and Clinton C. Duncan. Frank Walker had not assisted since the appeal.

John Rutherford rose and approached the jurors. The lawyer showed the telltale signs of exhaustion. His complexion was pale. He had lost a great deal of weight, and, in regular conversation, his voice was weak and hollow. Folsom marvelled. Rutherford was literally sacrificing his own life to save Tom Woolfolk's. The defense attorney stood leaning against the jury box for a moment as if mustering his strength. He then pushed himself away.

"The crime is a most horrible one, and it is exceedingly unnatural as charged against Tom Woolfolk. The defense will show that not one person, but several, had committed the crime." His voice was loud and sharp as he continued to tell the jury the defense's theory that a number of black men had reason and opportunity to murder the Captain. His speech lasted three times that of the State.

"Tom Woolfolk did not kill his father," Rutherford said in closing and returned to his chair.

A side door opened, and the prisoner shuffled in escorted by Sheriff Cooper and a deputy. As Cooper unlocked his shackles, Tom stared at the floor. He would not make eye contact with anyone in the room. His chains removed, he dropped down into his chair. Folsom heard him sigh and noted it in his notebook.

The first witness called for the State was Joseph Dannenberg.

Rutherford objected. "Your Honor, Mr. Dannenberg's conversation with the defendant back in eighteen eighty-five is vague, indefinite and has no connection to this case."

Gustin overruled.

The witness proceeded to tell of his association with the defendant and of a conversation they had in his store four years earlier.

"Woolfolk told me he expected to inherit his father's property. I said, 'Your father must have made a will then, as you have sisters and brothers living.'"

"And what was his response?" the prosecutor asked.

"Well, he told me that no will had been made, but that he expected to get the property nonetheless."

"Mr. Dannenberg," Rutherford began his cross examination, "do you remember testifying during the first trial?"

The State objected and was overruled.

"Do you remember what you said?"

"Yes."

"And to the best of your knowledge is it the exact statement as to the one given now?"

"Well, maybe not exactly the same, but the same in context."

"To what context are you referring, sir?"

"That he asked me about the law, said that he was going to get the property, and that there was no will."

"Did you and the defendant get along?"

"Yes."

"Was he a good renter? Paid his rent on time?"

"Yes. I never had any trouble from him. He always paid on time."

"You were planning a trip prior to this trial, were you not?"

"Yes. My doctor told me I needed a rest...I was going to Europe."

"This trial made you change yours plans, is that correct?"

"Yes."

"So you should be pretty angry at the defendant for all this trouble he has caused you."

"I have cause to be angry at'im, yes...but I'm not."

The next and final witness for the day was Henry Brown whose testimony was similar to the one he gave at the Bibb trial. Folsom listened closely to what he had to say. The reporter recalled vividly how upset Tom had been after the witness' original testimony.

Brown told of receiving the news and going immediately to the Woolfolk's house where he found Tom lying on the porch.

"When I come up, Tom says to me, he says 'Whoever killed Pa couldn't have done it for money cause there ain't none.'"

"You were a member of the party that arrested the defendant were you not?" the State asked.

"Yes, sir, when we went up to arrest'im, he said that was what he wanted. Then he said he wanted an investigation. We took'im in side. I wouldn't let'im stand near the window though."

"Why was that?"

"Cause by then suspicions 'gainst him were pretty high."

The witness described the bodies, the blood, and how it looked as if there had been a struggle outside the girls' bedroom.

"But there weren't no body there," he added and then proceeded to tell about the bloody handprint.

"Did he offer any explanation for the print?"

"He said it musta been his own, when he...," Brown looked around, nervously wondering if he should continue. "When he, uh, went to the...when he...uh went to the toilet."

Laughter broke out in the courtroom prompting Gustin to tap his gavel. Tom did not react but continued to look at his clasped hands resting on top of the table.

"What was his explanation for the spot of blood you found in his ear?"

"He said when his pa got hit blood flew everwhere and couldn't help but get there."

Folsom looked at Tom. The prisoner did not move a muscle although the reporter suspected this was the statement Tom disagreed with the most, to the point of accusing Brown of lying on the stand in Bibb County.

"Tell us about his clothes. What did he have on when you first saw him?"

"He was wearing trousers and a shirt."

"Was there any blood on them?"

"No, sir. He said the clothes weren't his. That he didn't have no clothes there."

"When he was stripped, did his underclothes have blood on them?"

"No, sir."

"But there was blood on his leg, underneath the drawers, is that correct?

"Yes, sir. That's when he told us it musta been when he...you know.

The room again erupted in laughter. Gustin slammed his gavel loudly on the bench and glared at the audience.

"Go ahead, Mistah Brown," the Judge said.

"When he went to the toilet. Well, we checked the drawstring in his drawers..."

The prosecutor interrupted. "Was the string in the front or back?"

"In the front. When we looked at the string...it didn't have no blood on it."

Brown repeated his original testimony about Tom refusing to drink water from the well or eat food from the kitchen. These points seemed important to him. He had made a special effort during both trials to stress that such were unusual actions on the part of the accused. He then elaborated in detail about the stain on the floor in the defendant's bedroom.

"It looked like blood had been..."

The defense interrupted with an objection saying the witness was making an assumption. The Judge overruled.

"It looked like blood had been scrubbed up in several places in his room."

"And how did he explain that?"

"He said he had spilt some salts on the floor and tried to wipe'em up."

The witness identified the clothes brought up from the well and was then shown the axe.

"Do you recognize this?"

"Yes, sir. It's the same one I saw beside the door in the Captain's room."

Monday, the third day, Folsom walked into the courtroom and sat down. Although he was late leaving the Perry Hotel across the street, he had no difficulty getting a seat. Only five other people were in the audience. The room was virtually empty. A small number of reporters milled around the lobby. Pea Jay returned to Atlanta after the first day. Attendance at the trial was surprisingly low.

Houston County was rural, populated largely by farmers and laborers. Perry and Fort Valley, twelve miles away, were country towns whose populations together totaled less than Macon's. During this trial, the attitude of the audience seemed to reflect a lack of seriousness and respect for the situation. Although the majority of the community knew of the Woolfolk family, many knew Tom's uncle John Woolfolk who lived in the county, and were aware of the murder. The tragedy had not apparently hit as close to home or strike the emotional nerve as it had in Bibb County.

He glanced around the room. It was quiet. Court officials wandered in and out. The clerk arranged papers on the Judge's bench. Folsom's gaze stopped at the defense's table. There, purposefully placed in front of Tom's seat, was a single, red rose.

Court convened with Rutherford cross-examining Henry Brown. Although the witness admitted his testimony was not exactly the same as in the Bibb trial, he was, nonetheless, telling it as best as he could remember.

William H. Smith and then George Yates took the stand and identified themselves as the first white men to go to the house after the alarm was sounded. They both gave the same testimonies as were given to the coroner's jury and during the first trial. Rutherford tried but was not able to get Yates as flustered as before.

Because he had lost his notes, John Clay, the undertaker, was not as detailed and precise as he was in Macon. He could not remember the number of wounds. He recalled seeing blood on the floor, walls and ceilings. The information he supplied was considerably less than before.

During his cross examination, Rutherford showed him the axe the undertaker identified as the one he saw at the house.

"Mr. Clay, is it possible that another axe similar to this one could have made some of the wounds?"

"Well, we know that one in particular did because it had blood and brains on it."

"Yes, but, is it possible that some of the wounds were made by an additional axe of similar size?"

"I suppose so, yes...a similar axe could have made some of the wounds."

The large double doors in back opened. Folsom turned to look. Tom's sisters and aunt filed down the aisle to their seats. Each leaned over and gave him a kiss. The defendant accepted their greetings without a word or response.

Dr. Howard Williams testified he saw the shirt after it had been drawn from the well and that it looked as if it had blood and brains on it. He stressed he was not an expert and could not positively identify the blood to be human.

When William A. Davis rose to take the stand, Rutherford jumped to his feet in adamant objection and asked that the jury be removed. The court obliged, and the twelve men left the room.

Rutherford argued that Davis' testimony concerned evidence obtained after the defendant had been stripped against his will. The attorney then stated that Tom had been threatened with force by the coroner's jury had he not cooperated. The State countered. The Judge overruled Rutherford's objection.

Houston County Courthouse, Perry, GA
(Photo courtesy of Billy C. Horne)

CHAPTER TWENTY-ONE

*"He said that Tom loved him better
than any of the other children."*

The next morning, Flo rose from her seat and greeted her brother with a kiss. "How did you sleep?" she asked.

Tom laughed. "I rested well last night." He smiled and nodded a greeting to Folsom sitting a few rows back. "A crazy woman in the cell next to mine kept me awake three nights." He explained to the reporter. Folsom chuckled. Tom grinned back and continued, "The woman went to the asylum yesterday."

Shackleford patted him on the shoulder while his aunt kissed him and gave him a bowl of fruit. Lillie then leaned over and handed him a small bouquet of flowers. Folsom watched the genuine warmth and love flow back and forth across the bar between the prisoner and his family.

The overwhelming emptiness of the room caused the bailiff's voice to echo as he called everyone to their feet.

"The State calls R. H. Barron," Solicitor Felton announced. Rutherford and Miller jumped to their feet in loud objections. Gustin sent the jury out.

"Your Honor," Rutherford argued, "Mr. Barron was on the jury that rendered a verdict against the defendant. His evidence is inadmissable and contrary to the very policy of the law."

Alexander Miller agreed vehemently and then added, "The impartiality of the trial would be impaired by the testimony of a man backed up by a verdict to which he was a party."

"The impressions of the witness gathered as a juror at the former trial is not allowable," the Judge ruled. "But he is competent to testify to facts. Bailiff return the jury to the box."

"Proceed counselor," Gustin ordered.

Felton picked up the familiar underdrawers and asked if the witness recognized them. Rutherford and Miller objected. Gustin overruled.

Barron took the garment, looked it over, and then handed it back.

"Yes, its the same pair of drawers used at the former trial."

Rutherford and Miller objected. Gustin overruled.

"Can you tell us more about these drawers?" Felton asked.

"Well, they had blood stains on them at the courthouse in Macon. Some of the stains were the imprint of a hand..."

The defense interrupted with objections and were again overruled.

"Well...like I said there was a bloody imprint of a hand...with fingers pointing in and up on the leg."

"And were these the same drawers shown to you at the former trial?"

Rutherford and Miller again exploded to the floor with loud objections and were overruled. The witness answered 'yes'. The defense's incensed objections to the second witness, Asher Ayres, another former juror, were also overruled. Ayres supported Barron's testimony.

The third witness for the State was Jerry Hollis. The witness recalled graphically the positions of the bodies. He told of pulling the shorts up from the well and taking them home with him with plans to take them to the Sheriff as soon as possible. It was there, he said, he discovered the print matching the one on Tom's leg.

During his cross-examine, Rutherford asked if the witness thought the defendant guilty.

"Yes, sir, I do."

"But what if evidence was presented in this court room that proved the defendant's innocence, would you still think him guilty?"

Hollis thought for a moment. "Yes, sir, I would. The angels in Heaven can't change my opinion on this...only my God can."

"You say you had the drawers in your custody before taking them to Macon and turning them over to the Sheriff. Is that correct?"

"Yessir."

"And during this time did you do anything to them?"

"No, sir. I examined them closely, that's all."

"Did anyone else have access to them?"

"No, sir. No one messed with them. I'd a known."

"Mistah Hollis, I want you to look at these drawers very, very carefully. Now, tell me, are you absolutely certain, one hundred percent sure before your God and this court that those are the same exact drawers you pulled from the well?"

The witness examined the garment closely. "Yes, sir,…uh …well…"

"Do you swear before God and this court that those are the identical pair of drawers you took from the well and gave to the Sheriff?"

"Well…these have a tear and the pair I had didn't."

Rutherford whirled around and objected to the admissability of the altered garment as evidence. Gustin overruled.

Sheriff Westcott was next sworn in and testified that the evidence had been stored in accordance with the law. When questioned about the tear he explained the garment must have been torn accidently.

"Now Sheriff, would you mind telling the court about a certain bribe…"

Rutherford interrupted with an objection, and Gustin ordered the jury out of the room.

"Tom Woolfolk offered me five thousand dollars if I would place him in a particular cell in the hospital ward of the jail so he could escape. I asked him about the money. He said he would get me five hundred dollars and that Captain Rutherford would arrange the balance. He said that Rutherford wanted him free. He told me to go see Rutherford about it. Well I refused him, of course. He begged me not to say anything about it."

"I must protest Your Honor!" Rutherford shouted. "I have never heard of this. I would never speak to my client on such a subject and would reprove him if he ever attempted such an escape."

"Your Honor, it's not the intention of the State to cast a negative shadow on Colonel Rutherford," Felton offered.

"Your Honor, this testimony is obviously intended to imply indirect admission of guilt on the part of the defendant."

"I will reserve ruling on this. Bailiff, return the jury to the box."

Greene Lockett repeated his testimony given in the first trial and was turned over to the defense.

"How far are you from the Captain's house?"

"Say that again, Mistah Ruthe'ford. I don't zactly understand."

"How far is your house from the Captain's house?"

"Well after the last time you axk me that, I went back and I figgered it out. I lives 'bout thirty yards from the house."

"So you live near the Captain's?"

"Yassuh. Mine's the closest to the big house."

"So...when you are standing on the porch of the Captain's house you could easily hear the children playing down at, oh...let's say...Emma and Aaron Jones?"

"Yassuh."

"And what about children playing at...well, let's say over at the Gilbert Place."

"Yassuh."

"And down at your place?"

"Yassuh."

"So voices carry well around that hill?"

"Say that again, Mister Ruthe'ford. I didn't zactly understand."

"Sounds from one house carry to another around there?"

"Uh...yassuh, they do."

"What did you hear that night, Mister Lockett?"

"I hears Mister Tom callin' for me."

"Nothin' else?"

"Well...I hears d'mean ole dawg of d'Cap'ns...but that's all."

"Were you the only hand on the place?"

"Say that again, Mister Ruthe'ford. I don't zactly understand."

"Were you the only negro man on the farm that night?"

"Oh, nawsuh."

"Who else was on the farm, Mister Lockett?"

"There was...uh...Aaron Jones and...An'son James."

"Were the three of you the only negro men on the farm that night?"

"...nawsuh."

"Who else?"

"Say that again, Mister…"

"Who were the other negro men on the farm that night in addition to you, Jones, and James, Mister Lockett?"

"I cain't rightly say."

"Do you know the names of the other black men who worked and lived on that farm with you?"

"Yassuh."

"So would you please give us the names of the other men on the farm that night in addition to three of you?"

"I cain't rightly say who was there that night."

"Mister Lockett, do you own a short handled axe?"

"Nawsuh."

"You don't own a short handled axe with a string that runs through the handle?"

"…Nawsuh."

"A short handled axe…"

"Your Honor, I object," Felton interrupted. "The defense is badgering the witness. Mr. Lockett has already stated that he does not own such an axe."

"Sustained."

Before the witness was dismissed, Felton wanted to redirect.

"Mr. Lockett, do you recognize this axe?"

"Yassuh."

"And where did you see it last?"

"Hit was in the Cap'n's house by the doe."

"And before that, where did you see it?"

"…I saw Mistah Tom with a short handled axe same as that one."

The fourth day began with Anderson James' testimony. In careful detail, he retraced his movements just before and after he went to Greene Lockett's. During his cross examination, Rutherford attempted to get him confused. Anderson became frustrated and angry.

"What prompted you to go to Greene Lockett's house before daylight?"

James reacted as if he did not understand the attorney's terminology and asked him to repeat the question. Rutherford did.

"I can't follow you around your way," James said. "You might carry me wrong. I won't say anythin' I don't know."

"What were you doing in the area so early in the morning?"

"I done told you. I heard someone callin' and hit woke me up."

"Who was it?"

"I don't know who. I just heard someone callin' and then I heard a ruckus at Greene Lockett's. So I goes over there to 'vestigate."

"Who were they calling? You?"

"Nawsuh, not me. I dunno who they was callin'."

"All right. You said you went to Lockett's to investigate and found Tom Woolfolk at Lockett's front door. What happened then?"

"Mistah Tom says to me 'Go to the lot and git the horse and go after Mistah Chambless, somebody's killed pa and ma.'"

"I says 'Good God' and sits down."

"You said 'Good God'?"

"Yessuh. Well...I was 'fraid to go to the lot."

"Why?"

"I has to go right by the house. So I goes the other way and I runs into Mistah Smith...ridin' in."

"Other than Aaron Jones, Greene Lockett, and yourself, who were the other negro men on or about the farm that night?"

"I ain't followin' where yer goin' with that."

"Would you mind tellin' the court the names of the other men who were about the place, in addition to yourself, Mister Jones and Mister Lockett?"

"I don't know who else was there. Aaron and Greene were the only ones I seen."

Jim Foster recalled his original testimony to the State.

"What exactly did you tell Mistah Smith when you reached his house?" Rutherford asked.

"I told'im that someone had broken into the Cap'n's house."

"You didn't tell him that the Captain had been killed?"

"Nawsur."

"Do you recognize this axe?"

"Yassur, that's the one I use to chop wood wid. I's the one that cut off the handle like that."

"Why did you do that?"

"It was all worn out 'n all."

"Did you use this axe the day before to cut wood?"

"If I could've found it where it 'pose to be."

"Do you recall Mrs. Woolfolk preparing several baskets of food for the picnic?"

"Nawsur."

"Where were you that night?"

"Got in purty late. Uncle Greene was already in bed."

"When did you last see Tom Woolfolk?"

"I seen'im sick day 'fore the killin's. He was lyin' down in the hall."

"During your last testimony, you said he was lyin' down in the barn. Where was he, Mister Foster, lying in the hall or in the barn?"

Jim Foster hesitated a moment.

"In the hall, like I said."

"Where were the other negro men around the place that night...besides you and Greene Lockett?"

"Don't know where anybody else was."

"You sure?"

"Like I said, I don't know where dey was that night."

I.P. Davis repeated his testimony. Rutherford tried to provoke him into admitting he would sometimes make up stories to attract attention and that he was involved in an ongoing battle between his wife and mother. The State objected and the court instructed the defense to adhere to the questions relating directly to the case.

A surprise witness was W.D. O'Connor who identified himself as a peddler from Atlanta. Tom spoke softly to his attorneys, shaking his head. It was obvious to the Folsom, the prisoner did not know the man.

In a strong Irish brogue, O'Connor testified he met Tom Woolfolk at a bar one night in Macon a few months before the murders. Tom was already drunk but volunteered to have another drink with the witness. The witness recalled that during the course of the conversation the defendant said that at one time he had a great deal of money.

"He said he would have more soon. He said, 'Father's made a will in favor of his last wife, but I intend to have the property in Macon...or I'll kill everything on the place.'"

The stir his last statement caused seemed to rattle the witness. Rutherford rose to cross-examine.

"You say you ran into the defendant in a saloon...a bar."

"That's right. He was already drunk."

"What about you?"

The State objected and was sustained. Rutherford attempted to rephrase the question.

"Are you a drinkin' man, Mr. O'Connor?"

"Your Honor, I object. The defense is attacking the witness' personal life that has nothing to do with the case."

"Your Honor, I am simply trying to establish the reliability of this witness."

"Sustained. Be careful counselor."

"How many wives do you have?"

The prosecutors jumped to their feet in objections. The witness grabbed the chair arms and raised himself up. "Yer Honor, Mistah Rutherford here's tryin' to spring somethin' on me."

"Sustained. Mr. Rutherford, I will not allow you to badger the witness nor make any reference what so ever to his private life."

John Owens shifted in his seat and waited for the cross-examination. He had just told the State the same story he originally told the coroner's jury and then again at the first trial. Rutherford stood up and approached the witness.

"You said the defendant walked up to you and praised your paint job?"

"Yassur, he said 'John, you're gettin' along pretty well.'"

"That statement sounds a bit familiar. What would you say your relationship would be with the defendant?"

"Friends."

"Friends?"

"Yassur. Good friends. He always hung around with us. He'd go with us for a little devilment."

"No further questions," Rutherford said and returned to his chair. Felton stood up and asked to redirect.

"Mr. Owens, define the word 'devilment'."

John Owens grinned, "You know...girls."

Fannie Crane buried her audible gasp with her handkerchief. Tom did not move a muscle.

Crawford Wilson told the jury of talking with the defendant a few months before the murder. "I was workin' on a bridge, and Tom rides up. I told him what a nice girl Pearl was. He got real angry and said 'Anybody could be nice livin' off somebody else's money.' He said, 'They're sittin' on my dead mother's property and before I stand it I'll see them all dead and in hell...and I'll wade knee deep in their blood.'"

The room rumbled with whispers. Gustin tapped his gavel. Tom did not move a muscle. He continued to watch the witness closely. Wilson would not make eye contact with the defendant.

"And what did you say?" Felton asked.

"Well, I said. 'If you think that way about your family, I'd advise you to leave.'"

"What did Mr. Woolfolk say to that?"

"He said, 'I expect to leave, but I'll leave with revenge.'"

Again, the room reacted with hushed whispers.

Rutherford rose to cross-examine. He walked up to the witness box, looked Wilson directly in the eye, and then turned back towards the audience. The witness waited.

"Mr. Wilson, what else did you talk about that day on the bridge?"

"Uh...can't rightly say."

"Surely you talked about other things...the weather or maybe about the fine horse the defendant was riding?"

"I don't remember."

"Why don't you remember? You were able to recall in incredible detail parts of the conversation. Why then can you not recall the other parts?"

Felton objected and was overruled.

"I just don't remember, that's all. After we talked, I forgot all about it."

"What refreshed your memory?"

"When I heard about the murders."

"Did you tell anyone else about this conversation?"

"Yessir, I told Captain Woolfolk."

"You did? What was his response?"

"He told me not to talk like that about Tom. He said Tom loved him better than any of the other children."

"My name is E.J. Parker," the next witness told the court. "I'm a farmer in Hazzard District and uh…was a friend and neighbor of the Woolfolk family."

Parker proceeded to recall how he learned of the murders and hurried to the Captain's house. He told about washing the Captain and Richard Jr. and preparing them for burial. In a low, steady voice he described cutting off their clothes and wiping the blood from their bodies.

"What did you do with the clothes you cut from the bodies?"

"I wiped up some blood from the floor with'em and then…I burned'em."

"Your witness."

Rutherford rose half way from his chair. "I have no questions for this witness."

"Mr. Howard," Felton questioned Charles Howard. "As the administrator of your sister's estate, would you tell the court the value of her property."

"Her estate is worth about nine thousand dollars."

"And the Captain's?"

"About seven thousand."

"So your sister actually owned the majority of the property?"

"Yes. Our father gave her a substantial dowry when she married. She was also good with business transactions and accumulated more land on her own."

"So whoever inherits the property will inherit a great deal?"

Rutherford objected that the State was asking for an opinion. Gustin sustained.

"Would you describe the Captain and young Richard's physical strength?" Felton continued.

"Well, the Captain was bigger than Tom and was in pretty good health. Richard wasn't as developed as Tom. He was as tall but not as strong."

"Your witness."

"No questions."

Tom looked at his attorney. Two witnesses for the State had not been cross examined. Rutherford sat with his feet stretched out in front of him. He twirled his pencil back and forth between his fingers and was deep in thought.

P. H. Dixon testified that the clothes pulled from the well could not have been from the victims as no one would have been able to put anything in the well during the day without being seen. Rutherford could not get the witness to change his testimony.

As Elizabeth Black was being sworn, Frank Walker joined his former colleagues at the defense table. Forced to resign from the case due to a lengthy illness, Tom's original attorney informed them he was there only to observe and to testify and could not actively participate.

Mrs. Black repeated her original testimony about her mother's deafness. Rutherford was able, however, to get her to admit that contrary to what she said at the first trial, her mother could actually hear loud noises and would wake when touched.

John Howard told about receiving a gold watch and some money found in the house; thus, weakening the defense's argument that the original motive was robbery.

Rutherford did not cross examine.

Sarah Hardin recalled under oath that she washed Thursday and ironed Friday before the murders. The State showed her the garments pulled from the well. She explained how she knew the socks and drawers were not the property of either of the murdered men. As before, she identified the shirt brought out from the well as belonging to Richard.

She started to explain how Mattie Woolfolk did not want her to wash the shirt and told her to leave it where she found it when the defense objected and asked that the jury be removed. Once the twelve men left the court room, Sarah was instructed to continue her statement.

"Miz Mattie said, 'Leave that shirt for Tom to sleep in. He's too dirty to sleep in my bed.' So I flung it back down."

The court ruled the statement inadmissable.

It was obvious to Folsom that the prosecution learned its lesson from the appeal and was covering every point originally objected to. When the State called Julia Woolfolk to the stand he knew the matter of the wool hat was about to be explained. She identified the hat as the same one she had bought for her son and explained how it fell in the well by accident.

"How do you know how it fell in the well?" Rutherford asked during his cross-examine.

"I was there."

"When the hat was brought out of the well...what happened to it?"

"I don't know what happened to it. All I knows is I got it from Greene Lockett. I give it t'Jeff, Silas' boy, and he wore it a long time 'fore they come and takes it for the trial."

"So, this hat was in your grandson's possession for a length of time before it was retrieved for trial?" Rutherford looked curiously at Hardeman and did not wait for her answer. "Exactly when did the hat fall in the well?"

"Don't know 'xactly when."

"A day, a week, a month, maybe a year before the murders?"

"Don't know when, but there weren't no blood on'is hat when it fell in the well."

"I seem to recall that you people have your society meetings at the church on Friday nights."

"Yassur, but I didn't go to no 'ciety meetin' that night. The meetin' had done broke."

Folsom jerked. The woman completely contradicted her original testimony.

"George Caldwell is your son-in-law, is that not correct?"

"Yassur."

"Why was he put on the chaingang?"

"Stealin' one a'da Cap'n's oxes."

"When did you see him last?"

"He come down the road one night, 'fore d'boss was killed."

Folsom was again astonished.

"Didn't Silas say Captain Woolfolk owed him money, was ahead of him, but that he would get even?"

Felton jumped to his feet in objection and was sustained. Gustin instructed the witness and jury to disregard the question.

Jim Foster was recalled to the stand to clarify facts concerning the hat.

"When was the hat recovered from the well?" Felton asked.

"When we drugged the well that day."

"What day?"

"The day of the killin's."

"And what did you do with the hat?"

"Miz Chambless told me t'give it to Greene Lockett...he gave it to Jeff Woolfolk."

Sam Chambless' widow Amanda was sworn in for the State.

"Miz Chambless, who was responsible for obtaining the clean clothes that were placed on the bodies?" Felton asked.

"I was."

"And where did you get them?"

"I got them from a pile of clean clothes in Pearl's room."

"And when you put them down did you put them where they could have gotten blood on them?"

"Oh, no. I made sure I put them where they would stay clean."

"You were given the clothes cut off of the men, were you not?"

"Yes. They were cut open at the front, the sleeves, and the legs."

"Weren't you also given the responsibility of cleaning some of the victims?"

"Yes...Pearl."

"When you cleaned her hands...did they have blood on them?"

"Yes."

"And what were the size of her hands?"

"I would say a fair size."

Nat Birdsong took the stand against the fervent objections of the defense. Rutherford asked the court to decide the admissability of the jailer's testimony in the jury's absence. The jury left the room and Gustin asked for Birdsong's statement.

The jailer explained to the court his responsibility of guarding the defendant.

"One day I asked him who's gonna get the inheritance. He says that his sisters probably would but that he'd settle that question at the proper time."

"Did the defendant ever say anything else that seemed...ah...let's say unusual or peculiar to you?"

"Yes sir. One night I heard him mumbling like he was prayin'. He said 'Lord have mercy upon me for what I've done. The only thing I regret is killin' my father.'"

Soft, muffled sobs attracted Folsom's attention. Alone, behind her brother's chair, Flo Edwards sat crying.

The Judge overruled the objection and ordered the jury back in.

During his cross-examination, Rutherford asked if the jailer heard the entire prayer or only a part.

"He could've said somethin' in prayer before I went up...but I didn't hear him."

The State asked to have the jury removed. Gustin ordered the bailiff to again escort the jury from the room and instructed

Rutherford to proceed with his line of questioning to determine admissability.

"Have you heard other prayers of the prisoner professing his innocence and asking forgiveness for those who unjustly accuse him?"

"Yes," Birdsong answered.

The State argued that the question was inadmissable, and the court agreed. The jury returned to the box and the state rested.

CHAPTER TWENTY-TWO
"I told him it was too late."

The first witness for the defense was R. H. Bailey. Rutherford handed him the underdrawers.

"Have you ever seen these?"

"Yes, sir. I saw'em at Jerry Hollis'."

"And you're sure they are the same ones?"

"Well...other than this here tear right here...yeh, I'd say they're the same ones. But I didn't see no bloody handprint on'em then.

"You didn't, what did you see?"

"Just an ole worn out pair of underdrawers."

"How long were they at Mistah Hollis'?"

"Several days. He had'em in a shed with some other men's clothes. One colored boy had a whole suit in there."

"No further questions."

"Mistah Bailey," Felton asked, "are you certain these are the same pair of drawers?"

"Yes, sir. Hollis pointed to the left leg and said there was a handprint, but I didn't see it."

"How is it that you are a witness for the defense?"

"I went to Mistah Rutherford and told him I heard Hollis say he wouldn't believe an angel from heaven if they said Tom wasn't guilty."

"Are you a friend of Mistah Hollis? Do you like him?"

"I object, Your Honor."

"Overruled."

"Mistah Bailey, would you mind telling the court what you think of Mistah Hollis."

"Well...I...don't have the best of feelings towards'im, I guess. He owes me money for rent."

"No further questions."

"Redirect, Your Honor?"

"Go ahead, Counselor."

"Mistah Bailey, why didn't you appear at the first trial after you were summoned?"

"I...I didn't want to."

"Are you a willing witness now?"

"No...I don't want nothin' to do with this."

"Thank you. I have no further questions for this witness. Your Honor," Rutherford walked across to his table and picked up a sheet of paper, "I would like to retain the following State witnesses, James J. Holly and W.D. O'Connor."

The defense then called Emma Jones followed by Luanna Cooper. Both women repeated their original testimonies with no discrepancies. When Rutherford asked Luanna where John Jeff was that night, the State objected loudly. After a bitter argument from both sides, Judge Gustin disallowed the question.

When word that the bailiff could not locate O'Connor, the Irishman who testified against Tom, leaked out, Folsom hurried to the hotel where he last saw the man.

"He skipped town," the hotel clerk informed the reporter. "Left without paying for twelve days and ten dollars, he did."

"What happened?" Folsom asked.

The clerk shook his head in disgust. "He said his first wife was actually livin', and that he's got another wife and son livin' over in Stark. It seems before the trial and the newspapers printed what was said, she didn't even know he had a first one."

"So...he cut out to avoid being arrested for bigamy." Folsom was astounded.

The morning of June the 14th began immediately with arguments, in the jury's absence, over the admissability of various testimonies. Although O'Connor's disappearance seemed to support the defense's claim that the witness was not reliable, the testimony had been admitted by the court and was thus on record. The prosecution, on the other hand, vehemently blocked Rutherford's plan to present evidence concerning John Jeff's whereabouts that night as well as threats he had lodged against the Captain a few days before.

As it became obvious he would not be allowed to pursue the line of questioning he had planned, the defense attorney seemed to panic. In a sense of rage, he ignored the prosecution's objection and continued to plead his case. Finally, the Judge ruled John Jeff was not the person on trial, and, unless it was proven he committed the murders, any hearsay about him or, for that matter, any confession he might have made, was inadmissible.

John Rutherford's posture seemed to become slightly stooped and took on the appearance of a man beaten by a greater foe. He returned to his chair and waited as the jury entered. His brow was deeply carved. A vein protruded in his neck. Folsom watched and wondered if such a man so dedicated to the defense of his client could endure the strain.

Tom sat in his chair casually reading the book Folsom loaned him. The day before, the prisoner requested something to occupy his mind and the reporter gave him a book entitled "Napoleon and His Marshals".

Frank Walker took the stand and testified that he saw John Jeff during one of his visits to the murder scene.

"I had him go in the house with me.

"And how did he act?"

"He was excited and seemed anxious to get out. I was examining Pearl's room and began to question him. He said he had some chickens to feed and walked out closing the door behind him."

"Did he answer your questions at all?"

"At first, but then later after he contradicted himself several times, he shut up and wouldn't talk at all."

"What were some of his contradictions?"

The State objected and was sustained. Angry and frustrated Rutherford said he had no more questions and returned to his seat. Felton remained seated and asked Walker the status of the house.

"It's closed up."

"It's unoccupied then...no one living in it?"

"No one is living in it."

Foster Shi next took the stand and identified himself as living near Hazzard District in Monroe County.

"Right after I heard about the murders, I went to the house and talked to John Jeff. I mentioned the killings...John got nervous and excited."

"Did he tell you anything about what he did the night the murders occurred?"

"He said he had gone to church and went right to bed when he got back. Said he didn't hear about it until around sunup. He said if he'd been there, he'd been in it."

"What else did he say?"

"He said that if anything had happened at the lot when he was at home he'd have heard it and gone to see about it."

"How close did John Jeff live to the Captain's house?"

"His lot was right in back of it."

The State unsuccessfully attempted to manipulate the witness into contradicting himself. Felton finally gave up and was about to release Shi when he stopped and asked, "How nervous would you say John Jeff was when you saw him?"

"He was pretty nervous."

"About as nervous as you are now?" the solicitor asked with a smile.

"Yeh...about this nervous," Shi smiled back.

When his name was called, Henry P. Cowan patted Lillie's hand, stood up slowly and entered the bar. He placed his hand on the Bible and swore to tell the truth.

Cowan identified himself as the Captain's son-in-law and executor of his estate. The defense asked if his responsibilities required him to spend time on the farm after the murders. The witness stated that it had.

"Did you happen to see John Jeff on the farm?"

"Yes, I did, several times."

"And were you able to converse with him, ask him any questions?"

"Yes, but he'd answer with a question of his own."

"You mean, he never gave you a straight answer."

"That's correct. He'd respond with a question."

"How did he act?"

"Excited...but not overly nervous."

The moment Rutherford called Sam Pennington to the stand, Hardeman rose to his feet and requested that the jury be removed. The familiar heated argument concerning the witness' testimony followed. Finally, Judge Gustin asked if any information other than what was originally discussed in the Bibb County trial would come from the testimony. Rutherford tried to convince the Judge that there were to be additional facts.

"I am ruling inadmissable the admissions or threats or sayings of a person not on trial but being implicated in a crime." The Judge sustained the objection and recalled the jury.

"Mistah Pennington," Rutherford began, "do you remember seeing John Jeff at the Bibb County Courthouse?"

"Yes, sir."

"How did he appear to you?"

The State objected and was overruled.

"He was nervous and very embarrassed."

"Did he say anything to you?"

The State objected. Judge Gustin sustained and instructed the witness not to answer the question.

"When was the first time you saw John Jeff?"

"In Macon, a few days before the murders. He helped me with a lunatic."

"And do you remember a statement Jeff made about..."

The State's objection was sustained. Gustin warned Rutherford he would no longer tolerate his attempts to manipulate the court. Rutherford stated he was finished with the witness.

"Mr. Pennington, do you remember identifying John Jeff during the first trial?" Hardeman asked.

"Yes, yes, I do."

"As you will recall, you mistakenly identified another man, Greene Lockett, as John Jeff."

"That is not true. I said they looked alike, but that Jeff was taller."

"Do you remember saying that the person you were looking for could have been Jeff's twin?"

"I didn't mean it the way you took it...I meant..."

"No further questions."

Sam Pennington walked over to the defense table, leaned over and asked if he could go home to La Grange. Miller looked at Rutherford who responded by saying under no certain circumstances was he to leave Perry. The attorney then returned his attention to the court and again tried to have I.P. Davis' testimony thrown out. He presented a number of witnesses who discredited him. The court refused.

Finally, after several expert witnesses testified on and jostled with the State about the blood on the clothes pulled from the well, the day came to an end.

Folsom hurried from the train depot to the Bibb County Jail. The detective he ran into the week before sent word that Jack Dubose was being transferred to Perry. The reporter wanted to interview the prisoner first.

The detective escorted him to Dubose's cell. The man's appearance surprised him. He was expecting the tattered attire of a transient and instead was greeted by a clean cut man wearing a suit.

"Dubose, this is Folsom from the Atlanta Constitution. I promised him an interview with you."

Folsom entered the cell and sat down. Dubose sat on the cot and watched as the reporter took out his notebook and made a few notes.

"Are you the same Jackson Dubose we have heard so much about?" Folsom asked.

"That's me."

"The one arrested by Sheriff Kitchen in Cherokee County?"

"That's me."

"Tell me about yourself."

"Well...I's born right cheer in Georgia. Sent to d'chaingang five years for watchin' out for some people fire Judge Pottle's house over in Warrenton. Wus workin' in d'gang b'low Macon on d'railroad when m'time was up."

"When was that?"

"Eighty-seven."

"What time of the year?"

"Summer." The man closely watched as Folsom wrote down what he said.

"And after your sentence expired, what did you do then?"

"Walked through d'country. I's headin' for Monroe County...come to d'Woolfolk place a day or two 'fore d'killin'."

"Did anyone see you at the Woolfolks?"

"Kept hid most time. Some of d'colored folks brung me m'food."

"Did you ever see the Woolfolk men?"

"I saw Tom Woolfolk. That Friday mornin'. I saw'im take a drink a whiskey."

"From a bottle, a jug,...what?"

"One of them..uh..," Dubose could not think of the correct word.

"Flask? A small bottle you can keep in your coat?"

"Yeh. One of them. I saw'im take a swig from a flask."

"Tell me about the murders."

"D'killin's happened several hours 'fore light. I was in d'yard at d'Woolfolk house."

"What were you doing there at that time of night...two or three hours before light?" Folsom wrote furiously. The sound of his pencil scratching against the paper seemed to echo in the cell block.

"I went to d'orchard t'get some apples. I saw Green Lockett's wife and another niggah go in d'house by d'back doe."

"How did they get inside?"

"Tom Woolfolk unlocked d'doe for'em. They helped do d'killin'. I saw Tom Woolfolk jump through d'winder, and he passed so close by me where I wus b'hind a bush...I coulda touched'im."

"Why didn't you say something to him?"

"Nawsur. He'd a knocked me in d'head like he did his folks and carried me in d'house and laid me down with all them dead people and then swear that I done d'killin' and he attacked 'n killed me."

Folsom pushed the tablet away, leaned back against the bars, and stared at the prisoner. Dubose said nothing. He looked the reporter directly in the eyes and waited for him to start writing again.

"It is said that you did the killing," Folsom finally said.

Dubose stiffened. His eyes flashed his anger. A muscle in his lower jaw twitched. "Nawsur. If anyone down there in Perry tries to make out that I killed them Woolfolks...I'll, I'll pick up a chair and kill d'Judge and anybody else that troubles me."

"What became of you after the killing?"

"I left them parts and walked up into north Georgia. Wus 'rested in Cherokee and sent to A'lanta. Mistah Walkah, he seen me and had my picture took. He told me I better skip 'way as fast as I could. I told Sheriff Kitchen I wus in d'Woolfolk yard on d'night of the murder and seen Tom Woolfolk jump out d'winder. When I's r'leased from prison, I wandered all about d'country...and landed in Alabama. I went t'work for a feller on a farm near Carrollton and then I stopped work. I's a'rested for vagrancy and put in jail. One day Sheriff Hudgins gets a letter with m'picture that Mistah Walkah had took when I's in d'Cherokee Jail. D'letter told 'bout d'Woolfolk murder. Sheriff Hudgins compared d'picture to my face and seen it suited me. He said he'd keep me in jail 'til he heard from Macon. Then...I's brought here."

"Jack, how did you say Tom Woolfolk killed his people?"

Dubose looked around the cage, scratched his head, and exhaled. "He...," the prisoner started slowly and then grinned broadly, "he...blew'em up wit dynamite."

Folsom pondered Dubose's statement while riding the train back to Perry and decided he was either as crazy as everyone said or acting.

Court convened Saturday, June 15th with Alexander Miller of the defense inquiring about O'Connor. The Sheriff stated he was unable to find him and Felton admitted he was very much alarmed that the witness left.

"Maybe pressure had been brought to bear on him, although I am not implying that the pressure came from the defense or any individual in the court. He probably expected to be arrested," Felton added.

"Your Honor, yesterday Mr. O'Connor approached me and asked to be recalled. He said he would swear that he was mistaken when he identified Woolfolk," Miller remarked.

"And what was your response to that?" Gustin asked.

"I told him it was too late."

The jury remained sequestered while the court investigated the matter further. Witnesses were presented who testified that O'Connor admitted he did not know the defendant. It was also stated that he actually had two wives neither knowing of the other's existence. A letter written by an informant named Jones was compared to a letter written by O'Connor and was determined to be by the same hand. It was also noted that he had requested to be a witness for the State.

Gustin ordered an investigation pending prosecution of the witness. Miller announced that the defense would not participate in the matter. The Judge sent for the jury and instructed the defense to proceed with its case. Miller called Henry Cowan.

"Mr. Cowan, did you have a conversation with Mr. O'Connor yesterday?" Miller asked.

"Yes, he came to me and said he made some mistakes on the stand and wanted to fix it. He said that the defense did not question him correctly, and if he was put back on the stand he would testify that he did not know Tom Woolfolk as the man who made the threats."

Felton approached the bench. "Your Honor, so there will be no doubts, the State would like to withdraw O'Connor's testimony."

"I object," Rutherford responded. "The State obviously placed a witness on the stand it should have known was not honest. The testimony was presented by the State as reliable and true and was heard by this jury. There is no guarantee that withdrawing the testimony would repair the damage caused by this gross miscarriage."

"The testimony will stand. Continue counselor."

"The defense calls Nancy Bird," Rutherford announced. Folsom looked up from his notes. During the two years since the murders he had never heard the name nor did he recognize the woman being sworn in.

"Now Miz Bird, would you please tell the court where you were the night of August 5, 1887."

"I was at the Woolfolk place."

"When did you arrive there?"

"I got there 'bout sundown," the woman answered quietly trying to hide her nervousness.

"And where did you stay?"

"I spent the night at Greene Lockett's house."

"Would you mind telling us about that evening?"

"Well," she hesitated, "Greene, Greene was there at supper, but he...he went out right after that and didn't come back 'til late." She stopped.

Rutherford smiled politely.

"I hears these screams and a dawg howling and some more screamin'. Just after d'first screamin', Greene come in d'house and lays down cross his bed."

"Go on."

"Then I hears Mistah Tom callin' for Greene. He gits up and goes to d'doe. I hears Mistah Tom tell'im that someone had broken into d' house and killed his pa and ma."

"Where were you at the time?"

"I was in d'big room."

"What happened then?"

"Greene come in and tells Little Greene t'go t'Mistah Yates and tell'im 'bout d'trouble at d'Cap'n's house."

"Did you see Jim Foster that night?"

"Nawsur."

"Did you see Anderson James that night?"

"I don't know no Anson James. I don't know nobody there 'cept Greene's family."

"What happened then?"

"Well...after Mistah Tom went back up to d'house, this barefooted colored man come up and talks to Greene."

"What did they say?"

"I couldn't hear'em...they talk real low. Then d'nigga goes away."

"Where did he go? Back up to the house?"

"Nawsur, he went d'other way, 'way from d'house. After while I see Mistah Yates and d'other white men come."

"What did you do after that?"

"I waited til light and I went home."

"Why didn't you hang around and tell the Sheriff what you saw?"

"I didn't see anythin'. Inways...I was skeered."

"Your witness."

"Miz Bird," Felton said from his seat, "when did you arrive in Perry?"

"Wednesday night." The woman was apprehensive.

"Where did you stay?"

"In a stable."

"And do you recall having a conversation with me and Mr. Hardeman there yesterday morning where you told us you weren't on the Woolfolk's place that night...that you were at home in Monroe County?"

"If I told you so...I was skeered," she answered.

"Did we do anything to scare you?"

"Nawsur...but I was skeered anyhow."

Augustus Trippe, the former slave of Judge Robert Trippe from Forsyth, Georgia, took the stand.

"Is it true, Mister Trippe, that you used to live on the Woolfolk plantation?"

"Yassur. I lived there three months last year."

"And who did you live with?"

"I lived at Tom Banks."

"This is after the farm was closed down? Who else lived there?"

"Greene Lockett and John Jeff."

"Do you see Judge Robert Trippe sitting in the audience?"

"Yassur...he's right over there," the witness answered and pointed to his employer.

"Do you remember telling the Judge about a conversation you had with Anderson James?"

"Nawsur."

"You never told him that Anderson James told you about the killing?"

"I never said nothing to d'Judge about no killin'. I...I heard Anderson say d'Cap'n was a fine man."

"Did James ever threaten you...say that he'd kill you if you told about the murder?"

"Nawsur. He ain't never threatened me."

"What did you say to Judge Trippe?"

"I object!" Felton jumped from his chair. "A conversation between third parties concerning a crime is not pertinent to the case."

"Sustained. The witness and jury will disregard the question."

"Your Honor," Rutherford reacted in astonishment, "I request hearing on this matter."

"After the jury is retired, counselor, I will permit arguments."

Slowly, one by one, the jurors filed out of the courtroom. Rutherford waited until the door closed behind them.

"Your Honor, the conversation between the witness and Judge Trippe is directly related to the case. The jury has agreed to hear all the truth, but the rule of the court has excluded part of the truth. Augustus Trippe told the Judge that Anderson James told him exactly how each member of the family had been killed. Afterwards, when confronted, the witness denies this. We intend to prove it by placing Judge Trippe on the stand. The witness is clearly withholding evidence out of intimidation from other parties."

"The testimony is inadmissable. The witness will not answer the question," Judge Gustin ruled.

Miller and Rutherford both shouted their objections in unison. The Judge tapped his gavel.

"The court has ruled the evidence inadmissable. Bailiff, recall the jury."

"The defense calls William McKay."

"Your Honor, the State requests the jury retire as this evidence is hearsay."

"The jury will retire."

"Your Honor!" Rutherford said pleadingly.

"The jury will retire so that the court can consider the admissability of this testimony."

After the jury left the room, McKay recalled buying an ox from George Caldwell. "He had stolen it from Captain Woolfolk," the witness explained. "The Captain asked me to prosecute because he was afraid Caldwell would do him harm."

"What happened to Caldwell?" Rutherford asked.

"He was prosecuted and convicted but he knocked the jailer down and escaped some time before the killin'."

Judge Gustin ruled that the witness could make his statement to the jury but would not be allowed to quote the Captain. Rutherford objected. Gustin overruled and ordered the jury back in.

The defense then presented three witnesses–R.L. Bradley, Wiley Jones, and Mrs. S. M. Fletcher–who testified that Tom always spoke highly of his father, stepmother and her children. Tom lived at Mrs. Fletcher's boarding house prior to going back to the farm.

"He said he loved his stepmother as well as he could have loved his own mother," Mrs. Fletcher stated. "He would often praise Pearl and said Rosebud was a very sweet child."

The first member of the family to take the stand on Tom's behalf, Flo Edwards, was unable to hold back her tears. The emotional strain she was under was evident to everyone in the room. She struggled to answer the defense's questions about her brother and her family. No longer able to hold up to the stress, she began to cry. Rutherford waited for her to regain control before continuing with his questions. The sobs continued.

When it became apparent her sister was losing control on the witness stand, Lillie rushed up to her and helped her from the chair. Rutherford turned to the Judge.

"Your Honor, the defense requests a postponement of Mrs. Edwards' testimony. She is not well."

"Granted."

Fannie Crane and then Love Shackleford were called to the stand. Both reiterated their testimonies from the original trial.

Edgar Ross took the stand and identified himself as a farmer who lived ten miles from the Woolfolk plantation. A side door opened, and Jack Dubose walked in escorted by a deputy. The witness stopped talking and watched the prisoner walk over to a chair that was strategically placed within the bar and sat down. The deputy remained at his side. Quiet whispers drifted across the room.

"Mr. Ross," Rutherford continued, "do you recognize this man?" he asked, pointing to Dubose.

"Yes, I do. His name is Jack Dubose."

"How do you know Mr. Dubose?"

"I had hired him to work on my farm."

"When was that?"

"It was the Monday after the murder."

"So, you are testifying that this man was on your property, ten miles away from the Woolfolk plantation three days after the Woolfolk family was killed.

"Yes."

"How long did he work for you?"

"Half a day."

"What was he wearing?"

"He had on trousers, shirt, a slouch hat, and no shoes."

"Had you ever seen this man before that day?"

"No."

Two additional witnesses, Spencer Zachery and Cilla Darden, testified they also saw Dubose around that time and dressed as described. Mrs. Darden added that she saw scars on Dubose's ankles.

"Now then, Mrs. Darden, would you please tell us what Jack Dubose said about the Woolfolks?" Rutherford asked.

The State objected and was sustained. Gustin instructed the jury to disregard the question.

Rutherford called Washington A. Kitchen to the stand who identified himself as Sheriff of Cherokee County, north of Atlanta. The witness pointed Jack Dubose out and recalled arresting him.

The court would not allow testimony about Dubose admitting he was on the plantation the night of the murders and seeing Tom Woolfolk jump out of the window. The jury was removed, and Rutherford proceeded to reiterate vehemently his argument on why the testimony should be heard.

"Your Honor, absolutely no effort was made by the authorities to find out if suspicion was directed to men other than Thomas Woolfolk."

Hardeman rose to his feet. "That is not true, Your Honor. No information of the arrest of Dubose and his confession reached me except through the newspapers as interviewed by Frank Walker."

Court refused to allow the testimony.

Rutherford recalled Nancy Bird who denied she had contradicted her testimony. The defense then submitted excerpts from the transcripts of the first trial.

"There were discrepancies in testimonies, Your Honor. These contradictions, however, were not made by this witness," Rutherford announced. "No. Your Honor, let the record show that the contradictions in testimony were made by George Yates, I.P. Davis, James J. Holly, Henry Brown, Greene Lockett, Jim Foster, and Jerry Hollis."

CHAPTER TWENTY-THREE

"Richard rushed in ahead of me...
and saved my life."

Sunday, June 16th, Folsom visited the Houston County Jail.

"Tom?" he called out as he entered the cell block.

"Folsom," the prisoner responded, getting up from his cot and walking over to the bars, "its good t'see ya."

"So...how do you think the trial's going for you?"

Tom propped a hand against the bar, cocked his right foot crossed his left and stared down at the floor for a moment. Folsom waited patiently.

"Well...I tell ya...I believe that I'll come out all right."

"You do?"

"Yeh...you know, a man shouldn't be judged by the lies told about him. All they say in court don't amount to anything. The lawyers talked about the horror of this thing...and it was...then a lot of lies were sworn to...then some more horror talk and more lies were sworn. But we can bust some bombs, too, as you'll see tomorrow."

After visiting with the prisoner a few minutes more, Folsom made his exit through the cell block. At the end of the aisle, he looked in a cell and saw Jack Dubose pacing back and forth.

"Hey, Dubose. Come here," Folsom called out.

The prisoner glared at him. His deep, close-set eyes shot daggers at the reporter. Folsom took a step back and called him again.

"I said get over here, boy. I want to ask you a few more questions," he said with authority.

Sheriff Cooper instructed him earlier to refrain from discussing the trial with Dubose as he was still considered a witness. The reporter agreed to the conditions.

"What do ya want t'axk me?" the prisoner finally responded.

"How old are you?"

Dubose let out a sharp laugh. "I'm a hundred and fifty years old."

"How long you been out of the pen?"

"Two years...and I don't know a damn thang 'bout this thang."

"So, why are you here?"

"They wants my blood 'cause my hair's short...but they won't git it. I'll make'em smell hell in d'courthouse t'morrow...the Judge and all. I'll floor'em with a chair." The prisoner stopped, looked around, and then put his face against the bars. "I saw somethin' in d'office...I'm gonna git it." He looked around again.

"How?" Folsom humored him.

"Take it...just like I gits everthang else I wants."

Rutherford began the ninth day of trial by adding to the record the original testimonies of Sarah Hardin, Julia Woolfolk, and Joseph Dannenberg showing the contradictions they also made in their more recent testimonies. He then called Lillie Cowan to the stand.

Lillie repeated the testimony she gave at the first trial and was turned over to the State for questioning.

"Did you not say, at the home of Mrs. Edwards, in the presence of Mrs. Stewart, the Friday after the killing, that Tom evidently did the killing?"

Rutherford and Miller exploded to their feet and shouted their objections. Beneath it all, Folsom heard Lillie faintly answer 'No'. The defense requested the jury be removed for argument. Rutherford contested the admissibility of the question. District Attorney Guerry responded by saying she made the statement. Lillie jumped to her feet.

"I positively deny it," she cried and then collapsed into the chair crying bitterly. Tom shifted in his seat and turned, pleadingly, to his lawyers. His sister's tears caused him to become agitated and angry.

Guerry looked at the witness and then back at the Judge.

"We propose to prove it," he said calmly.

"I will not allow the question," Gustin answered.

"Your Honor," Guerry continued, "the State presents a motion to rule out any testimony made by family members as to the defendant's attitude toward the family."

Gustin overruled the motion, recalled the jury, and instructed it to disallow the previous question. Lillie was excused, and Flo was called.

"Now, Mrs. Edwards, would you please tell the court the circumstances that brought about Tom going to your father's the Saturday before the killing?" Rutherford asked.

"Tom was living at the Southern Hotel in Macon. Father sent for him. Tom was unwilling to go but did anyway. He didn't carry any clothes."

"So he wasn't intending to stay?"

The State objected. The defense was asking for an opinion. The court sustained.

"What was your brother's feelings towards the stepfamily?"

"I would say it was the same as any other brother. He called our stepmother 'mother'."

"Did he claim any property from your real mother?"

"No."

Felton began his cross-examination by standing up, adjusting his vest, and casually walking towards the witness stand. Flo waited patiently. There was no residual symptoms of her emotional collapse the day before.

"Mrs. Edwards," he began, "didn't you say, in the presence of Mrs. Stewart..."

Tom again bolted up right in his seat and, again, the defense attorneys loudly objected. Gustin sent the jury out of the courtroom and ruled the inadmissibility of the questions. He then recalled the jury. Tom called Rutherford over to the table and huddled in an intense conference with his three attorneys. As the jurors reentered the room, Rutherford looked up, asked that the jury again retire, and requested a moment of privacy to consult with his client. Gustin granted the recess and excused the witness.

Tom sat down in the witness chair. He held a Bible. The room was deadly quiet. He turned to face the jury. He pulled a sheet of paper from the book and began to speak in a calm but sincere voice.

"Gentlemen, I am an innocent man. I went to my father's from Macon a week before the killing at his request. I expected to stay a day or two. He insisted, and I remained and went to work on the farm.

"The night before, I talked with my father about the sawmill he sold Birch Horn, who mistreated him. We retired to our rooms about nine. I took water and washed in the room where Richard and me slept. Richard went to town Wednesday or Thursday. I asked him to bring my clothes from my sister's and a bundle from the hotel. He brought the bundle only...one suit and a shirt. I put on that shirt the night before the killings...didn't change the drawers.

"About two the next morning, I was awakened by a noise in my father's room. I jumped up and started in. Richard rushed in ahead of me...and saved my life." He paused. His elbows were resting on the chair arms. No one moved.

"I heard a blow...and Richard fall. I jumped out of the window, ran to Greene Lockett's, told him to get the gun and help me protect the family, somebody had broken in the house. He wouldn't go. I was frightened myself.

"I met Anderson James and asked him to go with me. We started, but, half way, Anderson said he heard somebody in the house, and he ran back. I was scared nearly to death, and sat down on the ground. I heard the murderers run out of the house...dogs barking...and back gate slam. They went to Tom Banks' house.

"When all was quiet...I walked cautiously into the house...still very frightened. I had no sense hardly. I went into my father's room. I picked mother up and put her on the bed...her face was nearly on the floor...her legs on the bed. Can't say I picked anybody up in the hall. I...I think I picked Pearl up and placed her on the bed." He shifted in his seat and continued.

"I tried to find matches and see if they were all dead, thinking I might save the little one. Got blood on my hands. I slung it off and half way washed my hands and wiped them on the towel. I was...I was...uh, troubled with my bowels. Went out, took my drawers down and got the blood on my thigh. I went back to try to get the children out.

"I went back to Lockett's and asked him to go in the house with me. He wouldn't. Said he heard a noise and guessed I did. I went in the house again. Came out and called Lockett...who said he was sick. The others came up. I told Smith there is blood on my hands and feet, and would go and wash. I drew water from the well and washed in my room. The second time I used a towel. About half way washed, I had on my shirt and drawers...went in the room...put on the clothes. I laid down on the porch.

"Mrs. Chambless, a relative of the prosecutor, came up and accused me of killing the family and told others I did it. The coroner's jury took my shirt off...saw the blood on it...and no blood on my body. They asked for the shirt I pulled off the night before...got it behind the box. The shirt and drawers were not too large.

"I thought the blood on my thigh was dirt...but remembered putting my hand there, and explained how the blood came there. I told the jury I didn't know why the strings on the drawers were not bloody." He stopped and cleared his throat.

"I never had that conversation with Dannenberg. He testified from malice. I would not let him take the store I rented from him and rent to Worsham for a higher price. The clothes taken from the well are not mine...John Owens is a bad character...he's cut two men...been in the chaingang for stealing. I heard him say he'd paint the house red. I didn't say what he testified.

"I pray every night. I don't care who hears me. I am innocent and could not have said what Birdsong said I did. I never talked with Crawford Wilson about the family...he lied. Bone Davis is a liar. I didn't talk with him as he said I did.

"I declare to the jury I am innocent of this crime. I couldn't get justice in Bibb, but hope I will get it here. I want justice...but I don't ask for mercy. If you are afraid to say I am innocent...have the manhood to say so. If you think I am guilty...say so. I am not tried before a king. Don't let prejudice govern your verdict. Don't regard the wishes of Bibb County people, nor any people here, but do right. I trust my life to your honor."

He folded the paper he used only a few times as a reference, stood up, and walked back to his seat. Folsom, as did everyone, watched him sit down. He seemed relieved somewhat. Rutherford stood up.

"The defense rests, Your Honor."

Tom had his say ,but it was not over. Felton stood and called the State's first rebuttal witness, Tom's cousin, Sallie Woolfolk, Major Thomas J. Woolfolk's daughter.

"Now, do you recall a conversation you had with the defendant in June of eighty-seven?" Felton asked.

"Yes, I do."

"Would you please tell us about it?"

"I was at Flo Edward's house. Tom was there and somehow we began talking about Aunt Mattie. Tom said that she had her finger in my eyes but not his. He said she was as mean as the devil, and that he hated her as if she was a devil."

As a result of that statement, an argument ensued that lasted two and a half hours. In the end, the defense asked that statements about Mattie Woolfolk be disallowed.

"Your Honor, the defendant is on trial for killing his father...not his stepmother."

"I will allow the line of questioning, Mistah Rutherford," Gustin said and ordered the jury back in.

Three additional witnesses were presented–Tom's cousin, Millie, who was Sallie's sister, Millie's husband, Ben Stewart, and Mary Reese–who each testified to various statements Tom made in anger about his father and stepmother.

The testimonies of Nancy Bird and Sam Pennington were challenged by witnesses. The State then clarified contradictions made by Greene Lockett.

Folsom remained in his seat as the courtroom emptied. He was exhausted and emotionally drained. The detective who had been guarding Dubose sat down beside him.

"Just thought you'd like to know," he looked around and then continued in a low voice, "Dubose's been charged as an accessory to murder."

Folsom looked at him is total amazement.

"The Woolfolk murder?"

"The Woolfolk murder," the detective answered.

Top: Left, Millie Woolfolk Stewart; Right, Ben Stewart.
Bottom: Sarah (Sallie) Woolfolk
(Photos courtesy of Millie C. Stewart)

CHAPTER TWENTY-FOUR
"He showed no grief."

Tuesday morning, June 18, Tom took his place at the defense table, picked up his book and began to read. The State continued in its rebuttal by presenting five witnesses supporting the honesty of Crawford Wilson and I.P. Davis followed with George Yates and William Smith countering parts of Tom's statement. Jerry Hollis clarified parts of his testimony. Immediately upon his release as a witness, however, he was arrested and charged with selling property he did not own.

The superintendent of the Bibb County chaingang verified that George Caldwell was in his custody during the night of the murders. The original trial transcript was studied and the charge of discrepancy overruled. The owner of a farm in Monroe County swore Nancy Bird was home the night of the murder.

By mid-afternoon, the State closed. Rutherford began his sur-rebuttal by calling six witnesses who testified that Nancy Bird had not been coerced into testifying. A little after four, however, he had to request a recess so Pennington could be located. Gustin granted the time but warned that he had until the morning. If Pennington was not found and the sur-rebuttal involving him not presented, the final arguments would begin.

That evening Folsom looked in on Tom in his cell.

"So...whatta you think?" he asked.

Tom smiled. "I hope to be acquitted."

"What about the other eight indictments?"

"Well...if Bibb County can stand it...I can."

Sam Pennington was not located and final arguments began the morning of June 19, 1889.

The court room was full and overflowing. Flower arrangements were placed on the defense and prosecution tables as well as the Judge's bench. Tom's cousin, Mrs. Ben Stewart, gave the prosecutors a bouquet while Fannie Crane pinned a flower to Tom's lapel. The Woolfolk clan was divided.

Felton was the first to speak. For four hours, the fair haired, clean shaven man talked about the murders and the evidence. He then proceeded to point out those areas in the defense's case that gave him problems.

"Three quarters of an hour elapsed between the time of the murder and when he called Greene Lockett. He made no suggestion to the neighbors who came that a search should be made for the murderers. He showed no grief."

At 2:25, Clinton C. Duncan rose for the defense. He defined circumstantial evidence and for an hour argued that the State's case was built on presumptions, hearsay, lies, and prejudice.

Next, John Hardeman approached the jury box. The former solicitor towered over the jurymen as he described in minute details the mutilation, the horror, the blood.

Folsom looked around the room. He had never seen so many women, especially young ones, at a trial. The handsome, quiet defendant with the dark eyes was an attraction for many a feminine heart. All members of the audience were visibly shakened. Tears filled eyes. Muscles twitched in tightly clinched jaws.

Tom appeared anxious. His motions were jerky and nervous. He picked up his book and then put it down. He looked at the audience, smile weakly and then turned back around. When facing front he rocked back and forth, slowly, as if responding to some silent beat. Moments later, he picked up the book and the cycle began again.

Someone gasped. The reporter's attention was suddenly jerked back to Hardeman.

"... in a death struggle with Pearl," the attorney was saying. "she desperately clutched her brutal assailant, leaving the imprint of her bloody hand upon his thigh. His thigh!" Hardeman yelled, pointing at Tom.

The next day Alexander Miller continued with the defense's argument, "The issue here is one of life or death, gentlemen of the jury. There can be no half way ground, but an unqualified verdict of guilt or…innocence." Four hours later, after adamantly declaring Tom Woolfolk innocent, he turned the floor over to Rutherford.

The room shifted forward. No one spoke. Not a sound was made. Rutherford began quietly.

"Gentlemen, I am a stranger to you and you to me…but we are here for a common purpose…to ascertain the truth." Heads nodded in agreement.

Tom leaned forward and focused his attention on his attorney.

"This case is different from any other I have ever known where the man is first arrested and then evidence is searched for and found…instead of first finding the evidence."

Folsom furiously tried to record Rutherford's words as the attorney stormed around the room, yelling and gesturing wildly. He then calmed and said softly, "If he be proven guilty, no man will quicker than I join the cry, 'HANG HIM! HANG HIM!' But the evidence does not establish guilt."

The reporter pondered the point made by the defense. Tom had been arrested before any evidence implicated him. After he was placed in jail evidence was brought forward. Some of the clothing allegedly retrieved from the well was brought in more than a week later.

The authorities made no effort to look for other suspects. Tom was immediately assumed guilty.

The following evening, after Rutherford's day long speech, Folsom returned to his hotel room. He was tired. In addition to his regular news beat he had for two years obsessed about Tom's case. Just as Walker had to resign from illness and Rutherford was on the verge of a relapse, the reporter was nearing exhaustion.

He picked up the Atlanta Constitution, read his report first and then proceeded to peruse the paper. On page two an article caught his attention. Recently, the State of New York was considering electrocution as a more humane means of execution over hanging. "Hanging is brutal," a Judge was quoted. "It is repulsive. It does no good by force of example more than death by other means would do…and it is horrible to the extreme.

"I infinitely prefer electricity," the quote continued, "it is a clean, speedy and humane death...and may not be compared to the brutality of hanging..."

Folsom shuddered and closed the paper. He would read no more of hanging and execution. He needed to sleep. He wanted rest.

John Rutherford looked exhausted. For a day and a half he relentlessly and dramatically presented the defense's case. Saturday morning, June 22, he again rose to his feet to continue to plead for Tom Woolfolk's life.

"Nothing is so certain as the unexpected," he said. "The reasoning of the prosecution is wrong...fitting the man to the circumstances instead of the circumstances to the man."

He then spoke for another six and a half hours. "Gentlemen, I thank you," he finally said. He bowed slightly to the Judge, turned around, walked over to the table, picked up his brief case and walked out of the courtroom.

The Perry Hotel
(Photo courtesy of Harold Green, owner of the New Perry Hotel)

Folsom slept late Sunday and spent the day resting in his room. By evening he was ready for a stroll. The reporter walked along slowly, breathing the cool night air. Beneath an open window he stopped and listened. Above his head members of the jury, sequestered together at the Perry Hotel for the night, were singing a hymn.

"There is a fountain filled with blood."

A chill shot through his body. He pulled his coat tightly about him, tilted his hat down to his eyebrows, and walked away.

The State concluded its argument with Dupont Guerry, Monday, June 24. The prosecutor spoke a total of six and a half hours.

"I hope and pray he may make peace with his Maker," Guerry said in closing, "and prepare for the great change to come. We ask nothing in the spirit of vengeance. We simply ask that you, gentlemen of the jury, rise up in your majesty as representatives of society and the country. We ask the just performance of your duty. That is all we ask, and think we have the right to demand it. Render a verdict in accordance with the facts...and we will be satisfied with your judgement."

Guerry returned to his seat. Gustin charged the jury with its task, explained the law, defined certain legal phrases, and sent them to chambers. Forty five minutes later, the twelve men returned.

Folsom watched Tom as the guilty verdict was read. The defendant seemed to jerk slightly. His skin paled. He blinked as tears filled his eyes. Behind him Flo, Lillie, Love and Fannie remained still.

No one in the audience moved. The room was deadly quiet. Rutherford stood up and announced the defense would appeal. Gustin dismissed the jury.

"A recess is declared," he announced, "until nine o'clock tomorrow morning when sentence will be passed." Having so adjourned the proceedings, the Judge left the courtroom.

A deputy walked over and began placing the leg irons on Tom's ankles while Sheriff Cooper shackled his wrists. Rutherford grasped Tom's hand.

"I told you before the verdict would not stand. I tell you now ...this verdict will not stand. You can rest as easy as if at home in your bed, so far as this verdict is concerned."

The ankle bracelets secured, Cooper took his prisoner by the elbow and waited patiently. Tom turned and smiled weakly at his lawyer.

"Oh...I ain't afraid."

CHAPTER TWENTY-FIVE

"Dubose told him that the old man's name was Woolfolk."

Jackson Dubose, escorted by Nat Birdsong and manacled at his ankles and wrists, hobbled through the cell block. Charged as an accomplice to the Woolfolk murders, he was brought back to Macon to await his trial.

He walked along slowly, looking in each cell as he passed. He stopped and stared at a prisoner chained at the neck to the wall of a cell. The two men looked at each other for only a moment before the tethered prisoner dropped his eyes. Dubose stayed rooted to the spot. Birdsong reached up and gave him a slight push.

"Git goin'," he barked.

Dubose stumbled slightly, righted himself, and walked on. The jailer opened a cell door and pushed him inside. Dubose waited until his shackles were removed and Birdsong left before calling out to the other prisoner.

"Hey," he yelled, "what you in here for?"

There was no response.

"I'm talkin' t'you."

"What you want?" Came the reply.

"What's your name?"

"Joe Warren."

"What you in here for, Joe Warren. What you do?"

"Made some money."

"Made money? Why they put you in jail fo makin' some money?"

"Not that kind of money. Counterfeit."

"What they give you for som'n like that?"

"I's a federal prisoner. Got six years."

"Why they got you chained up like that?"
"Hell if I know."

Folsom locked his trunk and surveyed the room a final time before sending his luggage on to the depot. Exhausted, he had decided to take a trip to Saint Simons Island off the coast of South Georgia for a much needed rest. Originally planning to go immediately after the trial, he was delayed a few days settling a sensation caused by an article Pea Jay had reported in the Constitution.

The report that a black woman was admitted to Tom's cell, in Perry, and allowed to stay with him several hours was, of course, a rumor. The scandal it caused, nevertheless, resulted in a scramble by Houston County officials to adamantly and vehemently deny it. Along with Sheriff Cooper, thirty one respected citizens of the area endorsed Folsom's follow up article with the publication of their names.

The reporter pondered the events associated with the trial and chuckled slightly to himself. The very name of Woolfolk evoked a sensation and anyone associated with him in any way was given notoriety. Some used it to their advantage. It appeared to him that Sam Chambless, John Hardeman, and even William Felton had gained some political ground.

Others were affected in other ways. With Major Thomas Woolfolk's daughters testifying against Tom, the Woolfolk family was torn apart. The sisters and other relatives lost their privacy and in some cases the friendship of their neighbors while the local law officers enjoyed a new sense of community respect and appreciation. Jailer Birdsong, in particular, was given widespread support when he was charged with contempt of court and fined by a United States judge for chaining the federal prisoner, Joe Warren, by the neck.

When Folsom asked Westcott about it, the Sheriff explained that the prisoner was hostile and unruly. The reporter reflected on Tom's imprisonment. During his entire stay at the Bibb County jail, while awaiting his trials, he was also chained in a similar although less severe fashion. Tom, himself, admitted he gave his keepers a hard time that probably resulted in the chaining. Folsom could tell the chains caused him serious discomfort and anxiety.

Finally, at the expense of Joe Warren, the extreme measure was made known to a federal judge who penalized the jailer and put an immediate stop to the practice.

Even though it would be by train, hack, and finally boat, the reporter looked forward to his journey to the Golden Isle. The late night hack ride to the depot through the rain gave him a sense of escape. Reining the buggy onto Fourth Street, the driver brought the horse to a steady trot.

"What's the hurry?" Folsom asked.

"I got's to git over t'the jail after I drops ya off. The Sheriff wants me to carry him 'n a deputy back to the depot t'pick up an important prisoner comin' in."

"Where's he coming from? Do you know?"

"I b'lieve he's comin' in from Fort Valley."

"Tom." Folsom muttered to himself. "Driver, I've decided not to go just yet. I'll go on to the jail with you."

"If you say so, boss."

The buggy rolled passed the depot and crossed the tracks. Lights at the jail house reflected activity as the driver pulled into the yard. Folsom hopped down.

"Tell the Sheriff I'm here when he needs to go."

"I will," he answered, ran up to the door, and rapped loudly. Birdsong opened it and shook his head.

"I'll be damn. Folsom. How is it that yer here this time of the night?"

"I want to be here when you bring Tom Woolfolk in."

"Tom…who says he's comin' back t'night?"

"I've got my sources. Sheriff Westcott," Folsom called out to the Sheriff. "What time are you going to the depot to pick up Tom Woolfolk?"

Westcott looked at Folsom then Birdsong. Birdsong protested his innocence. The Sheriff shook his head.

"You beat all Folsom. You know that?"

"So…it's true Tom Woolfolk's comin' in tonight."

"Yeh. Judge Gustin notified me yesterday that he ordered Sheriff Cooper to deliver him to me tonight."

"Why are ya'll bringing him back here?"

"I guess the Judge don't like the treatment he gets in Houston County."

"You talking about that woman? You know as well as I do that was nothing but a lie...probably to make Cooper look bad."

"I know, but the Judge didn't like all the publicity it caused. True or not, it didn't sit well with him. So he's ordered Tom back here where we can keep a close eye on him."

"Mind if I tag along with you? I'll be sure to stay outta you way."

"Sure. Come on."

Westcott put on his hat, took a shot gun from a cabinet and joined his deputy at the door. The deputy raised a pair of shackles signaling he was ready. The three men climbed aboard Folsom's buggy and rode away.

At the depot Folsom did as he had promised and stood at a distance. He watched as Sheriff Cooper, his deputy, and Tom Woolfolk climbed down from the train. The prisoner wore only handcuffs. Westcott greeted the Sheriff with a handshake and conversed while the Bibb deputy kneeled down and put leg irons on Tom's ankles. Westcott waited for the Houston deputy to remove his bracelets. He then locked on a pair.

Tom remained quiet. He did not look around. He said nothing. The Houston County officers each shook his hand, told him goodbye, and then boarded the train. Westcott took Tom by the elbow and escorted him through the rear of the depot to the waiting hack. Folsom joined them there.

"How ya doin' Tom?" the reporter asked quietly.

Tom looked at him, nodded a greeting, and then climbed into the buggy. The loudly clanking of his chains forced Westcott to cautiously look around. They had not attracted attention. After all were on board, the driver whipped his horse to a gallop and raced the party back to the jail.

Folsom climbed down, followed by the deputy, Tom, and then Westcott. Birdsong opened the door and the group filed inside. There was no conversation. Tom remained totally subdued.

"Well...I'll see ya Tom," Folsom said and reached out to shake his hand. Tom smiled weakly but said nothing. He grasped the reporter's hand tightly.

Folsom donned his hat and made his exit. He hurried back to the depot. He had missed his train but needed to get a message as soon as possible to the Constitution and tell them the news. Tom Woolfolk was back in the Bibb County jail.

On the fifth of July, Jackson Dubose was escorted to the courthouse for his trial. Other than the Judge, his clerk, and the bailiffs no one else showed up. There was no one to prosecute him, no one to defend him.

The Judge, aware that Dubose had been held against his will weeks before actually being charged, was determined to rectify the situation. After an hour conference with the prisoner he decided to drop the charge of accessory to the Woolfolk murder. DuBose was then tried on a writ of lunacy, declared insane, and sent to the asylum.

Folsom walked along the dark beach and marvelled at the sounds and smells of the ocean. The silver rays of the moon glistened between the storm clouds in the distance and reflected upon the water. He stopped and examined a dead jelly fish washed ashore. It's crystal clear body moved in synchronized motion with each wave. He prodded it with his walking stick. The gelatin mass wiggled and wobbled but did not rupture.

The reporter straightened up and filled his lungs with the warm night air. His depression was preventing sleep. The nightly walks were necessary to calm his thoughts. A single streak of lightning shot across the horizon. He stopped and waited for the distant thunder. The soft rumble was lost in the waves.

In front of him the flare of a match as an unknown hand brought it to a cigarette alerted him to the stranger's presence.

"Hello," he called out as he approached the dark figure perched on the half buried bow of a wreck. Startled, the man started to jump down.

"I'm sorry. I didn't mean to disturb you. Please. Go back to what you were doing."

The man cautiously settled back into his seat. Folsom looked around, shoved his hands deep into his pockets, and sighed. The broad beam from the light house rotated across the sky periodically illuminating the area enough for him to see the well dressed man sitting nearby.

"Gonna rain," the stranger finally said.

"Yes, yes it is. Mind if I join you?" the reporter asked.

"Not at all. I like to come out hear and watch the waves at night. It helps me think. Know what I mean?"

"I sure do," Folsom said, sitting down beside the man.

"You from around here?"

"No...I'm from Macon, Georgia. I write for the Atlanta Constitution."

"I read your paper alot during the Woolfolk trials."

"Do you think Woolfolk will hang?" Folsom asked.

The stranger pulled a long drag from his cigarette and slowly exhaled the smoke. He flicked the ashes away.

"I don't think anything about that," he finally answered. "I know positively that Woolfolk will hang."

"How do you know this?" Folsom asked studying the man closely.

"Well...," he began cautiously, tossing the cigarette into the ocean, "I've a secret which I've kept many a year. One I thought to keep through my life."

"If you know something about the case...something not generally known...I'd wish you'd tell me. I can promise you total anonymity."

"Well...as you insist...I'll take you into my confidence. I was living near there when the news of that horrible butchery spread like wild fire across the country. It was but a few hours to the scene of the murder. I was in the company of several friends and started out for the Woolfolk plantation." The man stopped and shuddered.

Folsom listened as he recalled his vivid memories of that day two years earlier. The reporter was impressed with the man's articulation. He was well educated. His accent was refined Southern.

"The coroner's jury was preparin' to render a verdict and I had started to walk away...when someone handed me a note which said, 'You are requested to attend a meeting in the oak grove just behind the house. Don't come unless you are every inch a man.'

"I proceeded at once to the spot and to my surprise found twenty six men in solemn counsel. I knew at a glance what it meant.

I knew that this band of men proposed to do away with the tediousness of court proceedings by handling Tom Woolfolk on the spot."

Folsom's jaw dropped. The man was sincere. The reporter believed what he was telling him.

"I joined'em...heart and hand and after makin' some arrangements...which I won't tell you...we all returned to the house for the purpose of carryin' out our plans...but the officers were too shrewd. They suspected this....and hurried their prisoner to Macon.

"Well...we mounted our horses and went in hot pursuit, but...Woolfolk had been in jail a full fifteen minutes before our arrival. I heard nothing further of this until the trial came off in Macon. Towards the close...I received a short letter saying that my presence was needed there. I returned by the first train and again found the same twenty six waiting.

"The last day of the trial...various conjectures were made in regard to the verdict...every member was in the courtroom when the jury returned. We were armed to the teeth...had that jury acquitted Tom Woolfolk...he would have been riddled by twenty seven bullets."

Folsom leaned against a protruding beam. Lightning danced about the sky. Thunder grew louder. The storm was near. The man continued talking, choosing his words carefully.

"The jury pronounced him guilty...and we went away thinking that justice would soon be satisfied. Some time ago I received another communication tellin' me that I must go to Perry. I went...and if Woolfolk had not been pronounced guilty again, I would have been one of the twenty seven who had made it their business to put an end to this...this...brute."

Pea Jay hurried to the jail house and was permitted to see Tom.

"Woolfolk, got some news for ya," he said loudly as he walked up to the cell door.

Tom was lying on his cot, reading a book. The reporter peered through the bars.

"I said I got news for ya."

Tom ignored him and continued to read.

"It's about your wife Georgia…did ya know she's filed for a divorce?"

"No…I didn't know. But it doesn't surprise me."

"So, would you like to make a statement?"

"No. No statement," he said not looking up from his book.

"Nothing at all?" the reporter asked.

Tom ignored him. Pea Jay tried again.

"How's it feel…knowin' you're going to hang soon."

Tom slammed his book with a loud bang and bolted from his bed. His hands grabbed the bars before Pea Jay had a chance to jump back.

"I will never hang," the prisoner growled. "You can rest assured of that fact."

The date of Tom's scheduled hanging, August 16, came and went. Tom remained in his cell. His attorneys continued the appeal process. The family received the news with solemn acceptance.

Folsom, still at the coast, sat on the veranda of his hotel and watched the morning waves break into endless rows of white foam. A waiter refreshed his drink and handed him a copy of the Brunswick Times. The reporter casually looked it over and then bolted from his chair.

"Porter," he called, "get me a hack."

Folsom hurriedly put on his coat and hat and followed the uniformed man through the lobby and out the front door.

"Get me to the ferry as fast as possible," the reporter yelled up to the driver.

"Yassa, boss," the driver answered and laid a whip across the rump of his horse.

News that Tom had not eaten for six days greatly alarmed the Woolfolk clan. Love Shackleford immediately went to Macon to see about his cousin's health. Birdsong opened the door to the cell block.

"Go on in. He's down at the end."

"Thank you," Shackleford said and walked between the rows of cages until he came to Tom's cell. The prisoner was thinner but did not look ill.

"Tom?"

Tom looked up and smiled. "L.A.," he said, "what're you doing here?"

"I heard you've decided to starve yourself. That true?"

"Well...I'm not going to eat anymore of the swill they serve here. I told them I wanted food from the Lanier House...I'd even paid for it myself."

"Food that bad here?"

"Bad enough for me not to eat a bite for a week."

Jailer Birdsong walked up.

"I brought ya alittle somethin' t'eat Tom."

Tom looked at the tray. It held a little rice, gravy and a biscuit.

"That all?"

"You shouldn't eat anymore than this with your stomach empty so long," the jailer answered.

"He's right, Tom," Shackleford offered.

"I'll be damned...you bring me a cup more of rice and four more biscuits and I'll eat."

"This is all you're gittin' Tom."

"Then...take it away. I'm not eating until you learn to feed a man right."

The jailer looked at Shackleford and then back at Tom. The prisoner turned his back to the door and dropped back down onto his cot. The two men walked away.

Folsom rushed into the Brunswick Times front office and asked the clerk if he could speak with the author of the article, entitled "The Woolfolk Tragedy." Minutes later a young reporter walked out.

"My name is Montgomery Folsom from Macon. I'm with The Atlanta Constitution."

"Ed Lambright," the reporter answered politely and extended his hand. "What can I do for you?"

"I'd like to know more about this article."

The reporter glanced to see which one Folsom was talking about and then smiled broadly.

"Yeh...I guess you would, wouldn't ya. Well, what is it you want to know?"

"Is it true?"

"As best as I can tell at this point, the colored man's story checks out."

"Can you tell me where he is?"

"Well...I don't know."

"Tell you what, I'll send this article on to my paper, complete with your by-line if you'll just let me talk with the man."

"Why would you want to talk with him?"

"I just want to. Can you arrange it for me?"

"I'll see what I can do."

Immediately after reading the article, Rutherford sent an associate, R.C. Jordan, to Brunswick on the next train. Folsom met the young lawyer and drove him directly to the paper.

"Wasn't able to locate the man. Guess he got scared and ran off...or hid out," Folsom informed him.

"That's too bad. With Tom's case going to the Supreme Court soon, it would have helped if we had him."

"Probably thought he'd be arrested."

"And he would have. What do you know about this?"

"Just what was in the paper. A black man by the name of John Richards told two reporters from the Times that he knew who killed the Woolfolk family."

"Did you line up a notorary so we can get affidavits?"

"There's one waiting for us at the paper."

Lambright's statement astounded Rutherford. In addition, Folsom and Jordan were able to locate a witness to the conversation between the man and the two Brunswick reporters. Everything checked out. John Richards was probably telling the truth when he told Lambright that he knew Jack Dubose. Rutherford read the reporter's sworn statement again.

"He said his name was John Richards and that he lived in Americus in 1887 until about two months before the Woolfolks were killed. He said there was a negro working with him named Jack Dubose and that they were good friends.

"One day Dubose went to Macon and Richards didn't see him again until he himself went there. He ran into a crowd of men at the depot and saw Dubose. He said he called out to him and Dubose asked him what he was doing there. Richards answered that he was just there for fun. Dubose asked if he wanted to make a raise. He asked what kind. Dubose told him there was an old man living in the country who kept money in his house. He asked Richards to go with him.

"Dubose told him that the old man's name was Woolfolk. Richards finally agreed to go. Once on the plantation they met a man Dubose knew named Anderson. Richards tried to back out and Anderson told him to shut up. He said he saw the two men, Dubose and Anderson, go in the house and then he saw a white man jump out of the front window. Richards said he heard screaming, got scared and ran away."

Jordan looked at Rutherford's expression and realized the obvious. Unless they could find the man named John Richards and get his statement first hand, the courts would not allow the evidence.

CHAPTER TWENTY-SIX

"I'd rather die than remain in prison another year."

The headlines said it all. Jefferson Davis was dead. Fannie Crane felt the decades old heartache rekindle inside her. The old chieftain was the last flicker of the glorious cause for which so many of her friends and relatives had died.

The death of Davis, December 6, 1889, marked the complete passing of the crown from the old order of Southern leaders to the new. All were gone–Robert Toombs, Howell Cobb, Alexander Hamilton Stephens, Robert E. Lee, Ben Hill, and finally Jeff Davis. The impact rattled the hearts and minds of Southerners everywhere as profoundly as the earthquake rattled the buildings in Macon two months earlier.

Tom received the news in stride. He did not care for the Lost Cause that destroyed his family's wealth. It had not been his war but that of his father and uncles. His life had been reduced to a five by eight cell. Davis' passing meant nothing to him. He felt no remorse, no sense of lost.

After Judge Gustin refused to grant Tom a new trial, he resigned his judgeship. Rutherford's efforts to have Tom's case presented to the Georgia Supreme Court were thwarted by endless postponements. Although Rutherford's health continued to fail, he was relentless.

Tom continued to maintain a low profile in jail. He no longer aggravated his keepers. He stayed deep in thought, withdrawn and said very little.

When word that the Supreme Court had postponed, yet again, the hearing for a new trial reached the jail house, Birdsong hurried to Tom's cell. The prisoner was lying down.

"Tom," the jailer called out.

"What do you want Nat?" Tom said turning over.

"The Supreme Court's postponed your case."

"How do you know that?" he responded, putting his feet on the floor.

"I heard the news from Atlanta today."

"Is that all you woke me up for?" the prisoner asked between a yawn and a stretch. "I'm going back to sleep."

Birdsong watched through the bars as Tom climbed back in bed. "What do you think about the postponement, Tom?" he asked.

"It doesn't bother me any. I reckon I'll just roll in and finish my nap," Tom said wrapping his blanket around him.

Birdsong considered telling him that his wife had been granted a divorce, but decided against it.

Pea Jay examined the razor closely. The tip of the blade was broken and wedged in the handle so it would not retract. The handle was wrapped tightly with string and coated with wax. The maker of the weapon put a great deal of time and energy in constructing it.

"Where did you get this?" he asked the jailer.

Birdsong nodded towards the cell block. "A colored prisoner, Joe Paul, says he got it from Tom Woolfolk."

"Woolfolk? Really? It looks like it's been handled quite a bit." The reporter handed the razor back over. "You believe'im?"

"Nothin' surprises me anymore. Could be Woolfolk's. He's been known to get knives before, y'know."

"I know. What's this colored man in for?"

"Assaultin' an officer."

"And how did he happen to come by the razor?"

"Says he stole it from Tom's cell."

"Does Woolfolk know it's missing?"

"He don't act like it. Probably was plannin' to keep it hid until he got the chance to do me in."

"But I thought Woolfolk's been sick."

"Probably just an act. If you ask me, he was plannin' to kill me or...if all else failed...kill himself. That man swears he ain't gonna hang."

"I guess he's desperate enough to do anything."

Tom sat in the large wash tub and scrubbed with a brush. Nearby, Birdsong hung a clean change of clothes on a nail.

"Tom...they refused to give you a new trial."

"Is that so? Well...I guess it's all right," Tom continued washing. "I thought they would've given me one...but Colonel Rutherford's here yet. I don't believe I'll ever hang."

Birdsong walked over to the clothes Tom had been wearing and began to search through them. As he unrolled the sleeves of the shirt, a small knife fell out.

"Tom!" Birdsong barked.

Tom did not respond. He dried himself and began putting on the clean clothes. The jailer confiscated the weapon and escorted Tom to his new cell, the one directly over Birdsong's living quarters. A guard was already waiting for them.

"What's he here for?"

"He's called the death watch, Tom. Now that the Supreme Court's through, we're gonna keep an eye on you 'til yer hangin'."

"Two juries having found the defendant guilty, and the Judge who presided in the court below being satisfied with their finding, and there being sufficient evidence to uphold the verdict, this court does not feel authorized to disturb it." With those words, the Georgia Supreme Court ruled in favor of the State.

Tom's shoulders dropped. The single paragraph, dwarfed by the thousands of pages of argument sitting on the table, penetrated his heart as would a bullet fired at close range. Rutherford stood nearby and waited for a response.

There was none.

"As I told you, Tom, we're taking this to the United States Supreme Court." He waited but still no response. "And if the court of last resort goes against us...we'll make an appeal to executive clemency."

"So...what now?" Tom finally asked, not looking up from the paper.

"Well, it goes before Judge Lamar. If he should decide that there are grounds for an appeal that would, of course, hold up the sentence, for a considerable time, perhaps three or four years."

"What are my chances for that?"

"I'm not going to mislead you, Tom. Time is running out. The Houston County Superior Court will be convening in October to resentence you. We have until then to get your appeal in motion. I'm going to appeal to executive decision."

"Who you gonna make it to, Gordon or Northen?" Tom asked referring to the newly elected governor.

Rutherford stopped and pondered the question. "I'll appeal to both. It'll either be Gordon's last official act or Northen's first...either way...it must be done."

The third anniversary of the murders prompted Pea Jay to visit the Bibb County Jail. The reporter, however, was not allowed access to Tom. No one accept his lawyers had permission to see him. Pea Jay decided to question the jailer.

"You remind Tom of the anniversary of the killings?"

"Yeh."

"What was his response?"

"He said he hadn't thought much about it. He said he don't let himself think about it any more than he can."

"What's it been like guarding him?"

"Well...I tell you...I've had a hard time keeping Tom all this time, but I've done it and I ain't gonna let him get away from me now..."

Folsom walked into the post office and greeted the postmaster with a handshake.

"Got here as soon as I could. What can I do for you?"

"Read this," the postmaster said and handed a letter over to the reporter. Folsom opened it up and looked over it. The writing was difficult to read and the spelling at times impossible to understand but he managed, nonetheless, to read it.

> *"September 2, 1890, Lake City. I do a sert that I will write the facks on the Woolfolk case, as you do entend to brake the neck of Woolfolk's. I will beg the people to turn him luce, for I an two more men don the killing of the Woolfolk famley to get monney, an wode of killed Tom Woolfolk if we only could cont him, an I say more.*
>
> *"We put his close in the well, so it wode fassen the crim on Tom an Tom run out at gate an gout a way. We all pledge our selfe to not tell the way of it entell they went to kile Woolfolk. We ask you to turn him go, for you will never get us. All for one is ded, an the other, I dont know, but if you kill Woolfolk, you will kill a ensson man.*
>
> *"We will not tell what couler we are, you can gess it for your self, and I beg the papers to publies all in this letter, and gave the ensson man a canch, for he out to be free an we are sorry that he has suffered an our a count a minet. We never did enteen to let him be kiled on the count of that mudred. Well I mus close by begen you all papers to publies all that is in this letter. I will send this letter to the postmaster in maken Ga ...please publies at wonce. I again tell the worl that he is ensson as a ded man do not dlay save a ensson man."*

"This is incredible," Folsom muttered, handing the letter back. "What do you intend to do?"

"Just what he asks."

"You want me to publish this? Do you think it's for real?"

"I have no way of knowing. But if you publish it, as he requested, then I will be done with it."

October 6, 1890, Sheriff Cooper went to the Bibb County Jail and escorted Tom back to Perry. The Houston County Superior Court had convened.

Upon Gustin's resignation, Alexander Miller was appointed to replace him. Miller, having served on Tom's defense, however, was immediately disqualified and in his place sat Judge G.F. Gober of the Blue Ridge Circuit. John Rutherford, confined to his bed at his parents' home in Athens, was too ill to attend. Clinton Duncan and Winter Wimberly sat with Tom.

Judge Gober asked if the defense had anything to say before sentencing. The two defense attorneys said they did not. Tom rose to his feet and faced the Judge.

"Thomas G. Woolfolk, do have you have any reason why sentence should not be passed upon you at this time?"

"I have nothing to say except that I am innocent of the crime charged. I didn't do it, but I would rather be in my grave than be alive under the circumstances that surround me. I am an innocent man."

The editor of the Houston Home Journal, John Hodges, met Folsom in the lobby of the Perry Hotel. The two men sat down.

"Thank you for seeing me," Folsom said and pulled out his notebook.

"My pleasure," Hodges answered politely.

"I understand you recently interviewed Tom Woolfolk in jail."

"Yes, right after his sentence. I had quite a long talk with him. Got my notes right here with me in fact," he said, reaching into his inside coat pocket and pulling out a small notebook.

"Would you mind sharing them with me?"

"Not at all. Right after Tom was returned to his cell, I was permitted to see him. Judge Gober has set the execution date for October 29th, you know."

"Yes, I am aware of that."

"Any way I asked Tom if he had a statement to make to which he said, 'I've got nothing to say beyond what I have said time and again. I'm an innocent man and will protest my innocence to the last. I didn't do what they say I did.'"

Folsom wrote Tom's statement down in his notebook. Hodges waited until he was through.

"He said, and I quote, 'Life in prison is a life of torture, and I am ready to die. I'd rather die than remain in prison another year.'"

"What else did he say?" Folsom asked not looking up from his notes.

"Well he said he reads his Bible every day and night and prays regularly. I said, 'Tom, you are the most philosophical man in the face of death I ever saw.'"

"What did he say to that?"

"He said," the editor looked at his notes. "'Yes because I expect to die on the 29th and I am ready. I am trying to lead a Christian life, and I have repented and received forgiveness for my sins. I have given my heart to God, and my entire trust is placed in the mercy of my Savior, Jesus Christ.' Does he have a particular religious affiliation?"

"Baptist, I think. Did he say anything about a continuance?"

"No, except that he doesn't expect any further intercession in his behalf. He repeated his claim that he was ready for execution and that he prefers death to continued confinement without hope of final release."

"Where do they plan to hang him?" Folsom asked.

"Just on the western limit of town, near where Fanny Gresham Branch empties into Big Indian Creek. It's a valley of about five acres, surrounded by hills on three sides. A natural amphitheater."

After the editor excused himself and left the lobby, Folsom continued writing in his notebook.

"Many believe that Woolfolk will confess to having committed the crime with which he stands charged, despite his incessant protestations of innocence. He is certainly a changed man, and he says continued imprisonment for more than three years would change any man for the better who believes in a God and a future life. He does not use profane language now, whereas eighteen months ago oaths frequently escaped his lips."

Folsom closed his notebook and stuck it inside his coat pocket. He walked over to the hotel clerk and asked directions to Fanny Gresham Branch where it emptied into Big Indian Creek. The clerk pointed to the west.

"It's about a half mile that way. You can't miss it. The cemetery overlooks the valley."

The reporter thanked him, put on his hat, and left the hotel. He walked until he came to the top of a hill. To his left was the cemetery. Below him a road crossed Big Indian Creek. Nearby was a clearing. Hodges was right. It was a natural amphitheater.

Sheriff Cooper entered the cell block. Tom met him at the cell door.

"You wanted to see me, Tom?"

"Yeh...uh...the gallows you hung Johnson and Butts on."

"Yes...what about them?"

"That the same one you gonna hang me on?"

"Yes. It's out in the jail yard."

"Can I see it?"

"You sure you want to see it?"

Tom hesitated a moment and then answered, "Yeh."

Cooper unlocked the cell door and walked Tom to the yard. Tom looked up at the structure.

"Is that what you're gonna hang me on, Mr. Cooper?" he said softly staring up at the tall wooden structure.

"Yes, Tom."

"Well...I don't much like the looks of it," he said and walked back into the jail house.

Sheriff Cooper returned Tom to his cell, locked it, and then went back out into the yard. A group of laborers who had been waiting in the shade, walked over to him.

"I want the gallows moved over to the place I showed you yesterday. The prisoner's requested to have it whitewashed. See that it's done before Wednesday."

Yawning broadly, the night death watch F. A. Jobson leaned his chair against the wall, folded his arms, and settled deeper into his seat.

"Mr. Jobson?"

"Yes, Tom?"

"Tell me about the noose."

"What do you want to know about it?"

"How they tie one of them thangs?"

"Well...first they grease the rope and test its strength. Then they make the loop, tie the knot and wrap it thirteen times."

"How's it supposed to kill ya?"

"It breaks the neck instantly...that is...if it's set right."

"Mr. Jobson?"

"Yes, Tom?"

"Have they made mine yet?"

"Yes, Tom."

Tom climbed out of bed and began pacing the floor of his small cell. Jobson, the death watch, continued to lean back in his chair. A few minutes later, the prisoner approached the cell door.

"Mr. Jobson?"

"Yes, Tom."

"I'll give you five hundred dollars and a written history of my life...if you let me get out of here."

Jobson shifted in his chair and chuckled to himself. Tom returned to his pacing.

"Mr. Jobson," he again addressed the guard.

"Yes Tom, what is it?"

"I'll give you a hundred dollars and a history of my life for a bottle of morphine."

"You know I can't do that."

"I don't want it all at once. Just give me alittle at a time...I won't let anyone know."

"Sorry, Tom."

Love Shackleford helped Flo from the train. Waiting for them on the platform were Lillie and Henry Cowan. The sisters tearfully embraced each other and then were helped into the carriage by their menfolk.

The short ride to the jail was made in total silence. No one felt compelled to enter into light conversation, and no one wanted to talk about what was ahead of them.

Minutes later, the carriage pulled to a stop at the small Houston County Jail. Outside, a small crowd had gathered. The arrival of Tom's sisters stirred them to reaction. Flo looked at the group and swallowed her tears. Lillie gasped loudly. Love and Henry hopped down, surveyed the crowd, and reached up to help the sisters. Flo's hand trembled as she took Love's. Lillie collapsed into her husband's arms. Together they walked into the jail.

Inside, Folsom sat waiting. He arrived at the jail that morning and found himself not wanting to get very far from the ongoing story. He stood up when the family entered and approached them politely.

"Mrs. Edwards, Mrs. Cowan. Is there anything I can do?" He asked quietly.

Flo looked up at him and smiled weakly. "No...but thank you for your kindness."

The jailer escorted the four back into the small cell block. Folsom remained out front. An hour passed before they reemerged and went to the courthouse. Minutes later, Sheriff Cooper left the courthouse, walked over to the jail, entered the cell block, and unlocked Tom's cell.

Unshackled, the prisoner accompanied by the Sheriff walked over to the courthouse. Folsom followed and watched from a respectable distance. Sheriff Cooper picked up some paper, pen and ink, walked over to a table and sat down. Tom sat down across from him. Both Flo with her hand on her brother's shoulder, and Lillie remained at Tom's side.

Although Folsom was unable to hear what was being said the activity clearly indicated that the prisoner was dictating his last will and testament to the Sheriff. Cooper would write a few lines and then read them back to Tom who would either approve or amend. Sixty minutes later, Tom read the finished document and signed it, followed by Sheriff Cooper and a deputy as witnesses.

Tom turned to his sisters. Lillie threw her arms around his neck and sobbed. Flo stood a step away crying in a handkerchief.

Henry Cowan reached over and tenderly put his hands on his wife's shoulders. Lillie pleaded to stay. Tom reached up, pulled her arms away, and kissed her gently on the cheek. She turned and buried her face in Henry's chest.

Tom turned to Flo. The two stood looking at each other for a moment. He then leaned over and kissed her on the cheek. As he was pulling away, Flo embraced him tightly, kissed him on the neck, and started crying. Tom looked to Shackleford for help. Love walked over to the pair, put his hands on her shoulders and pulled her away.

Gently, the two men escorted the sisters from the room. Folsom, tears streaming down his cheeks, watched the two couples slowly walk down the hall and out of the building. A second later, Tom Woolfolk walked by, followed close behind by Cooper, and also disappeared into the darkness.

Millie, John Rutherford's sister tapped on his bedroom door. Doc Whaley opened it, looked over his shoulder at his sleeping patient, and then stepped out side.

"Doctor, this telegram just came for John."

Whaley took the telegram and read it.

"There's nothing he can do for Woolfolk now. He's too ill. I don't want him disturbed."

Millie looked down at the message from Flo begging her brother to try to get a stay of execution for at least twenty four hours.

"Will you see that he gets it, please."

"Millie, by the time John is able to read this telegram Woolfolk will be dead."

Flo read the answer she received from Judge Miller and wept. In total desperation, she sent telegrams to both Miller and Rutherford. Miller responded with sincere regrets. She still had not heard from Rutherford.

There was hope yet.

At the jail, Cooper permitted Folsom an interview with Tom and allowed them to talk in a side room. The reporter looked at the prisoner and marveled as usual at his composure.

"Tom...you ready?" he finally asked.

"Yeh, I'm ready to go. I've made peace with God, and this time tomorrow I'll be with Him in my heavenly home."

"You're ready to go?" Folsom reacted before realizing he had spoken the words aloud. Tom nodded.

"Yes...ready and anxious. I'd rather die tomorrow than to stay in jail another year."

"Suppose you could get a commutation or a life sentence?"

"I don't want it. I'd rather die than go to the penitentiary. I'm ready and don't want anyone to interfere."

"Your sisters are trying to get a respite of one day."

"I don't want it. I have put my trust in God, and I want to go." Tom stopped and looked at Folsom's side. "Say...what paper you got in your pocket?"

"Do you want it?"

"Yes, if you please."

"No," Cooper spoke up. "Don't give it to him...I'd rather he'd not see it."

Tom frowned and looked at Folsom. "Is there anything in it about me?"

"No...nothing. Why do you ask?" Folsom stammered.

"Oh, I want to know what they say about me. That's all."

"Tom...are you going to tell anything about this matter?"

"No, I have nothing to tell. They're going to kill an innocent man. That's all I can say. I'm ready to go though, and I want to go as soon as possible. I want it over."

"Would you get away if you could?"

"Yeh, if I could do it without hurting anyone."

"Wouldn't you take the chance in that?"

"Not at all. I wouldn't hurt Mr. Cooper for the world."

"Ah, go ahead and give him the newspaper," Cooper interrupted.

Folsom stood up, walked over to the Sheriff, and pointed out an article.

Cooper looked the article over and then shook his head.

"Is it something about me?" Tom asked.

"Nothing that would do you any good to see, Tom," Folsom answered sticking the paper back in his pocket.

Tom's night guard Jobson stuck his head in the door and was greeted warmly by his prisoner.

"Well..." Folsom said, "I guess I'll see ya in the mornin'."

"Yeh, see ya tomorrow," Tom answered, smiling.

Folsom turned to walk away.

"Uh...Folsom?" Tom called out. The reporter turned around.

"Yeh, Tom?"

Tom walked over to him.

"You haven't got anything against me, have you?" he asked.

"Of course not."

"Then...when you go to bed tonight pray for me. I know you don't pray much, but try it...tonight...for my soul."

CHAPTER TWENTY-SEVEN
"Are you ready to die?"

Folsom stood with the other members of the press waiting for their promised interview with the condemned man. Sheriff Cooper greeted each man with a handshake and escorted them into the cell block. Cooper asked the turnkey if the prisoner was still asleep.

He was.

The group walked slowly down the corridor and stopped at the door. Inside the dark cell, a man was sleeping. His chest rose and dropped, at a slow, steady pace.

"Tom," the sheriff called out. "Tom, it's time to get up."

The reporters waited for the prisoner to respond. He did not.

"He sleeps well," the Sheriff said and smiled, nervously. "If he is behind on sleep in this world, he won't have much time to make it up here. He'll soon have a chance to make it up somewhere else."

The Sheriff called Tom's name twice, but there was no response. He called out again, shaking the cell door. The sleeping man continued to sleep soundly.

"Hey, Tom!" the turnkey barked, hitting the heavy ring of keys against the bars. "Tom, come on and git up."

"Maybe he's drugged," Pea Jay remarked.

"Oh no," the Sheriff answered stiffly. "He was searched carefully and watched closely last night. I'll stake all I have on him being sound and well."

Grabbing the bars of the cell door tightly, the Sheriff yelled, "Come on, Tom, it's time to git up!"

The prisoner slowly opened his eyes. Raising up on his elbows he looked around, dazed and confused.

"Good mornin', Mr. Cooper," he finally said, pulling off the blanket and putting both feet on the floor. After he rubbed his eyes, he stretched. It was then he saw the group of reporters watching him.

Tom smiled and quickly stood up to greet them. During the three years since the murders, he had become friends with several.

"Mornin' Folsom," he said reaching through the bars and shaking the reporter's hand.

"Mornin', Tom."

The Sheriff spoke up. "Tom, get dress and I'll let you out. These gentlemen would like to talk to you."

"All right." He said and began to gather his clothes.

The party watched as he pulled on his pants, tucked in his shirt, and carefully laced his shoes. He dressed slowly and purposefully. His movements were controlled and deliberate, every detail was attended to.

"You'd think he was gettin' ready for his own damn wedding," Pea Jay whispered to Folsom. Folsom ignored him.

Tom put on his coat and picked up his hat. "I'm ready, Mr. Cooper."

Sheriff Cooper unlocked the door, and Tom walked out. Immediately, he reached out, took the Sheriff's hand, and gripped it tightly. He turned and again shook hands with Folsom who gently patted him on the shoulder. The Sheriff then introduced Tom to those he did not know. He shook each hand warmly.

Folsom was the first to speak up. "How do you feel, Tom? You aren't at all nervous, are you?"

Tom smiled and stuck out both hands. "Do you see any nervousness about me?"

His hands were steady.

"And how did you sleep?" Pea Jay asked.

"Like a log, after about two o'clock.," he answered. "I know what you are going to ask next, so I'll save you the trouble and tell you now that I did not dream."

He smiled at Folsom and then looked again at Pea Jay. "Somehow you always harp about my dreams. For your benefit, I'll tell you the only dream I ever had in this jail. Prisoners don't dream here because Mr. Cooper takes too good a care of them."

His guests laughed nervously.

"But my dream," he continued. "I dreamed a few nights ago that I had got away. I was having a big time of it. Every officer in the state was after me and I walked in among them and they didn't know me. I was just in clover, I tell you...but suddenly, when I was the happiest, Westcott and Cooper came into the dream, and I began to hide out. But it was no use. They caught me. Then I woke up and for the first time in my life...I was mad at Cooper."

Folsom watched his friend closely. He spoke softly. He was calm and relaxed. His smile was genuine, not forced, and it never left his face. The reporter was sincerely impressed with his strength and willpower.

Someone handed the prisoner a cigar. "Thanks. I like to smoke before breakfast."

Sheriff Cooper lighted it for him. After taking a few hardy puffs, Tom sat down in a chair the turnkey brought over. He took the cigar out of his mouth and looked it over. "That's a very good cigar," he said.

"When did you have a drink last, Tom?" Folsom asked.

Tom smiled, more to himself, and then looked sheepishly over at the sheriff.

Cooper smiled. "Tell him, Tom."

"I had a mighty good one last night, and then I had a small one earlier this morning."

Pea Jay spoke up. "Would you like another?"

"If you've got somethin' good." Tom smiled widely, looking around. "I wouldn't mind taking one."

"I'll give him all he wants," Cooper responded proudly.

"I've got some change, and if I want anything, Mr. Cooper'll get it for me." Tom added.

Folsom marvelled at the warm bond between the two men, the prisoner and his keeper.

"Would you like to have enough, Tom, to make you drunk?" He was asked.

Tom thought for a long moment before responding. "I...I don't know. No, I don't. I don't want to die drunk. I want to die sober, and that's what I'm going to do."

"Are you ready to die?" Pea Jay asked.

"I had just as well be because I've got to die and I'm thoroughly satisfied with it. I firmly believe that my sins have been forgiven, and naturally I'm ready," he said softly, looking sincerely from face to face. "I know there are those who don't believe this any more than they believe I'm innocent of the crime for which they're going to kill me."

"Are you innocent?" a reporter asked.

Tom stood up and looked at the men.

"I am," he said. He then sat back down.

Pea Jay finished writing a quick note in his notebook and looked up. Sticking out his pencil as if to accentuate his point, he said, "Tom, there are those who believe you innocent. If you are, why don't you write a card telling them so and let it be printed?"

The group waited for his answer. Tom looked intently at the floor in front of him. "No," he finally said. "I'm not going to write anything. I've got nothing to write."

"Or nothing to say on the scaffold?" someone asked.

"Nothing...only to confess my innocence."

The interview lasted more than an hour. Tom's manner eased the reporters' anxiety somewhat, making it easier for them to converse with the condemned man. He joked and laughed. At times, he would be quiet and pensive. He was never belligerent, never angry.

As the interview was coming to a close, he reached over and took Pea Jay's silk hat from his head. "Let me try that churn on," he said, putting it on.

The group laughed at his antics.

"That becomes you, Tom," Sheriff Cooper laughed.

"Does it? I used to wear one," he said and turned to Pea Jay who seemed uncomfortable at the sincerity in Tom's friendly demeanor. "I'll trade hats with you. I think I'd like to die in this one."

The room was silent. Tom looked at each of them and then broke out in a loud, hardy laugh.

Henry Cowan looked at his watch. It was a few minutes before nine. He had requested a visit with his brother-in-law and was granted it. Cooper came out and escorted him back to Tom's cell. Under the circumstances, the Sheriff was obligated to stay within ear shot.

Just as Cowan had been given the responsibility of administrator of the Captain's estate, Tom had asked him to attend to the matter of his burial.

"Don't give me any sort of a grave," Tom said after they had greeted each other warmly. "Have it walled up and put me away decently."

"Of course, Tom. Anything you want."

"...if any of my friends want to see me after I'm dead, let'em..." He stopped in mid-sentence. Cowan waited patiently for him to continue. "But...I don't want my sisters to see me," he said softly.

His brother-in-law was visibly shaken. Tears filled his eyes as he tried to write down Tom's instructions. His hands trembled.

"Well," Tom said, slapping his knees and standing up, "I guess that covers it."

Cowan stood up and nervously retrieved his hat and coat. Tom escorted him to the cell door. His hand rested gently on his brother-in-law's shoulder.

"Tom..." Cowan muttered weakly.

Tom smiled and embraced him warmly. Cowan smiled, put on his hat and walked out of the cell.

Sheriff Cooper walked in. "Now, Tom," he said firmly, "I want to have a last talk with you, and this will be your last chance to have a private talk with me. I want you to be honest."

"Okay," Tom said, blankly.

"Tom, people generally believe you are guilty, and, for my own satisfaction, I want to know the truth. I think you should say you are guilty, if you are, for the satisfaction of the judges, the lawyers, and the jurors."

"But I'm not guilty, Mr. Cooper," the prisoner answered softly.

"Well...that may be...but Tom, if you are and want to tell me, I pledge you my word never to breathe it until after you're gone."

Tom smiled. "I tell you, Mr. Cooper...I'm not guilty."

"Tom, have you given up all hopes. Do you think there is any chance for you to have your life prolonged?"

"Not at all and I'll tell you now…I don't want it prolonged and knowing that in a few hours I'll be in the presence of my God, with my sins forgiven or unforgiven, I tell you, I am an innocent man."

"All right, Tom. I'll send in your breakfast."

"Can I see Dr. Warren?"

"You have several preachers are waiting outside to see you," Cooper answered and walked out.

Folsom returned to the jail after breakfast in hopes of seeing his friend a final time. Sheriff Cooper informed him that the three preachers, E.W. Warren, Henry L. Morehouse, and Benjamin Brewton, had just been admitted in to see Tom. The reporter volunteered to wait.

Tom met the preachers in the cell corridor with sincere appreciation. He was most especially glad to see his advisor and friend Dr. Warren. Each man carried a Bible.

The prisoner reassured them of his spiritual state. "I believe that my sins have been forgiven, and that I am all right."

Through the small barred window in the door leading into the corridor from the jail's front office, Folsom could see the group praying around Tom, who was kneeling with his hands folded together beneath his chin. The reporter pressed the scene into his mind so he would never forget.

At the close of the prayers, Tom stood up and speaking softly and warmly embraced each man. The group turned away and walked down the corridor towards the exit. Tom walked back into his cell and closed the door.

Sheriff Cooper unlocked the corridor door and let the men out of the cell block. Their expressions were solemn and tight.

"He has requested that I meet him here," Dr. Warren said immediately to the Sheriff, "and go down to the gallows with him. Drs. Morehouse and Brewton are to meet him there on the scaffold. He would also like Mr. Folsom to accompany us."

The Sheriff nodded and turned to enter the corridor. Folsom quickly walked in behind him. Dr. Warren reached up and stopped the two men. "He is not as calm about this as he appears. He has yet to be able to bring himself to the point of saying the words 'gallows' and 'scaffold'."

Folsom turned and followed the Sheriff into the cell corridor. Tom was pacing about the cell. His hands were clasped behind him. His head was bowed.

"Tom?" the sheriff called out. "I guess you had better come out and wash and dress. The boy will help you to wash."

A black boy walked up with a foot tub of water.

"Never mind that," Tom responded, blankly. "I can do that myself. Where are my clothes? What are they?"

The Sheriff unwrapped a package and laid the new clothes on the cot. Tom looked at each piece closely. He had been given a new pair of underwear, shirt, collar, and socks. His black suit was hanging on a nail. He walked over and, taking it down, slapped out the wrinkles.

Folsom stood outside the cell watching as Tom dressed slowly, making comments, joking with his neighbors. When he was finished, he turned to the Sheriff.

"How do I look, Mr. Cooper?" Tom asked.

"Very nice," the Sheriff responded. "A barber will be here directly to shave you."

Tom rubbed his chin. "I believe I do need a shave. It would make me look better. Do you think I need my hair cut?"

The barber entered carrying a pan of water, a towel, and his tools. Tom seated himself. The towel was wrapped around his chest. His large mustache was trimmed, his cheeks and neck shaved. The small goatee beneath his bottom lip was shaped.

Folsom wanted to find him a mirror, but none was available. The barber removed the towel and shook it out. Tom stood up and smiled at the reporter who imprinted the man's handsome features to memory.

"I'd like to see Dr. Warren again and have a piece of paper. I want to write a statement," Tom said.

Sheriff Cooper turned to the boy waiting for instructions. "Go fetch Dr. Warren."

As the boy hurried away, Folsom took a piece of paper from his reporter's notebook and handed it to Tom.

"Thanks. You know, I don't think I've ever seen you without a notebook," he said laughingly and walked over to a small table. He sat down and began to write.

Moments later, Dr. Warren walked in. Tom finished writing, folded the paper, and stood up. "I want you to read this on the..uh...well you know...down there."

The preacher took the paper and quickly looked at the contents.

"Certainly, Tom."

Sheriff Cooper looked at his watch. "It's almost noon, Tom. Is there anything you want? We'll be leaving soon."

"Just something to eat."

Cooper ordered the turnkey to have the prisoner served. "Tom, we won't read any death warrant. I've been instructed that it's not necessary."

Tom smiled. "Well...I'm glad of that."

The turnkey returned carrying a tray of food. Folsom, the Sheriff and preacher left to allow Tom some time alone.

The arrival of the militia the Perry Rifles prompted Folsom to look at his watch. It was 12:15 p.m. A large crowd had been gathering in front of the jail all morning. Pea Jay worked his way through the congestion and was given entrance into the front room.

"You wouldn't believe what it's like at the gallows," he said, walking over to Folsom. "It's like a damn circus out there. Photographers, street vendors. They even have bleachers and are selling tickets."

"I know," Folsom responded. "I hear there's going to be thousands turning out to watch him die."

"Well, it's about time, if you ask me."

"After all that came out in the trials, you still think he did it?"

"Hell yeh, I think he did it."

"But...what if he didn't?" Folsom asked. Pea Jay had already walked away.

A deputy hurried up carrying a rifle. "The carriage's out front," he said to Cooper.

Dr. Warren and the Sheriff entered the corridor. Folsom and Pea Jay waited in the doorway as the two men slowly walked between the rows of cells. The prisoners were quiet. Some were lying on their sides facing the walls. Others stood at the bars waiting for their famous neighbor to walk by.

"Well, Tom. Let's go," Cooper said as he walked up to Tom's door.

Folsom heard the prisoner say softly, "I'm ready."

Tom stood up and walked over to Cooper who was standing at the opened cell door holding a pair of handcuffs. The prisoner stuck out his hands and waited. Slowly, the Sheriff locked the bracelets around his wrists. Folsom saw the two men, prisoner and keeper, look directly into each other's eyes. Cooper pulled on the cuffs to confirm they were secure and then took the prisoner by the elbow.

The trio walked slowly down the corridor with Cooper on one side, holding tightly onto Tom's arm, and the minister at the other side, reading softly from the Bible. Tom stopped and looked back at the prisoners who watched him pass.

"Boys," he said. "Goodbye to all of you...and...God bless ya."

His neighbors nodded quietly and watched as he walked away.

In the front yard of the jailhouse, the crowd stood quietly waiting. The silence unnerved Folsom as he and Pea Jay also waited. Tom walked out accompanied by the Sheriff and preacher. They were escorted by an armed guard.

Out in the sunlight, Tom looked up and breathed the fresh air. He turned his face up towards the noonday sun and closed his eyes.

"It's a pretty, clear day," he said softly.

They walked by the reporters. Folsom joined the entourage. As it was the custom for a representative of the press to accompany a condemned man on his ride to his execution, Tom selected Folsom, giving them both a final victory over Pea Jay.

Tom and Sheriff Cooper climbed aboard the carriage first and took their places on the back seat. Folsom and Dr. Warren then seated themselves in the seat facing them. The driver was an armed deputy.

The militia surrounded the carriage, and slowly the execution party began its trip to the gallows.

Folsom watched his friend closely. Tom sat with his hands on his lap. He looked around at the people lining the road but said nothing. When someone called out to him by name, he would look in anticipation. If it was someone he knew, he acknowledged them warmly. If they were strangers, his jaw would tighten and he would look away.

The location of the scaffold was selected in order to accommodate the large crowd and allow for a clear public viewing. Originally it was planned to be a private hanging, attended by a small select group. The national attention the execution brought, however, changed the officials' minds. For days, every hotel in the area was filled to capacity. Special trains were scheduled to bring the people from Bibb County. The event could no longer be private.

The gallows were constructed in a slight valley-like depression surrounded on all sides by small hills on the outskirts of town. As the carriage reached the top of one, the passengers were given a panoramic view of the countryside and the valley below. Folsom was shocked at the number of spectators that had gathered during the morning. The hillsides were covered with people. In the center, surrounded by a three foot high single rail fence, sat the scaffold. The bright sun reflected off its white paint.

"Is that the place?" Tom asked.

"Yes, Tom. It is," Cooper answered softly.

As the carriage neared the bottom of the hill, the preacher began to counsel the prisoner.

Sheriff Cooper looked over. "Be brave, Tom. Be calm," he said.

Tom looked reassuringly at his keeper. "Oh, I'll go through it all right. Don't be bothered about that."

The passengers were then quiet. The crowd lining the road was silent. The only sound came from the grinding of the carriage wheels, the crackling of saddle leather and the breathing of the horses.

"Don't make it too long," Tom said politely to the Sheriff. "Get through as soon as you can."

A wave of silence flowed through the crowd as the carriage pulled up to the entrance of the cordoned area. Surrounded by their armed escort, the party climbed down from the carriage. Every eye was on the prisoner as he walked up to the steps of the scaffold and stopped. The guards encircled the gallows, turned, and, with their bayonets shining in the bright noon sun, they faced the crowd. The crowd of spectators hurried to places high enough to see the proceedings.

Tom acknowledged the presence of Drs. Morehouse and Brewton with a nod. Standing beside them was Sheriff Westcott who turned around and climbed the steps to the top of the scaffold. Tom followed. Cooper allowed him to go up unassisted, but stayed close behind him.

At the base, Folsom looked up and into the face of the condemned man. He was calm but not relaxed. The mood of the group was reverent and solemn. The crowd beyond the wall was quiet.

Sheriff Cooper unlocked Tom's handcuffs. His hands free, he looked out beyond the gallows and could see the Perry Cemetery with its tombstones shining brightly in the noon day sun.

"Tom, have you anything to say?" Cooper asked.

"I would like Dr. Warren to pray."

The preacher stepped forward and asked those attending to bow their heads for prayer. Folsom watched Tom as he listened. The prisoner looked nervous for a moment then his calm returned.

Next, Tom asked Dr. Morehouse to pray and then Dr. Brewton. Each man prayed for Tom's soul. Only Dr. Brewton mentioned the murders. The crowd was visibly affected by the service.

As Dr. Brewton said his final 'Amen', Dr. Warren walked to the edge of the platform again and addressed the crowd. "Mr. Woolfolk has made a statement in writing, which he requests me to read, and I will do so now."

The crowd moved forward. All ears were tuned to the minister's words. Everyone suspected that the long awaited confession was about to be read.

The preacher raised the paper in front of him and began. "I, Thomas G. Woolfolk, realizing the existence of an infinite, wise and holy God, so as to meet Him, knowing all that I have ever done, and fully understanding that I must stand before the judgement bar of God, and that today, in a few hours, I shall be called into His presence, do solemnly declare my innocence, and I leave as my last declaration that I did not take the life of my father, or any member of his family, or have any knowledge of the person or persons who did the murderous deed. Signed, Thomas G. Woolfolk."

Folsom watched as Tom became visibly anxious. His jaw twitched slightly. He clinched his fists. The reporter could see his chest rising and falling in jerks as if quietly sobbing. The prisoner, however, made no sound.

The mob had not been given its expected confession. A low, soft growl rose up from its midst.

Tom straightened up and looked out at the spectators. Folsom watched closely as he regained his now infamous stoic demeanor.

Sheriff Cooper turned to the prisoner. "Have you anything more to say, Tom?"

"Nothing...only I'd like to pray myself."

"All right."

Tom stepped forward. Sheriff Cooper stayed close at his side. The prisoner looked around at the hills covered with thousands of people. He looked down at Folsom, standing at the base of the gallows. He dropped his head back and closed his eyes.

"Oh, Thou Omnipotent Being who presides over all things, hear this my last petition to Thy throne of Grace. Thou knowest the innermost thoughts of my heart. Thou knowest the sins I have committed, and for them I ask forgiveness. Oh, God, now have mercy on my soul, which I now entrust to Thy keeping. Make it pure and clean," he spoke clearly with a slight tremor in his voice.

"God bless my sisters. Bless those who have gone before me. Forgive all those who have abused me, and accept my soul, for Jesus' sake. Amen."

Again, a murmur went through the crowd. There was no confession. Folsom looked at the faces of some of the officials standing beside him. They had tears in their eyes.

Sheriff Cooper took Tom by the elbow and guided him to his position behind the hangman's noose. With the help of his deputy he began to tie the prisoner's arms and feet.

Tom looked over at Sheriff Westcott.

"Please. Move that rope. It's in my face."

Westcott stepped forward and pulled the rope aside. Tom thanked him.

"Gentleman," Cooper said when he was finished binding the prisoner, "please leave the platform."

One by one, the men walked up to Tom and quietly told him goodbye. The most visibly shaken was Dr. Warren. Tears streamed down the sides of his face. There were no tears in Tom's eyes.

Folsom watched as each man slowly came down the stairs. Just above his head the reporter could see the prisoner's knees shaking. Tom took a deep breath and braced himself. The shaking stopped.

Cooper reached over and pulled the noose over his head.

"Mr. Cooper," Tom said in a low, soft voice, "after the doctors say I'm dead, let me hang four or five minutes. I want it certain that I am dead before I go in the ground."

The Sheriff did not respond but tightened the knot.

"Tie me right, Mr. Cooper. Don't make any mistakes. I want it done right."

Cooper looked at Tom and said quietly, "I'll do my best, Tom."

The Sheriff reached over and took the black hood from the deputy's hand. "Now, Tom, I'll say goodbye."

"Goodbye, Mr. Cooper, and God bless you. I appreciate your position and sympathize with you in this work. You've been good to me."

Cooper unfolded the black hood and began to put it over Tom's head. The two men looked deeply into each other's eyes and saw each other's tears.

"Does the rope choke you?" Cooper asked.

"Well, not much, go on," Tom muttered. "Am I standing where you want me, Mr. Cooper?"

"Yes, Tom."

The black hood secured over his face, the noose tight around his neck, his arms and feet tied, Tom waited.

"Well, Mr. Cooper," he said with his voice muffled by the hood, "you have been kind to me and I want to part as friends."

"I've done all I could do for you," the Sheriff responded warmly.

A low murmur came up out of the crowd. The spectators were beginning to grow restless. Someone yelled out for Cooper to stop stalling and get it over with.

Cooper walked over to the lever, placed both hands on it, and tensed his arms.

"Mr. Riley?" Tom called out to Cooper's deputy.

Cooper eased up on the lever. Deputy Riley walked over to Tom.

"What is it, Tom?"

The possibility that Tom may yet confess caused everyone to strain to hear what he had to say. They all waited in silence.

"Goodbye, Mr. Riley. That's all."

"Goodbye, Tom."

Sheriff Cooper again tightened his grip on the lever. Folsom watched as he began to pull and then hesitate. Instantly, he took a deep breath and snatched the lever back with all his strength. The trap door fell and Tom's feet dropped out from under him.

It was over.

Newspaper sketch of Tom Woolfolk's body on the gallows.

Tom's body swung from the gallows; the crowd began to slowly dissipate. Photographers continued to take pictures. Love Shackleford looked at his watch. It was 1:31 p.m. Beside him stood Flo's brother-in-law Henry P. Cowan. The two men represented the Woolfolk family. Across from them on the other side of the scaffold stood the Howards, Mattie's brothers, including the one who led them in the fight to have Tom convicted and executed, Charles W. Howard.

From the beginning, the majority of the Woolfolks, excluding Major Thomas J. Woolfolk's daughters, stood by the Captain's eldest son believing in his innocence. The Howards were convinced of his guilt and applied continuous pressure on the courts, the newspapers, and the general public. In the end, they had won.

Love Shackleford and Henry Cowan watched his body twirl around on the end of the rope. At the base of the platform, the hearse containing his casket sat waiting. Every few minutes, the doctors would walk up and check his heart. Seventeen minutes after Cooper sprung the trap door, Tom's chest still moved. The attending physicians would not declare him dead.

Everyone waited.

Folsom walked over to the hearse and looked at the casket. He reached over and ran his hand along the fine rosewood. On the lid was a silver plate with the words, "AT REST" engraved on it. The reporter looked up at the body of the accused mass murderer who had become his friend and watched it twirl back and forth, the rope grinding loudly as it continued to stretch from the weight.

At eleven minutes after two o'clock, the three doctors listened to Tom's heart a final time and told the deputy to cut the body down. Deputy Riley climbed back up the steps to the platform over their heads and cut the rope.

Gently, the three men lowered Tom's body to the ground where they made their final examination. Sheriff Cooper walked over to them as they supervised the placing of the body in the coffin.

"Sheriff," one of the doctors said, "the condemned man Thomas Woolfolk is dead of slow strangulation."

"What?" Cooper said, astonished.

"The prisoner did not die of a broken neck but of slow strangulation. I am afraid, sir, the noose was not set properly."

Cooper sadly watched as the lid was nailed shut. Cowan and Shackleford approached the Sheriff.

"Can we take Tom now?" Shackleford asked.

Cooper looked up. "Yes...we're done here."

Folsom walked over to Shackleford and shook hands with him. Tears filled their eyes as they watched the hearse slowly pull away. The two men walked out of the stockade behind it.

"Where is he going to be buried?"

"Flo and Lillie have a family plot in the Orange Hill Cemetery in Hawkinsville. Tom wants to be buried there."

"Will his sisters attend the funeral?" Folsom asked, not as a reporter but as a friend of the family.

Shackleford nodded. "Yes. Tom asked them not to go. He wanted to protect them as much as possible...but they both insist on being there." He placed his hand on Folsom's shoulder and continued. "There'll be a small service opened only to relatives and close friends. Why don't you go...I'm sure Tom would have liked that."

"No...I'm sorry. I wish I could, but...I have a story to write. For once let's keep the press away from him. None of us need to be there."

"I understand. Well, if you'll excuse me." Shackleford reached out, took the reporter's hand and squeezed it. "Thank you."

"I wish there was something I could have done."

"We all do. You know...I'm sure Tom is innocent," Shackleford said. He let go of Folsom's hand. "I will never believe otherwise."

"Neither will I," the reporter said as he watched the hearse slowly disappear over the hill.

EPILOGUE

Mattie's elderly father, Benjamin F. Howard, did not witness Tom's execution. He died April 4, 1890 and went to his grave not knowing if Tom would in fact be punished for the murder of his daughter, son-in-law, grandchildren, and Temperance West. His unmarked grave is in an isolated, wooded area near Bolingbroke, Georgia.

Charles W. Howard was given the rope used to hang Tom Woolfolk. He divided it into sections and gave the pieces to members of his family. A portion of this rope is still in the possession of a descendant. Family tradition says that Howard grieved the death of his sister until his own death on April 14, 1928. He and his brother John D. Howard who died eleven years later are buried near each other in Rosehill Cemetery.

Tom's aunt Fannie Crane lived out her life in Athens, Georgia and died March 16, 1927. She was eighty-five and is buried beside her husband John Ross Crane in Oconee Hill Cemetery, Athens, Georgia.

Tom's wife Georgia Bird Woolfolk married Reuben Lamb, a Macon policeman, on August 14, 1892 in Macon, Georgia. Her second husband died in Macon on March 3, 1922. In 1931, she married Bryant Holcomb who was reportedly an alcoholic and abusive. In less than a year, on June 22, 1932, Georgia Bird Woolfolk Lamb Holcomb was dead. She is buried at Riverside Cemetery in Macon.

A year after her brother's death, Lillie Woolfolk Cowan gave birth to a daughter and named her Susan after her mother. Three years later, a second daughter was born and was named Mattie. Lillie and her husband Henry moved their family to Macon where Henry died on July 11, 1919 and Lillie on August 22, 1936. They are buried in the Cowan's family plot in Riverside Cemetery, Macon, Georgia.

Floride Woolfolk Edwards married Love Shackleford in Athens, Georgia, July 8, 1893. They later moved to Hawkinsville where Love died February 24, 1938. Flo, who out-lived every principal participant in this tragedy, followed him in death seven years later, passing away June 1, 1945. They are buried side by side at the head of Tom's grave in Orange Hill Cemetery, Hawkinsville, Georgia.

Immediately after Judge George W. Gustin resigned his position as judge of the Macon Circuit Court, he went back into partnership with prosecutors Dupont Guerry and Joseph Hall and became the senior partner. His firm played a major, leading role in bringing new industry from the North into the Piedmont Region of Georgia. Judge Gustin died suddenly May 5, 1895. His pallbearers included Solicitor General William H. Felton and Attorney General Clifford Anderson. He is buried in Rosehill Cemetery in Macon.

In 1894, the first solicitor-general to prosecute Tom, John Lumsden Hardeman, was appointed Circuit Court Judge and served two years. He then returned to his private practice in Macon and died June 19, 1919. He is buried in Riverside Cemetery, Macon.

His judicial adversary, defense attorney Frank R. Walker, Tom's first lawyer, continued practicing law in Atlanta and was listed with his wife, Mary, as well as his son, E.G., also a lawyer, in the 1905 city directory. Little else is known.

Defense attorney Alexander Lawton Miller served as judge for the Macon Circuit from January 1890 through 1893. He was elected mayor of Macon in 1907 and served one term. In 1913, President Woodrow Wilson appointed him special ambassador to Ecuador. He died March 10, 1934 and is buried in Macon, Georgia.

At the same time Tom's execution was taking place, Solicitor General William Hamilton Felton, the prosecutor who was finally successful in obtaining and keeping a conviction of Tom Woolfolk, was in Rome, Georgia, campaigning for election to the House of Representatives. He lost but continued to serve as Solicitor General from 1889 through 1896. He was then appointed the youngest judge of the Macon Circuit and served for sixteen years. He died suddenly while reading on the back steps of his home in Macon, October 20, 1926.

In the 1960s, a dam was constructed on Tobesofkee Creek which flooded the Captain's original 1,000 acre plantation. Today,

Lake Tobesofkee is a popular recreation area in middle Georgia. The hill upon which "The Homeplace" once stood is all that remains above water. Residential development is rapidly encroaching from the urban sprawl of Macon, Georgia.

On the summit of the slight hill over looking the lake is a giant holly tree, still marking the grave of Tom's mother Susan Moore Woolfolk. All that remains of the Captain's house nearby is the rubble of two large chimneys and the well. Where the site was once well hidden in the thick woods, now much travelled paths lead the curious, the touched, and the related as they sojourn once again to the place where this tragedy began.

John Cobb Rutherford never regained his health and died March 30, 1891, five months after Tom Woolfolk's execution. He is buried with his family in Athens, Georgia, in the Oconee Hill Cemetery. His descendents still talk of how 'Uncle Johnny' gave his life for Tom Woolfolk.

Luanna and London Cooper, Emma and Aaron Jones, Silas and Julia Woolfolk, Anderson and Annie James apparently lived out their lives as sharecroppers near the "Homeplace" and by January 1891, black churches in the area were presenting dramatic reenactments of the Woolfolk murder that would end with the execution of Tom Woolfolk.

At the turn of the century a children's song was sung throughout Hazzard District. A single verse is still remembered a century later: *"Woolfolk, Woolfolk, look what you've done... You killed your family and didn't fire a gun."*

Montgomery Morgan Folsom's reputation for responsible journalism made him one of the Constitution's most respected reporters. His personal writings, however, reveal his overwhelming sense of sadness following Tom's execution. "Recollection," he once wrote, "doth but grieve me. Memory waketh but to weep." In another letter he wrote, "When a man has done all that he can to atone for the sins of the past, can't you leave him alone?"

An author of two books of prose and the father of five, Folsom suffered a massive stroke shortly after the contents of the Cooper Diary were made public. He died July 2, 1899 and is buried in historic Oakland Cemetery in Atlanta, Georgia. He was 42 years old.

Immediately following the murders, London Cooper's son Simon Cooper left Hazzard District and stayed out of the spotlight generated by the case. Shortly after Tom's first conviction, he disappeared.

In 1897, newspapers in South Carolina reported the horrendous axe murder of the Wilson family in Sumpter County. The attack, almost identical to the Woolfolk murder ten years earlier, occurred before sunrise on January 5, 1897, when Simon Cooper with his hand-picked gang of three reportedly planted a lookout in the front yard and boldly entered the house of Benjamin Wilson. A neighbor heard the commotion and saw Cooper attack a farm hand who was responding to family's cries for help. The blood-bath lasted only minutes but resulted in the deaths of five people. The last victim was found in the road way in front of the house. A short handled wood axe was where Cooper had left it, still imbedded in the man's head.

Cooper literally terrorized the black and white communities around Sumpter, South Carolina, days before and after the Wilson murders. A total of six people were dead and five were wounded.

His lookout Isaac Boyles surrendered to the sheriff and reported that Cooper boasted of raping Mrs. Wilson and of learning the art of mass murder ten years earlier in Macon, Georgia.

His half-brother secretly notified the sheriff of the location of Cooper's hideout, and a posse surrounded the log cabin. On the morning of January 8, after holding off the posse for hours and wounding some of the men, Cooper gave himself up.

In his hideout, he left behind a bundle of letters, a will, and various weapons.

When the deputy took him into custody, he found a blood covered knife hidden in his boot. While in the posse's possession and still covered with the blood of his victims, Cooper reportedly bragged to them about the murders and his ten year career as a murderer. Although his weapon of choice was the axe, he boasted that he also used knives, rifles, pistols, his bare hands and then repeatedly threatened members of the posse by name.

The grandson of a white man in Charleston, South Carolina, who was known for his brutality towards his family and subordinates, Cooper, a powerful six-foot-six, two hundred plus pound man, was reportedly argumentative and combative during his arrest. Cursing the posse, bragging of his murderous exploits and threatening them with certain death if he got free, Cooper incited the posse into an angry mob. It was when he started providing details of his murder of Mrs. Wilson that someone lost control and shot him in the head.

The deputy and newspaper editor, who tried desperately to protect the prisoner, were overpowered and tied to a tree. Unable to walk but still very much alive, Cooper argued for the right to kill the relative who had turned him in, his half-brother. A chain was tied around his throat. The deputy last saw him being dragged into a nearby swamp.

The next morning his bullet-ridden body was found on the side of a road. Back at Cooper's hideout, the sheriff found his will, and the bundle of letters revealing that he was literate, obsessed with his own power and his intense hatred for all white men.

Newspapers reported that his death was celebrated by both blacks and whites of the region. His body was refused by his relatives. Finally, the sheriff convinced a local church to bury him.

One elderly black man, while looking at Cooper's body, commented, "Well...he mighta been a monster. But he's a hero now."

His lynching was condemned by newspapers and politicians across the country, and, for a brief period Simon Cooper was indeed a hero to beleaguered blacks fighting an oppressive, hostile, white society.

When his will was probated, a trunk was bequeathed to a friend in Macon, H. S. Young. The trunk reportedly was left behind when he fled the state. Inside authorities found a memorandum notebook Cooper maintained while in Georgia. In it were details of his many crimes including some mysterious murders in both Georgia and South Carolina.

According to the reporter referencing the diary, Cooper was boastful of his numerous crimes and his uncanny ability to get away with murder. His notations on the Woolfolk murders correlate with Tom's version of the story.

One notation from the diary, however, provides a chilling epitaph to this story.

"Tom Woolfolk was mighty slick, but I fixed him. I would have killed him with the rest of the damn family, but he was not at home."

Tom's grave in Orange Hill Cemetery, Hawkinsville, GA
Date of death is in error. Tom was executed October 29, 1890.
(Photo courtesy of Sandy Kallas)

Following the publication of the first edition of this book, thousands of people have visited Tom's grave in Hawkinsville, Georgia. Although his tombstone still bears the scars of vandalism from the years when legend and myth blamed him for the murder of his family it is now reverently watched over by the locals. Descendents of the Gilbert family pay homage to his memory by maintaining the grave site. And finally, descendents of the surviving Woolfolks, so long burdened with the family's humiliation, guilt, and social ostracism have since re-united with descendents of Charles W. Howard to proudly declare their belief in Tom Woolfolk's innocence.

BIBLIOGRAPHY

(Editor's Note: The following is a partial bibliography provided for the readers' convenience. A complete bibliography of all sources used by the author over the last twenty five years of research would be too lengthly for inclusion in this book.)

PRIMARY SOURCES

NEWSPAPERS
(Atl. Const. = Atlanta Constitution; Macon Tele. = Macon Telegraph; Aug. Chron. = Augusta Chronicle).

1887
Pre-murder notes:
Death of John Rutherford's uncle—Atlanta Constitution, Feb. 25,1887, p.2.
Moore Mobbers — Atlanta Constitution, April 15, 23; May 28; June 6,7,8.
August:
7th — The Murder—Atl. Const., pp. 5, 8; Macon Tele., pp. 1,2,5; Aug.Chron., p.1;
   New York Times, p. 1
8th — The Funeral—Atl. Const., pp. 1, 2, 7; Macon Tele., p. 1
9th — In Atlanta—Atl. Const., p. 3,7; Macon Tele., p. 1
10th — Capt. Woolfolk/Fannie Crane Interview/Judge Nisbet refuses case—
Atl.Const., pp. 3,4,7; Macon Tele., p. 5
11th — Susan's Grave/Tom in Atlanta—Atl.Const., pp. 3,8; Macon Tele., p. 4
12th — William H. Felton/Tom's relationship with his step-mother/Tom's personality—
   Atl. Const., pp. 2,3
13th — Tom's personality/sanity—Atl. Const., pp. 3,7
14th — Woolfolk Estate/Captain's business/Frank Walker—Atl.Const.,pp. 6,11; Letter
   to Editor/Folsom column—Atl.Const. p.16; Macon Tele., p.4
15th — Moore Mobbers—Atl.Const.p.3
16th — Tom's mood/Petition to Gov.Gordon—Atl. Const.pp.3,7
17th — Misc. on family—Atl.Const., p. 4,; Macon Tele., pp. 4,7
18th — Charles W. Howard—Atl. Const., p.4; Macon Tele.
19th — Drought/Walker—Atl. Const., pp. 3,7; Macon Tele., pp.4, 7
20th — Misc.—Atl.Const., pp. 4; Macon Tele., p. 7
21th — Tom reading Bible/Folsom column—Atl. Const. p. 5,16
23rd — Misc.—Macon Telegraph, p.7
25th — Socks in well—Atl.Const., p. 8; Macon Telegraph, p.7
28th — Family visits Tom—Atl. Const., p. 12; Macon Telegraph, pp. 4, 7
30th — Walker in Macon—Atl.Const., p. 3;
   Sisters' visit Tom—Macon Tele. p.1
31th — Walker in Macon—Atl.Const., p. 3
September:
1st — Walker in Macon—Atl.Const.,p.3
6th — Misc.—Atl. Const., p. 3
8th — Gustin—Atl. Const., p.5;Macon Telegraph, p. 4
14th — Misc.—Atl. Const., p. 3
19th — Misc.—Atl. Const., p. 3
20th — Dubose—Atl. Const., p. 3
21st — Dubose/Anderson James—Atl. Const., p. 7
22th — Walker and Dubose—Atl. Const., p. 5
27th — Rain/Funeral Bill—Atl. Const., p. 3

October:
1st — Dubose—Atl.Const., p. 3
4th — Hunger Strike—Macon Tele., p. 11
9th — Woolfolk Estate/John Owens' Arrest—Atl. Const., p. 10
18th — Pres. Cleveland in Atlanta—Atl. Const., p. 1
25th — Davis/Tom in Macon—Atl. Const., p.1; Macon Tele. p. 11
27th — Bribery—Atl. Const., p. 2
November:
6th — Misc./Tom in Macon—Atl. Const., pp. 10, 15
7th — Tom in Macon—Atl. Const., p. 2
8th — Tom in Macon—Atl. Const., p. 1, 8
9th — John Rutherford—Atl. Const., p. 3
10st — Tom's Wife—Atl. Const., p.2
12th — Tom is Indicted—Atl. Const., p.3
13th — Misc.—Atl. Const., p. 11
15th — Georgia Bird Woolfolk—Macon Tele., p. 10
16th — Misc.—Atl. Const., p. 3
22nd — Postponement—Atl. Const., p. 2; Macon Tele., p. 8
December:
5th — Trial—Atl. Const., p. 2, 8
6th — Trial—Atl. Const., p. 2, 8
7th — Trial—Atl. Const., p. 2
8th — Trial—Atl. Const., p. 2
9th — Trial—Atl. Const., p. 2
10th — Trial—Atl. Const., p. 2
11th — Trial—Atl. Const., p. 10, 12
13th — Trial—Atl. Const., p. 1, 2; Macon Tele., p. 1, 5, 6, 12
14th — Trial—Atl. Const., p. 2
15th — Trial—Atl. Const., p. 2
16th — Conviction—Atl. Const., p. 2
17th — In Atlanta—Atl. Const., p. 7
18th — In Atlanta—Atl. Const., p. 15
20th — Emma Jones & Luanna Cooper—Macon Tele., pp. 4, 6;
Atl. Const. p. 4
21st — Threat of Lynching—Atl.Const., p. 4; Macon Telegraph, p. 1, 4, 6
27th — Trial analysis—Macon Telegraph, p. 8
30th — Tom in Atlanta—Atl. Const., p. 2

Also see:
Athens Weekly Banner-Watchman — August 9th, p.3; 16th, p.1; 23rd, p. 2; September 27th, p.1; November 15th, p. 4; December 13th, p. 3;20th, pp. 1,2,3
Calhoun Times — August 11, pp. 1,2; September 8, p. 2
Greensboro Journal and Herald — August 12, pp. 1,4; December 9, p. 1
Oglethorpe Echo — December 23, p. 2
Perry Home Journal — August 10; December 15

————

1888
January:
1st — Tom praying in cell—Atl. Const., p. 10
3rd — Misc.—Macon Tele., p. 3
4th — Tom frees himself—Atl. Const. p.2
5th — Visitors from California—Atl. Const. p.2
8th — Hardemann represents Flo and Lillie—Atl. Const., p. 2
10th — Misc.—Macon Telegraph, pp. 1, 8
11th — Dr. E.W. Warren—Atl. Const., p. 2

14th — Jailer Birdsong—Atl. Const., p. 3
22nd — Sisters visit Tom—Atl. Const., p. 10
24th — Misc.—Atl. Const., p. 2, 8
31st — Appeal to Supreme Court—Atl. Const., p. 2, 4;
Misc.—Macon Tele., p.4
February:
6th — Misc.—Atl. Const., p.2
9th — Motion for Retrial—Atl. Const., p.2
10th — Motion for Retrial—Atl. Const., p.2
14th — Misc.—Atl. Const. p.2; Macon Tele., p.10
16th — Tom reputation—Atl. Const. p. 2
18th — Tom receives a warning/bribe's plumber—Atl. Const., p. 2
19th — Motion postponed—Atl. Const., p. 10
25th — Motion postponed—Atl. Const., p. 9
29th — Tom in jail/visitors—Atl. Const., p. 2
March:
5th — Macon Misc.—Atl. Const. p.2
9th — Motion postponed—Atl. Const., p. 3
13th — Misc.—Atl. Const., p. 3
23rd — Misc.—Atl. Const., p. 3
24th — Tom cuts free—Atl. Const., p. 9
27th — Misc. Macon Tele., p. 1
April:
1st — Misc.—Atl. Const., p. 2
24th — Misc.—Macon Tele., p. 2
May 10 — Misc.—Atl. Const., p. 2
June:
2nd   — Tom in isolation—Atl. Const., p. 2
17th — Misc.—Atl. Const., p.13
July 23 — Judge Gustin—Atl. Const., p. 5
October:
1st — Jack the Ripper—Atl. Const., p.1
7th — Jack the Ripper—Atl. Const., p.11
November:
10th — Jack the Ripper—Atl. Const., p.2
11th — Jack the Ripper—Atl. Const., p.2
30th — Jack the Ripper—Atl. Const., p.2
Dec. 19 — Death of Sam Chambliss—Atl. Const., p. 2, 5
Also see:
Calhoun Times, January 26, p.2

————

1889
January:
11th — Supreme Court—Atl. Const., p. 2
31st — Supreme Court—Atl. Const., p. 4
February:
2nd — Tom in good spirit—Atl. Const., p. 3
11th — Conversation with Tom—Atl. Const., p. 3
12th — Motion—Atl. Const., p. 8
14th — Jack the Ripper—Atl. Const., p. 2
March:
1st — Conviction Reversed—Atl. Const., p. 3
6th — Second Trial Convenes—Atl.Const., pp. 3,8
7th — Second Trial—Atl. Const., p. 3
8th — Second Trial—Atl. Const., p. 3

9th — *Mistrial Declare—Atl. Const., p. 3*
12th — *Third trial begins—Atl. Const., p. 3*
13th — *Third trial—Atl. Const., p. 3*
14th — *Third trial—Atl. Const., pp. 3,7*
15th — *Change of Venue Declared—Atl. Const., p. 3*
April:
20th — *Alexander L. Miller—Atl. Const., p. 3*
23rd — *Green Lockett—Atl. Const., p. 3*
26th — *Rutherford ill—Atl.Const., p. 2*
May:
10th — *Jackson Dubose—Atl. Const., p. 3*
11th — *Hardeman nominated—Atl. Const., p. 2*
23rd — *J.J. Dannenberg—Atl. Const., p. 3*
29th — *Perry, Georgia—Atl. Const., p. 3*
30th — *Tom in Perry—Atl. Const., p. 3*
June:
4th — *Fourth trial begins—Atl. Const., p. 3*
5th — *Fourth trial—Atl. Const., p. 3*
6th — *Fourth trial—Atl. Const., p. 3*
7th — *Fourth trial—Atl. Const., p. 3*
8th — *Fourth trial—Atl. Const., p. 3*
9th — *Fourth trial—Atl. Const., pp. 3, 15*
10th — *The jury—Atl. Const., p. 3*
11th — *Tom on trial/Jack Dubose in Perry—Atl. Const., pp. 1,3*
12th — *Green Lockett—Atl. Const., p. 3*
13th — *W.E.D. O'Conner—Atl. Const., p. 2*
14th — *Tom's defense—Atl. Const., p. 2*
15th — *O'Conner disappears/Trial—Atl. Const., pp. 3,4*
16th — *Jack Dubose/O'Conner—Atl. Const., p. 12*
17th — *Dubose—Atl. Const., p. 3*
18th — *Tom on the stand—Atl. Const., p. 3*
19th — *Final evidence—Atl. Const., p. 3*
20th — *Closing arguments—Atl. Const., p. 3*
21st — *Electrocution vs hanging/Rutherford—Atl. Const., pp. 2, 3*
22nd — *Rutherford—Atl. Const., p. 3*
23rd — *Rutherford—Atl. Const., p. 10*
24th — *Trial misc.—Atl. Const., p. 3*
25th — *Verdict—Atl. Const., p. 1*
26th — *Sentence—Atl. Const., p. 2*
27th — *Dubose in Macon—Atl. Const., p. 3*
29th — *Birdsong in Contempt/Dubose—Atl. Const., p 3*
30th — *Jailer Birdsong—Atl. Const., p. 16*
July:
3rd — *Misc.—Atl. Const., p. 5*
5th — *Tom/Dubose—Atl. Const., p. 3*
7th — *Tom/Sheriff Cooper—Atl. Const., pp. 2, 12*
20th — *Vigilantes—Atl. Const., p. 3*
22nd — *Georgia Bird Woolfolk—Atl. Const., p. 3*
26th — *Hunger Strike—Atl. Const., p.3*
August:
2nd — *Tom in jail—Atl. Const., p. 3*
11th — *Motion for retrial—Atl. Const., p. 12*
13th — *Misc.—Atl. Const., p. 3*
14th — *Tom in prayer—Macon Telegraph, p. 8*
15th — *Postponement—Atl. Const., p. 3*

392

29th — *John Richards and Dubose—Atl. Const., p. 3*
31st — *John Richards—Atl. Const., p. 3*
September 4 — Misc.—Atl. Const., p. 3
October 2 — Earthquake—Atl. Const., p. 2
December:
2nd — Fear of suicide—Atl. Const., p. 2
6th — Jeff Davis' death—Atl. Const., p.1

Also see:
Athens Banner-Watchman (the daily)—May 8, p. 1; May 19, p.1
Athens Weekly Chronicle—April 27, p. 2; May 8, p. 1; June 22, p. 2; June 29, p.2; August 10, p. 1; August 17, p. 3; August 23, p.1
Calhoun Times—December 5, p.2
Perry Home Journal—June 6, p. 1,2; June 13, p. 1,2

————

1890
January:
2nd — Misc.—Atl. Const., p.2
5th — Misc.—Atl. Const., p. 4
15th — Misc.—Atl. Const., p. 5
16th — Misc.—Atl. Const., p. 2
March 3rd — Supreme Court—Atl. Const., p. 2
April 6th — Tom's description—Atl. Const., p. 4
May:
11th — Supreme Court—Atl. Const., p. 14
13th — Supreme Court/Tom's divorce—Atl. Const., p. 3
14th — Tom's health—Atl. Const., p. 2
19th — Tom gets a razor—Atl. Const., p. 2
June 5th — Court Expense—Atl. Const., p. 5
July:
8th — John Rutherford/Supreme Court—Atl. Const., pp. 2, 4
29th — Retrial denied—Atl. Const., p. 6
August:
6th — Retrial denied—Macon Telegraph, p. 3
7th — Anniversary—Macon Telegraph, p. 3
23rd — Misc.—Atl. Const., p. 2
September:
4th — William H. Felton—Atl. Const., p. 1
13th — Letter of confession—Atl. Const., p. 2
17th — Misc.—Atl. Const., p. 3
27th — Bibb County Jail—Atl. Const., p. 2
October:
2nd — Bibb County Jail—Atl. Const., p. 3
3rd — Misc.—Atl. Const., p. 2
7th — Sentence—Atl. Const., p. 2
8th — Sentence—Atl. Const., p. 2
9th — Misc.—Atl. Const., p. 4
10th — Misc.—Atl. Const., p. 1
15th — Misc.—Macon Teleg., p. 2
25th — Editor John Hodges—Atl. Const., p. 3
26th — Death row—Macon Tele., p. 3
27th — Death row—Macon Tele., p. 3
29th — Eve of execution—Atl. Const., p. 1; Macon Tele., pp.1,7
30th — Execution—Atl. Const., pp. 1, 2, 3; Macon Tele., pp. 1, 2, 4; At. Journal,p. 1
31st — Funeral—Atl. Const., p. 2

November 5th — The murder discussed—Atl. Const., p. 5; Macon Tele., p.5

Also see:
Athens Weekly Banner—February 25, p. 3; June 16th, p. 1; August 5, p.4;
   November 4, p.5
Perry Home Journal–June 6, p.1; June 13, p.1
Greensboro Herald-Journal, October 31, p.1

Post-execution:
January 25, 1891 — Woolfolk Legend—Atl. Const., p. 15
March 11, 1891 — John C. Rutherford—Atl. Const., p. 2
March 13, 1891 — John C. Rutherford—Atl. Const., p. 2
April 30, 1894 — Judge James T. Nisbett—Atl. Const., p. 3
May 6, 1895 — Judge George W. Gustin—Atl. Const., p. 3
January 2, 1897--Simon Cooper--Atl. Const.
January 8, 1897--Simon Cooper--Atl. Const., Macon Tele. p1
January 9, 1897--Simon Cooper--Atl. Const., Macon Tele. p.1
October 20, 1926 — Judge William H. Felton—Atl. Const., p. 1
March 11, 1934 — Judge A. L. Miller—Atl. Const., p.1

OFFICIAL DOCUMENTS
1881, 1882, 1883, 1884 Monroe and Bibb County Tax Digests
Bibb County Deed Record, Vol. U, p.271; Vol.X, p. 243; Vol QQ, pp. 401, 481, 82;
   Bk 40, p. 430; Bk 42, p. 481; Bk 43, p. 742.
Georgia Reports, Woolfolk VS The State of Georgia, Vol. 81, pp 551-567; Vol 85,
   pp.75-109
Census Records — 1850, 1860, 1870, 1880, 1900, 1910 Bibb, Clark, Monroe, Jones,
   and Pulaski Counties
Bibb County Superior Court Minutes, Books 24, 25

Also see:
Macon City Directeries 1880-1900
Athens City Directeries 1860-1930
Atlanta City Directeries 1880-1905
Mt. Zion Baptist Church Record
Midway Baptist Church Record

SECONDARY SOURCES
1. E. Merton Coulter, THE WOOLFOLK MURDER, Georgia History Quarterly, v. 49,
   1965, pp. 115-156.
2. Young, Ida, et al, HISTORY OF MACON, GEORGIA, Press of Lyon, Marshalls, and
   Brooks, Macon, GA, 1950.
3. Buck, Paul, THE ROAD TO REUNION, 1865-1900. Peter Smith, 1959.
4. Cash, Wilbur J., THE MIND OF THE SOUTH. Alfred A. Knof, 1960.
5. Anderson, Nancy Briska, MACON: A PICTORIAL HISTORY. Donning, 1979.
6. Butler, John C., HISTORY OF MACON AND CENTRAL GEORGIA. Burke, 1879.
7. MONROE COUNTY HISTORY
8. Hynds, Ernest C., ANTEBELLUM ATHENS AND CLARKE COUNTY GEORGIA.,
   UGA Press, Athens,1974.
9. Davis, Harold E., HENRY GRADY'S NEW SOUTH: Atlanta, A Brave & Beautiful
   City., The University of Alabama Press, 1990.

Index

Davis, William A. 46, 176, 204, 293
Disroon, Frank 273
Dixon, P. H. 305
Dubose, Jackson 137, 144, 162, 169, 220, 232, 263, 283,
        316, 324, 327, 332, 341, 345, 351
Duncan, Clinton C. 288, 336, 358
Edwards, Floride Woolfolk 61, 67, 81, 86, 89, 105, 117, 125, 135,
        163, 173, 174, 196, 208, 230, 237, 239, 243, 255, 264,
        268, 295, 323, 328, 332, 339, 361, 363, 384
Edwards, Zachary T. 61, 81, 89
Felton, William H. 103, 160, 255, 258, 263, 270, 273,
        288, 295, 311, 318, 336, 342, 384
Fletcher, Mrs. S. M. 323
Folsom, Montgomery Morgan 59, 64, 67, 73, 78, 83, 89, 101, 133, 145,
        159, 167, 173, 187, 195, 199, 217, 230, 232, 248, 255,
        263, 268, 280, 285, 295, 312, 313, 327, 332, 335, 342, 345,
        362, 364, 367, 375, 385
Foster, Albert 99
Foster, Fred C. 162, 210
Foster, Jim 194, 196, 218, 300, 325
Frederick, J. M. 287
Gilbert, Mrs. Randolp 128
Gober, G. F. 358
Gordon, John B. 93
Grady, Henry 134, 143, 160
Guerry, Dupont 195, 203, 271, 328, 339, 384
Gustin, George W. 160, 167, 202, 219, 235, 236, 244, 249, 253, 255, 258, 263,
        281, 295, 312, 315, 319, 322, 339, 353, 358, 384
Hall, Joseph H. 271, 285, 384
Hamlin, Ben 184
Hardeman, John L. 48, 147, 159, 161, 174, 187, 191, 198,
        199, 208, 213, 217, 218, 224, 233, 235, 236,
        242, 253, 255, 288, 306, 315, 325, 336, 342, 384
Hardin, Sarah 97, 116, 132, 187, 306, 328
Harvey, Henry 238
Hill, Ben 353
Hill, W. E. 267
Hilliard, S. M. 194
Hodges, John 358
Hodnett, William 48, 50, 126, 133, 161, 265
Holcomb, Bryant 383
Hollis, Jerry 124, 175, 296, 311, 325, 335
Holly, James J. 54, 196, 312, 325
Howard, Benjamin F. 48, 63, 79, 83, 98, 163, 225, 233, 258, 268, 383
Howard, Charles W. 48, 102, 125, 147, 159, 161, 163, 197, 243,
        267, 268, 271, 304, 380, 383, 388
Howard, John D 48, 70, 82, 163, 268, 286, 305, 383
Hughes, W. S. 183
Jack The Ripper 263
James, Anderson 28, 31, 35, 53, 59, 83, 128, 193, 205, 264,
        299, 320, 322, 330, 385
James, Ann 49, 83, 385
Jeff, John 113, 206, 218, 219, 232, 256, 312, 313, 314, 315, 321
Jim Moore lynching 52

396

397

Order Form

Eagles Publishing Company
384 Bullsboro Drive # 339
Newnan, GA 30263
Phone: 770-252-4356 Fax: 770-502-0281

Yes! I'd like to order additional copies of

"Shadow Chasers"

Order online at www.eaglespubs.com or:

Fax this form to: 770-502-0281 or mail this form to the above address.

Soft-cover edition	Hard-cover edition
TOTAL	**TOTAL**
_____ **copies at $ 16.95** _____	_____ **copies at $24.95** _____
*shipping and handling** _____	*shipping and handling** _____

*Soft-cover shipping and handling charges		*Hard-cover Shipping and handling charges	
1 copy	$3.50	1 copy	$4.00
2 copies	$4.50	2 copies	$5.00
3 copies	$6.50	3 copies	$7.00
4-7 copies	$10.50	4-7 copies	$11.50
8-10	$15.50	8-10	$16.00

GA residents 7% sales tax	_____	GA residents 7% sales tax	_____
Sub total soft-cover	$_____	Sub total hard-cover $	_____

Total order $_____

Make all checks payable to Eagles Publishing Company

Charge to:___VISA   ___Mastercard   Account no. _____

Signature _____ Daytime telephone _____

Print name _____

Address   _____

City/State/Zip_____